Jesus in His Jewish Context

Jesus in His Jewish Context

GEZA VERMES

Fortress Press
Minneapolis

JESUS IN HIS JEWISH CONTEXT

Fortress Press edition 2003

An earlier edition of this volume appeared as *Jesus and the World of
Judaism* (London: SCM Press, 1983; Philadelphia: Fortress Press,
1984)

Cover image: "Christ Enthroned," wood engraving by Bernard
Solomon, from *The Zaddick Christ* (Greenwood, S.C.: Attic Press,
1973), copyright © 1973 by Bernard Solomon. Used by permission
of Attic Press.

ISBN: 0-8006-3623-6

07 06 0   2 3 4 5 6 7 8 9 10

Contents

Preface

My scholarly involvement with the historical Jesus began thirty years ago with the publication in 1973 of *Jesus the Jew: A Historian's Reading of the Gospels*, in which I sought to determine what kind of a person Jesus of Nazareth was by firmly setting this charismatic teacher, healer and exorcist in the real world of first-century Palestinian Jews. The pioneering volume was then further developed with a view to paying more and more attention to the doctrinal aspects of the message of Jesus and the nature of the Jewish religion that he preached and practised. This effort produced two further books at ten-yearly intervals, *Jesus and the World of Judaism* (1983) and *The Religion of Jesus the Jew* (1993). The three volumes add up to a trilogy demonstrating the authentic Jewishness of Jesus. The present collection of studies is meant to replace and enrich further *Jesus and the World of Judaism*. All three volumes intended for both scholars and a general readership are available from SCM Press, London, in Britain and Fortress Press, Minneapolis, in the USA.

In general, my contributions to the study of the historical Jesus have been received with sympathy in Britain and Europe. Nevertheless, they occasionally met with open hostility in the United States especially in the wake of some harsh words said about my method by Professor John P. Meier in *A Marginal Jew: Rethinking the historical Jesus*.[1] I usually do not respond to criticism and leave it to the readers to form their own judgement. 'Here is my pudding', I like to tell them. 'Taste it before you start finding fault with the recipe. The proof of the pudding is in the eating.' This time, however, I have been persuaded by friends and colleagues to make an exception.

Father Meier has raised two serious objections against my way of portraying Jesus. He has accused me of lacking 'methodology' and of making an 'acritical' use of the rabbinic sources.

His first charge is based on a misunderstanding of a remark, which I made on methodology. Professor Meier interpreted it *à la lettre* although it appeared in the context of a jocular piece of self-mockery. In *The Religion of Jesus the Jew* (1993, p. 7) I wrote, 'In my opinion, research aiming to be innovative should not be bound by strict, predetermined rules. Indeed, although the claim coming from someone, born in Hungary, educated in Belgium and France, and citizen of the United Kingdom by naturalization only, may strike a faintly amusing note, I nevertheless pride myself on being a true *British* pragmatist.'

Struck by my 'disdain for methodology' and 'preference for "muddling through"', a very British habit, Professor Meier thought it fit to lecture me on the rudiments of proper academic proceeding. 'Any scholarly investigation', I was told, 'that is not totally erratic operates by certain rules.'[2] It does indeed. Yet if this otherwise so meticulous researcher had taken the trouble to read, or even just glance at my essay, 'Jewish Studies and New Testament Interpretation: *Reflections of Methodology*', deliberately cited on the same page as the quotation which so upset him, he might have realized that I am not as unprincipled as he seems to imagine. The paper in question was my presidential address to the First Congress of the European Association for Jewish Studies.[3] I set out in it the programme of a 'dynamic' approach to rabbinic evidence.[4] This method seeks first to trace with the help of all the available data the evolutionary curve of a given theme, and then to determine the precise place on that literary curve of the various examples of this theme.

Instead of analysing the documents, Meier adopts a simplistic stand in his dealing with rabbinic literature. For him the date of a tradition is determined by the date of the literary source, which transmits it. So he simply declares Mishnah, Midrash, Talmud and Targum unfit for use in the study of Jesus because their redaction occurred after the composition of the New Testament (late first–early second century AD), namely between, say, AD 200 and 500. But scholars familiar with the works of the rabbis are well aware that a rabbinic anthology often contains teachings and interpretations, which are centuries older than the final compilation in which they are housed. They also know that it is possible to distinguish ancient elements from more recent material.

Professor Meier's second point of disagreement with me concerns my 'acritical' use of the rabbinic sources. The issue arises from my application to Jesus of the concept 'charismatic Hasid', which I have modelled mostly on the Mishnaic–Talmudic, but also partly on the Josephan, portrayal of two Jewish 'miracle workers', Honi (first century BC) and Hanina ben Dosa (first century AD). My approach to the figure of the charismatic Hasid was typological. I argued from features, which are attested and verifiable in *all the historical periods* of ancient Judaism from the age of the eighth century BC Old Testament prophets down to the Tannaitic and Amoraic rabbis in the early centuries of the Christian era. Anyone acquainted with my publications, which now stretch over more than fifty years, can see that I am fully aware of the time factor affecting the rabbinic sources and of the evolutionary process characteristic of them. After all, I spent more than twenty years on rewriting and re-editing *The History of the Jewish People in the Age of Jesus Christ*,[5] Emil Schürer's monumental classic, *the* textbook on the period of the Gospels.

Yet Professor Meier thinks otherwise (see vol. II, pp. 586–87). 'Despite the fact', he writes, 'that many of the traditions about Hanina ben Dosa do not find any literary attestation earlier than the two Talmuds, Vermes suggests that in some of the statements attributed to Hanina we may possess genuine sayings of "a remarkable personality living in first-century Palestine", sayings that "constitute the most direct insight we possess into the Hasidic mind and outlook." That Vermes can make this claim when discussing sayings attributed to Hanina in *Pirqe* [de-]*Rabbi Eliezer* [dating to the eighth or ninth century AD] leaves one speechless. . . . Ultimately, Vermes' acritical use of sources undermines his whole argument.' Some indictment.

John Meier is usually punctilious in giving page references, but for some reason he omits here to indicate the source of the statement which has left him speechless. The extract is borrowed from my essay, 'Hanina ben Dosa' (*JJS* 23, 1972, p. 50), in which among many other things I examine the surviving maxims attributed to this Galilean holy man. Here are my exact words, 'If the first three, and possibly four sayings [namely 1. Mishnah Abot 3:9a; 2. Abot 3:9b; 3. Abot 3:10; 4. Babylonian Talmud Berakhot 33a (baraita, i.e. a Talmudic text attributable to Tannaitic rabbis of the first or second century AD)] are accepted as genuine, they echo not only the voice of a remarkable personality living in first century Palestine, but also constitute the most direct insight we possess into the Hasidic mind and outlook, since the other much larger collection, that of the contemporaneous teachings of Jesus of Nazareth, is extant only in a foreign language and an alien arrangement.'

The two extracts from the early medieval Pirqe de-R. Eliezer (PRE) have been quoted in my article only for the sake of presenting a complete list of all the relevant doctrinal material extant in the sources. But I have deliberately and unequivocally excluded the PRE data from consideration in presenting the genuine teaching of Hanina. Indeed, I have explicitly called the two texts in question 'spurious' (ibid. p. 49). In the light of these correct facts, I invite the readers to decide whose argument, Professor Meier's or mine, is undermined by an 'acritical' handling of the evidence. Here I rest my case.

Meier has strongly objected to my way of employing the model of the charismatic prophet and the Elijah-like miracle worker in the study of the historical Jesus. Therefore let us now inquire how his '*marginal Jew*' is defined. Jesus, according to Professor Meier,[6] is an 'eschatological prophet' and a 'charismatic' similar to 'Elijah'. In other words, the 'marginal Jew' is the mirror image of the 'charismatic Hasid' delineated by me in *Jesus the Jew* twenty-one years before Father Meier. Thus unwittingly he vindicates my cynical remark published prior to the appearance of volume II of *A Marginal Jew* (1994). 'Methodology', I wrote, 'makes me see red perhaps because more than once I have been rebuked by transatlantic dogmatists for illegitimately arriving at the *right* conclusion, following a path not sanctioned by [their] sacrosanct rule book.'[7]

I am glad to say not all the American Gospel scholars share Professor Meier's ideas. To quote a couple of recent opinions, Paula Fredriksen, of Boston University, describes the Jesus trilogy as 'a groundbreaking series of studies on the historical Jesus' which 'have enjoyed great popularity'.[8] As for Ed Sanders, the leading transatlantic New Testament expert, he concludes his recently published review of *The Changing Faces of Jesus* with words, which almost make me blush. 'In Vermes,' writes the Arts and Sciences Professor of Religion at Duke University, 'Jesus has found his best Jewish interpreter.'[9]

Jesus the Jew

'Jesus the Jew' – which is also the title of a book I have written[1] – is an emotionally charged synonym for the Jesus of history as opposed to the divine Christ of the Christian faith that simply re-states the obvious fact, still hard for many Christians and even some Jews to accept, that Jesus was a Jew and not a Christian. It implies a renewed quest for the historical figure reputed to be the founder of Christianity.

In one respect this search is surprising: namely that it has been undertaken at all. In another, it is unusual: that it has been made without – so far as I am consciously aware – any ulterior motive. My intention has been to reach for the historical truth, for the sake, at the most, of putting the record straight; but definitely not in order to demonstrate some theological preconception.

Let me develop these two points.

If, in continuity with medieval Jewish tradition, I had set out to prove that Yeshu was not only a false Messiah, but also a heretic, a seducer and a sorcerer, my research would have been prejudiced from the start. Even if I had chosen as my target the more trendy effort of yesterday, the 'repatriation of Jesus into the Jewish people' – *Heimholung Jesu in das jüdische Volk* – it is unlikely to have led to an untendentious enquiry, to an analysis of the available evidence without fear or favour, *sine ira et studio*.

By the same token, when a committed Christian embarks on such a task with a mind already persuaded by the dogmatic suppositions of his church which postulate that Jesus was not only the true Messiah, but the only begotten Son of God – that is to say, God himself – he is bound to read the gospels in a particular manner and to attribute the maximum possible Christian traditional significance even to the most neutral sentence, one that in any other context he would not even be tempted to interpret that way.

My purpose, both in the written and the verbal examination of 'Jesus the Jew', has been to look into the past for some trace of the features of the first-century Galilean, before he had been proclaimed either the second

Person of the Holy Trinity, or the apostate and bogey man of Jewish popular thought.

Strangely enough, because of the special nature of the Gospels, a large group of Christians, including such opposing factions as the out-and-out fundamentalists and the highly sophisticated New Testament critics, would consider a historical enquiry of this sort *ipso facto* doomed to failure. Our knowledge of Jesus – they would claim – depends one hundred per cent on the New Testament: writings that were never intended as history but as a record of the faith of Jesus' first followers. The fundamentalists deduce from these premises that the pure truth embedded in the Gospels is accessible only to those who share the evangelists' outlook. Those who do not do so are – to quote a letter published in the *Guardian*[2] – 'still in the night . . . and so (have) no title to write about things which are only known to (initiates)'.

At the other extreme stands the leading spokesman of the weightiest contemporary school of New Testament scholarship, Rudolf Bultmann. Instead of asserting with the fundamentalists that no quest for the historical Jesus *should* be attempted, Bultmann is firmly convinced that no such quest *can* be initiated. 'I do indeed think', he writes, 'that we can know now almost nothing concerning the life and personality of Jesus, since the early Christian sources show no interest in either.'[3]

Against both these viewpoints, and against Christian and Jewish denominational bias, I seek to re-assert in my whole approach to this problem the inalienable right of the historian to pursue a course independent of beliefs. Yet I will at the same time try to indicate that, despite widespread academic scepticism, our considerably increased knowledge of the Palestinian-Jewish realities of the time of Jesus enables us to extract historically reliable information even from non-historical sources such as the gospels.

In fact, with the discovery and study of the Dead Sea Scrolls and other archaeological treasures, and the corresponding improvement in our understanding of the ideas, doctrines, methods of teaching, languages and culture of the Jews of New Testament times, it is now possible, not simply to place Jesus in relief against this setting, as students of the Jewish background of Christianity pride themselves on doing, but to insert him fair and square within first-century Jewish life itself. The questions then to be asked are where he fits into it, and whether the added substance and clarity gained from immersing him in historical reality confers credibility on the patchy Gospel picture.

Let us begin then by selecting a few non-controversial facts concerning Jesus' life and activity, and endeavour to build on these foundations.

Jesus lived in Galilee, a province governed during his lifetime, not by the Romans, but by a son of Herod the Great. His home-town was Nazareth, an insignificant place not referred to by Josephus, the Mishnah or the Talmud, and first mentioned outside the New Testament in an inscription from Caesarea, dating to the third or fourth century. Whether he was born there or somewhere else is uncertain. The Bethlehem legend is in any case highly suspect.

As for the date of his birth, this 'is not truly a historical problem', writes one of the greatest living experts on antiquity, Sir Ronald Syme.[4] The year of Jesus' death is also absent from the sources. Nevertheless the general chronological context is clearly defined. He was crucified under Pontius Pilate, the prefect of Judaea from 26 to 36 CE; his public ministry is said to have taken place shortly after the fifteenth year of Tiberius (28/29 CE), when John the Baptist inaugurated his crusade of repentance. Whether Jesus taught for one, two or three years, his execution in Jerusalem must have occurred in the early thirties of the first century.

He was fairly young when he died. Luke reports that he was approximately thirty years old when he joined John the Baptist (Luke 3.23). Also one of the few points on which Matthew and Luke, the only two evangelists to elaborate on the events preceding and following Jesus' birth, agree is in dating them to the days of King Herod of Judaea (Matt. 2.1–16; Luke 1.15) – who died in the spring of 4 BCE.

Let me try to sketch the world of Jesus' youth and early manhood in the second and third decades of the first century. In distant Rome, Tiberius reigned supreme. Valerius Gratus and Pontius Pilate were governing Judaea. Joseph Caiaphas was high priest of the Jews, the president of the Jerusalem Sanhedrin, and the head of the Sadducees. Hillel and Shammai, the leaders of the most influential Pharisaic schools, were possibly still alive, and during the life-time of Jesus, Gamaliel the Elder became Hillel's successor. Not far from Jerusalem, a few miles south of Jericho, on the shore of the Dead Sea, the ascetic Essenes were worshipping God in holy withdrawal and planning the conversion of the rest of Jewry to the true Judaism known only to them, the followers of the Teacher of Righteousness. And in neighbouring Egypt, in Alexandria, the philosopher Philo was busy harmonizing the Jewish life-style with the wisdom of Greece, a dream cherished by the civilized Jews of the Diaspora.

In Galilee, the tetrarch Herod Antipas remained lord of life and death and continued to hope (in vain) that one day the emperor might end his humiliation by granting him the title of king. At the same time, following the upheaval that accompanied the tax registration or census ordered in 6 CE by the legate of Syria, Publius Sulpicius Quirinius, Judas the Galilean and his sons were stimulating the revolutionary tendencies of the uncouth Northerners, tendencies which had resulted in the foundation of the Zealot movement.

Such was the general ambience in which the personality and character of Jesus the Jew were formed. We know nothing concrete, however, about his education and training, his contacts, or the influences to which he may have been subjected; for, quite apart from the unhistorical nature of the stories relating to his infancy and childhood, the interval between his twelfth year and the start of his public ministry is wrapped in total silence by the four evangelists.

Jesus spent not only his early years, but also the greatest part of his public life in Galilee. If we adopt the chronology of the Synoptic Gospels (Matthew, Mark and Luke) with their one-year ministry, apart from brief excursions to Phoenicia (now Lebanon) and Perea (or present day northern Transjordan), he left his province only once – for the fateful journey to Jerusalem at Passover. But even if the longer time-table of John's Fourth Gospel is followed, the Judaean stays of Jesus corresponded to the mandatory pilgrimages to the Temple, and as such were of short duration. Therefore, if we are to understand him, it is into the Galilean world that we must look.

The Galilee of Jesus, especially his own part of it, Lower Galilee around the Lake of Gennesaret, was a rich and mostly agricultural country. The inhabitants were proud of their independence and jealous of their Jewishness, in which regard, despite doubts often expressed by Judaeans, they considered themselves second to none. They were also brave and tough. Josephus, the commander-in-chief of the region during the first Jewish War, praises their courage, and describes them as people 'from infancy inured to war' (*BJ* iii.41).

In effect, in the mountains of Upper Galilee, rebellion against the government – any government, Hasmonean, Herodian, Roman – was endemic between the middle of the first century BCE and 70 CE, from Ezekias, the *archilēstēs* (the chief brigand or revolutionary) whose uprising was put down by the young Herod, through the arch-Zealot Judas the Galilean and his rebellious sons, to John the son of Levi from Gush Halav and his 'Galilean contingent', notorious in besieged Jerusalem for their 'mischievous ingenuity and audacity' (*BJ* iv.558) at the time of the 66–70 CE war. In short, the Galileans were admired as staunch fighters by those who sympathized with their rebellious aims; those who did not, thought of them as dangerous hot-heads.

In Jerusalem, and in Judaean circles, they had also the reputation of being an unsophisticated people. In rabbinic parlance, a Galilean is usually referred to as *Gelili shoteh*, stupid Galilean. He is presented as a typical 'peasant', a boor, a *'am ha-arez*, a religiously uneducated person. Cut off from the Temple and the study centres of Jerusalem, Galilean popular religion appears to have depended – until the arrival at Usha, in the late 130s CE, of the rabbinic academy expelled from Yavneh – not so much on the authority of the priests or on the scholarship of scribes, as on the magnetism of their local saints like Jesus' younger contemporary, Hanina ben Dosa, the celebrated miracle-worker.

These lengthy preliminaries done with, it is time now to turn to the gospels to make our acquaintance with Jesus the Jew, or more exactly, Jesus the *Galilean* Jew. I intend to leave to one side the speculations of the early Christians concerning the various divinely contrived roles of Messiah, Lord, Son of God, etc. that their Master was believed to have fulfilled before or after his death. Instead, I will rely on those simple accounts of the first three Gospels which suggest that Jesus impressed his countrymen, and acquired fame among them, chiefly as a charismatic teacher, healer and exorcist. I should specify at once, however, that my purpose is not to discuss his teachings. Few, in any case, will contest that his message was essentially Jewish, or that on certain controversial issues, for example whether the dead would rise again, he voiced the opinion of the Pharisees.

His renown, the evangelists proclaim, had spread throughout Galilee. According to Mark, when Jesus and his disciples disembarked from their boat on Lake Kinneret,

> he was immediately recognized; and the people scoured the whole country-side and brought the sick on stretchers to any place where he was reported to be. Wherever he went, to farmsteads, villages or towns, they laid out the sick in the market places and begged him to let them simply touch the edge of his cloak; and all who touched him were cured. (Mark 6.54–56)

Similarly, Mark, referring to events in Capernaum, writes:

> They brought to him all who were ill and possessed by devils . . . He healed many who suffered from various diseases, and drove out many devils. (Mark 1.33–34)

And both Luke and Mark report Jesus himself as saying:

> Today and tomorrow, I shall be casting out devils and working cures. (Luke 13.32)

And

It is not the healthy that need a doctor but the sick; I did not come to invite virtuous people but sinners. (Mark 2.17)

My twentieth-century readers may wonder whether such a person should not properly be classified as a crank. We must, however, bear in mind, firstly that it is anachronistic and, in consequence, wrong to judge the first century by twentieth-century criteria, and secondly, that even in modern times, faith-healers and *Wunderrebbe* and their secular counterparts in the field of medicine, can and do obtain parallel therapeutic results where the individuals who ask for their help are animated by sufficient faith.

To assess correctly Jesus' healing and exorcistic activities, it is necessary to know that in bygone ages the Jews understood that a relationship existed between sickness, the devil and sin. As a logical counterpart to such a concept of ill-health, it was in consequence believed until as late as the third century BCE that recourse to the services of a physician demonstrated a lack of faith since healing was a monopoly of God. The only inter-mediaries thought licit between God and the sick were men of God, such as the prophets Elijah and Elisha. By the beginning of the second pre-Christian century, however, the physician's office was made more or less respectable by the requirement that he, too, should be personally holy. The Wisdom writer, Jesus ben Sira, advised the devout when sick to pray, repent, and send gifts to the Temple, and subsequently to call in the physician, who would ask God for insight into the cause of the sickness and for the treatment needed to remedy it. As Ecclesiasticus words it:

The Lord has imparted knowledge to men
that by the use of His marvels He may win praise;
by employing them, the doctor relieves pain. (Ecclus. 38.6–7)

Jesus' healing gifts are never attributed to the study of physical or men-tal disease, or to any acquired knowledge of cures, but to some mysterious power that emanated from him and was transmitted to the sick by contact with his person, or even with his clothes. In the episode of the crippled woman who was bent double and unable to hold herself upright, we read that

He laid his hands on her, and at once she straightened up and began to praise God. (Luke 13.13)

Sometimes touch and command went together. A deaf-mute was cured when Jesus placed his own saliva on the sufferer's tongue and ordered his ears to unblock, saying:

Ephphatha (*'eppatah*): Be opened! (Mark 7.33–34)

There is nevertheless one story in which Jesus performs a cure *in absentia*, that is to say without being anywhere within sight, let alone within touching distance, of the sick man. Matthew's account of the episode reads:

> When (Jesus) had entered Capernaum a centurion came up to ask his help.
> Sir – he said – a boy of mine lies at home paralysed . . .
> Jesus said, I will come and cure him.
> Sir, – replied the centurion – who am I to have you under my roof? You need only say a word and the boy will be cured. I know, for I am myself under orders, with soldiers under me. I say to one, Go! and he goes; to another, Come here! and he comes; and to my servant, Do this! and he does it.
> Jesus heard him with astonishment, and said to the people following him,
> I tell you this: nowhere, even in Israel, have I found such a faith.
> Then he said to the centurion,
> Go home now. Because of your faith, so let it be.
> At that moment the boy recovered. (Matt. 8.5–13)

I quote this in full not only because of its intrinsic interest, but also in order to compare it with a Talmudic report concerning one of the famous deeds of Jesus' compatriot, Hanina ben Dosa. It will be seen from the second story how closely the two tales coincide.

> It happened that when Rabban Gamaliel's son fell ill, he sent two of his pupils to R. Hanina ben Dosa that he might pray for him. When he saw them, he went to the upper room and prayed. When he came down, he said to them,
> Go, for the fever has left him.
> They said to him,
> Are you a prophet?
> He said to them,
> I am no prophet, neither am I a prophet's son, but this is how I am blessed: if my prayer is fluent in my mouth, I know that the sick man is favoured; if not, I know that the disease is fatal.
> They sat down, wrote and noted the hour. When they came to Rabban Gamaliel, he said to them,
> By heaven! You have neither detracted from it, nor added to it, but this is how it happened. It was at that hour that the fever left him and he asked us for water to drink. (*bBer*. 34b)

Instead of ascribing physical and mental illness to natural causes, Jesus' contemporaries saw the former as a divine punishment for sin instigated by the devil, and the latter as resulting from a direct demonic possession. Therefore, by expelling and controlling these evil spirits, the exorcist was believed to be acting as God's agent in the work of liberation, healing and pardon.

Jesus was an exorcist, but not a professional one: he did not use incantations such as those apparently composed by King Solomon,[5] or foul-smelling substances intolerable even to the most firmly ensconced of demons. He did not go in for producing smoke, as young Tobit did, by burning the heart and the liver of a fish (Tobit 8.2), or for holding under the noses of the possessed the Solomonic *baaras* root, the stink of which, so Josephus assures us, drew the demon out through the nostrils.[6] Instead, Jesus confronted with great authority and dignity the demoniacs (lunatics, epileptics, and the like) and commanded the devil to depart. This act is usually said to have been followed by relief, and at least a temporary remission of the symptoms. (Even in the Gospels, the demons seem to have had an uncanny facility for finding their way back to their former habitats (Matt. 12.34–44).) So – we read in Mark

[Jesus and his disciples] came to the other side of the lake, into the country of the Gerasenes. As he stepped ashore, a man possessed by an unclean spirit came up to him from among the tombs where he had his dwelling. He could no longer be controlled; even chains were useless; he had often been fettered and chained up, but he had snapped his chains and broken the fetters. No one was strong enough to master him. And so, unceasingly, night and day, he would cry aloud among the tombs and on the hill-sides and cut himself with stones. When he saw Jesus in the distance, he ran and flung himself down before him, shouting loudly, . . . In God's name, do not torment me!
   For Jesus was already saying to him,
   Out, unclean spirit, come out of this man!
   . . . The people . . . came to Jesus and saw the madman who had been possessed . . . sitting there clothed and in his right mind; and they were afraid. (Mark 5.1–15)

Once more I must parallel the Gospel narrative with one concerning Hanina ben Dosa and his encounter with the queen of the demons.

Let no man go out alone at night . . . for Agrath daughter of Mahlath and eighteen myriads of destroying angels are on the prowl, and each of them is empowered to strike . . . Once she met R. Hanina ben Dosa and said to him,

Had there been no commendation from heaven, 'Take heed of R. Hanina ben Dosa . . .', I would have harmed you.

He said to her,

Since I am so highly esteemed in heaven, I decree that you shall never again pass through an inhabited place. (*bPes.* 112b)

Jesus, curing the sick and overpowering the forces of evil with the immediacy of the Galilean holy man, was seen as a dispenser of health, one of the greatest blessings expected at the end of time, when 'the blind man's eyes shall be opened and the ears of the deaf unstopped'; when 'the lame man shall leap like a deer, and the tongue of the dumb shout aloud' (Isa. 35.5–6).

But in this chain of cause and effect, linking, in the mind of the ancients, sickness to the devil, one more element remains, namely sin. Besides healing the flesh and exorcizing the mind, the holy man had one other task to perform: the forgiveness of sin. Here is the famous story of the paralytic brought to Jesus in Capernaum.

Four men were carrying him, but because of the crowd they could not get him near. So they opened up the roof over the place where Jesus was . . . and they lowered the stretcher on which the paralysed man was lying. When Jesus saw their faith, he said to the paralysed man,

My son, your sins are forgiven.

Now there were some lawyers sitting there and they thought to themselves.

Why does the fellow talk like this? This is blasphemy! Who but God alone can forgive sins?

Jesus knew in his own mind that this is what they were thinking, and said to them,

Why do you harbour thoughts like these? Is it easier to say to this paralysed man, 'Your sins are forgiven', or to say, 'Stand up, take your bed and walk'? But to convince you that the son of man has right on earth to forgive sins – he turned to the paralysed man –

I say to you, stand up, take your bed and go home!

And he got up, and at once took his stretcher and went out in full view of them all. (Mark 2.3–12)

'My son, your sins are forgiven' is of course not the language of experts in the law; but neither is it blasphemy. On the contrary, absolution from the guilt of wrong-doing appears to have been part and parcel of the charismatic style; this is well illustrated in an important Dead Sea Scrolls fragment, the Prayer of Nabonidus, which depicts a Jewish exorcist as having pardoned the Babylonian king's sins, thus curing him of his seven years' illness. In the somewhat elastic, but extraordinarily perceptive religious terminology of Jesus and the spiritual men of his age, 'to heal', 'to expel demons' and 'to forgive sins' were interchangeable synonyms. Indeed, the language and behaviour of Jesus is reminiscent of holy men of ages even earlier than his own, and it need cause little surprise to read in Matthew that he was known as 'the prophet Jesus from Nazareth in Galilee' (Matt. 21.11), and that his Galilean admirers believed he might be one of the biblical prophets, or Jeremiah, or Elijah *redivivus* (Matt. 16.14). In fact, it could be advanced that, if he modelled himself on anyone at all, it was precisely on Elijah and Elisha, as the following argument with the people of his home-town Nazareth, would seem to bear out:

> Jesus said,
> No doubt you will quote the proverb to me, 'Physician, heal yourself!' and say, 'We have heard of all your doings in Capernaum; do the same here, in your own home town.' I tell you this – he went on – no prophet is recognized in his own country. There were many widows in Israel, you may be sure, in Elijah's time . . . yet it was to none of these that Elijah was sent, but to a widow at Sarepta in the territory of Sidon. Again in the time of the prophet Elisha there were many lepers in Israel, and not one of them was healed, but only Naaman, the Syrian. (Luke 4.23–26)

Jesus was a Galilean Hasid: there, as I see it, lie his greatness, and also the germ of his tragedy. That he had his share of the notorious Galilean chauvinism would seem clear from the xenophobic statements attributed to him. As one review of *Jesus the Jew* puts it – a review written, interestingly enough, by the Gardening correspondent of the *Financial Times*! – 'Once he called us "dogs" and "swine" and he forbade the Twelve to proclaim the gospel to . . . Gentiles.'[7] But Jesus was also, and above all, an exemplary representative of the fresh and simple religiousness for which the Palestinian North was noted.

And it was in this respect that he cannot have been greatly loved by the Pharisees: in his lack of expertise, and perhaps even interest, in halakhic matters, common to Galileans in general; in his tolerance of deliberate neglect in regard to certain traditional – though not, it should be emphasized, biblical – customs by his followers; in his table-fellowship with publicans and whores; and last but not least, in the spiritual authority explicitly or implicitly presumed to underpin his charismatic activities, an authority impossible to check, as can be done when teachings are handed down from master to disciple. Not that there appears to have been any fundamental disagreement between Jesus and the Pharisees on any basic issue, but whereas Jesus, the preacher of *teshuvah*, of repentance, felt free rhetorically to overemphasize the ethical as compared with the ritual – like certain of the prophets before him – he perhaps could be criticized for not paying enough attention to those needs of society which are met by organized religion. As a matter of fact, this Pharisaic insistence on the necessity of faithfulness towards religious observances as well as of a high standard of ethics, has as it were been vindicated by a Christian *halakhah*, evolved over the centuries, that is scarcely less detailed and casuistical than our Talmudic legislation!

Nevertheless, the conflict between Jesus of Galilee and the Pharisees of his time would, in normal circumstances, merely have resembled the infighting of factions belonging to the same religious body, like that between Karaites and Rabbanites in the Middle Ages, or between the orthodox and progressive branches of Judaism in modern times.[8]

But in the first century circumstances were not normal. An eschatological and politico-religious fever was always close to the point of eruption, if it had not already exploded, and Galilee was a hotbed of nationalist ferment. Incidentally, there is no evidence, in my reading of the Gospels, that would point to any particular involvement by Jesus in the revolutionary affairs of the Zealots, though it is likely that some of his followers may have been committed to them and have longed to proclaim him as King Messiah destined to liberate his oppressed nation.

But for the representatives of the establishment – Herod Antipas in Galilee, and the chief priests and their council in Jerusalem – the prime unenviable task was to maintain law and order and thus avert a major catastrophe. In their eyes, revolutionary propaganda was not only against the law of the Roman provincial administration, but also murderously foolish, contrary to the national interest, and liable to expose to the vengeance of the invincible emperor not only those actively implicated, but countless thousands of their innocent compatriots. They had to be silenced one way or another, by persuasion or by force, before it was too late. As the high priest is reported to have said of Jesus – and it is immaterial whether he did so or not – 'It is more to your interest that one man should die for the people, than that the whole nation should be destroyed' (John 11.50). Such indeed must have been the attitude of mind of the establishment. Not only actual, but even potential leadership of a revolutionary movement called for alertness and vigilance. John the Baptist, who according to Josephus was 'a good man' and 'exhorted the Jews to live righteous lives', became suspect in Herod's eyes because of an 'eloquence' which might 'lead to some form of sedition . . . Herod decided therefore that it would be much better to strike first and be rid of him before his work led to an uprising'.[9] Jesus, I believe, was the victim of a similar preventative measure devised by the Sadducean rulers in the 'general interest'.

As Jesus hung dying on a Roman cross, under a *titulus* which read, Jesus of Nazareth, king of the Jews, he cried out with a loud voice:

Eloi eloi lema shevaqtani?
'My God, my God, why hast thou forsaken me?' (Mark 15.34)

Nothing, to my mind, epitomizes more sharply the tragedy of Jesus the Jew, misunderstood by friend and foe alike, than this perplexed cry from the cross. Nor was this the end of it. For throughout the centuries, as age followed age, Christians and Jews allowed it to continue and worsen. His adherents transformed this lover and worshipper of his Father in heaven into an object of worship himself, a god; and his own people, under the pressures of persecution at the hands of those adherents, mistakenly attributed to Jesus Christian beliefs and dogmas, many of which – I feel quite sure – would have filled this Galilean Hasid with stupefaction, anger and deepest grief.

I recognize that this sketchy portrait, and even the somewhat more detailed one given in my book, *Jesus the Jew*, does him – and you – less than justice. In particular, no biography of a teacher of the past can come alive if it is unaccompanied by a discussion of his essential message. As the Dean of Christ Church told me the other day in front of Thornton's bookshop in the Broad:

> My dear fellow, you are like an examination candidate who must answer several connected questions. So far you've only dealt with the first one: 'What kind of a Jew was Jesus?' You have advanced a theory. But I won't know whether it's true or not until you reveal your solution to the remaining parts of the puzzle.

Henry Chadwick was, of course, correct; *Jesus the Jew*, whether printed or spoken, is but the first part of a trilogy. I have the title for the second part: *The Gospel of Jesus the Jew*. But the rest has still to be written! The third will explore the metamorphosis of Jesus the Jew into the Christ of Christianity in the works of Paul, John and the rest of the New Testament writers. In the meanwhile I must accept that some of my readers will prefer to suspend judgement on my assessment of this remarkable man.

As I have already said, I began my search for the Jesus of history for its own sake, to prove that, by employing the right methods, something of the authentic image of the Master from Galilee can be recovered from the dark historical past. To my surprise and pleasure, however, at least one of my readers feels that the work may have some interesting side-effects. It has been said of *Jesus the Jew* by an anonymous reviewer that it

> poses a challenge to Christianity, though it may not be its primary purpose, or intended at all. The implied challenge is that, if Christians wish to return to the historical Jesus, they must also return, in some measure, to the Judaism in which he lived and moved and had his being.[10]

Rather less sure, but still encouraging, David Daube, perhaps the most influential Jewish voice on this subject, after assessing the book's contribution to the 'quest for the historical framework of Jesus's activity' and 'for his own concept of his vocation', goes on:

> Whether it will do much towards removing ill-will and distrust may be doubted. These attitudes are largely independent of scholarly data. Still with luck, it may do a little. The present climate gives some ground for hope.[11]

On the Christian side, reactions have been varied.

'Vermes's own "historian's reading of the Gospels" . . . is presented lucidly, persuasively and with humour' – writes William Horbury of Cambridge – 'but its cheerful elimination of *mysterium Christi* again and again raises the question whether the author is not neglecting evidence that cries out for historical interpretation.'[12]

A well-known English Jesuit, the late Father Thomas Corbishley, described *Jesus the Jew* as 'overcrowded' and its learning as 'oppressive'.[13] And one of his less prominent brethren finds, rather depressingly – in a review entitled 'Minus the Resurrection' – that this 'learned but tedious book' is a 'disappointment'.[14] An American Bible expert, reacting sharply to my comment that professional New Testament scholars often wear the blinkers of their trade, concludes his piece with the words: 'Jesus the Jew deserves better than this.'[15] A French lady, writing in an extreme right wing periodical, calls the book 'scandaleux et blasphématoire'.[16] On the other hand, the editor of a French theological quarterly ends his positive evaluation with an exclamation: 'Jésus ne sera plus le même pour moi après la lecture de (ce) livre.'[17]

In general, however, Christian academic opinion has been sympathetic yet not wholly convinced. As A. R. C. Leaney has put it in Oxford's own *Journal of Theological Studies*:

> The result is a valuable contribution to scholarship, but it is hard to assess exactly how successful it is.[18]

2

The Gospel of Jesus the Jew I:
A Historian's Reading of the Gospels[1]

Videtur quod non: such was the formula used by medieval theology in launching a debate. The schoolmen frequently initiated their discussions with arguments militating *against* their thesis.[2] In our case too, this *videtur quod non* – roughly, 'it would appear that such and such is *not*' – would seem most appropriate. Specifically, it would appear that the gospel of Jesus the Jew is *not* a suitable subject for historical enquiry.

The first, and on the face of it more reasonable, objection raised against pursuing such an undertaking is that a historical approach to the teaching of Jesus is unlikely to lead to any insight substantially new and worthwhile. A topic investigated and studied so intensely and constantly for some nineteen centuries must already have yielded everything accessible to the understanding.[3] If any further research is made, if it is sensible the outcome is likely to be commonplace; and if it is in any respect out of the way, its results cannot but be suspect.[4]

There is no theoretical answer to give to this, but the following considerations may be borne in mind by way of a preliminary defence. The bulk of New Testament research has been carried out by Christian theologians. In the present instance, it is conducted within a context of Jewish history, independent of later demands of creed and tradition, Christian or Jewish.[5] Again, contemporary New Testament study, unlike the broader theological scholarship of former centuries, views the pocket-book containing the sacred writings of Christianity as an autonomous object of study to which all other relevant ancillary material – i.e., the whole of Judaism and Hellenism – must be subservient.[6] It speaks of the *world* of the New Testament, to which Judaism and Hellenism furnish the *background*. Here, by contrast, Jesus and the gospels are regarded as parts and products of first century AD Palestinian Judaism. And since during the last three decades fresh archaeological and manuscript discoveries, as well as substantial progress in the reassessment of the classical sources of Judaism, have greatly improved our grasp of the society, culture and religion to which Jesus belonged, a new look at the gospels from this angle, by a Judaica specialist, should certainly add to what was known previously.[7] One other justification for my choice of subject is that a scholarly evaluation of the gospel of Jesus the Jew entails above all a balanced synthesis of the many known data; and here again, our new knowledge of the civilization into which Jesus was born opens up distinctly fresh possibilities.[8]

The second objection current among Gospel specialists may astonish the non-initiate. Arising from the acute pessimism of twentieth-century New Testament exegesis, it expresses with multiple variations a basic distrust of the interpreter's ability to establish the historicity of Gospel pronouncements, and in particular to trace to Jesus himself words placed on his lips by the evangelists. For many New Testament scholars, a historical exploration of Jesus' teaching is and must be essentially speculative.

On this point I am faced with a problem of presentation, for I have to deal with it in some detail and at the same time not lose the good-will and attention of the non-experts who read this book. I will do my best.

The key issue is the nature of the evidence supplied by the New Testament. In the old days, that is to say from the late first to the eighteenth century, people could speak without hesitation of 'the gospel truth'. It was inconceivable that anything in Matthew, Mark, Luke or John should be inaccurate or false; the veracity of the evangelists, in their story-telling and in their reports of Jesus' sayings, was guaranteed by heavenly warrant. Unlike Herodotus or Thucydides, Livy or Tacitus, the four narrators of the life of Christ bore the seal of God's approval. Indeed, for many, the evangelists were God's mouth-pieces; their Gospels were a divine dictation.[9]

The trouble is: we have not one gospel but four. And not only do the accounts given by these four represent four points of view; again and again they seem to vary in actual substance. The difference between the synoptics – Matthew, Mark and Luke – on the one hand, and John on the other, is particularly noticeable: two of the most glaring discrepancies are the duration of Jesus' ministry – given as one year in the Synoptics, with a single Passover, and two or three years in the Fourth Gospel – and the date of the crucifixion, which according to the synoptics followed the evening of the Passover supper, but according to John, preceded it.[10] Had the law commonly regulating the development of religious traditions been operative in the case of the Gospels, these divergences would have succumbed to the trend towards unification.[11] The same would have happened to them as to the four sources or traditions underlying the Pentateuch in the Hebrew Bible which, incorporated to form a single work, needed the brilliant scholarship of the nineteenth century before they were discovered. But although attempts made in the second century to merge all four Gospels into a single narrative known as the *Diatessaron* met with ephemeral success in Syria,[12] this *Four in One* failed in the long run to replace the separate original works. The principle of harmonization triumphed nevertheless. Discordances between the evangelists were carefully muted by means of an exegesis which took it for granted that the spokesmen of God could not possibly contradict one another. In the age of enlightenment and liberalism of the late eighteenth century, however, this attitude of mind was replaced by a spirit of criticism. Variants, and the concept of development in the Gospels, were no longer rejected in advanced scholarly circles, and from then on research concentrated on discovering the earliest, least evolved, and consequently most reliable of the differing accounts.[13] As you know, this turned out to be the Gospel of Mark. But since this slender volume includes a very limited amount of doctrinal matter, a separate source of sayings, one that had been used each in his own way by Matthew and Luke, was given the name of Q (short for the German Quelle = source) and proclaimed an additional document with a standing roughly equal to that of Mark.[14]

In other words, nineteenth-century New Testament scholarship, pursuing the old quest for 'gospel truth' with the help of critical tools, concluded that it can be found only in parts of the sources, and in a considerably reduced quantity.

With the turn of the twentieth century, the spirit of criticism gave way to one of scepticism. It began now to be argued by Christian New Testament experts, starting with Wilhelm Wrede, that not even Mark may be accepted as an unbiased reporter. His Gospel, too, is dominated by purposes of theology.[15] Its material is arranged to conform with doctrinal aims and is therefore not trustworthy as a historical framework.

Then, between the wars, any hope of recovering the historical Jesus apparently received its death blow, chiefly at the hands of Rudolf Bultmann, who categorically asserted the impossibility of reaching back to the teacher of Nazareth via the Gospels. These church documents, Bultmann said, afford no direct access to Jesus. Jesus was not a Christian; he was a Jew.[16] (The great Julius Wellhausen was of the same opinion.[17]) In an oft-quoted passage from his book, *Jesus*, published in 1926, Bultmann writes: 'I do indeed think that we can now know almost nothing concerning the life and personality of Jesus, since the early Christian sources show no interest in either.'[18] According to this leader of the school of form criticism, the Gospels represent, not the aims, aspirations and thought of Jesus, but doctrine to meet the spiritual needs of the primitive church, which actively participated in its formation. In particular, it is often alleged – though without much justification I think – that utterances in the name of the 'risen Lord' pronounced at liturgical gatherings by Christian 'prophets' – St Paul refers to such individuals a number of times[19] – are added by the evangelists to the sayings actually spoken by Jesus himself.

The task of the form critic is therefore to detect in the Gospel-accounts the discrete original literary units; to define their nature; to discover their *Sitz im Leben* (the particular church circumstances responsible for their formation); and to investigate, by comparing parallel attestations, the pre-history of the tradition, which may occasionally lead to the Palestinian church, or even to Jesus. In his classic *History of the Synoptic Tradition*, Bultmann devises a tentative method by means of which words or *logia* may, as he says, 'in a very few cases' be ascribed to Jesus with 'some measure of confidence'.[20]

The practical consequence of the impact of form criticism was to advise against, and even discredit, historical enquiry proper. Gone now were the days when serious New Testament exegetes could compose without scruple comprehensive presentations of the life and teaching of Jesus. The last characteristic example of this favoured genre was *L'évangile de Jésus-Christ* by the famous French Dominican, Marie-Joseph Lagrange, which was published in 1929. After Bultmann's *Jesus*, another thirty years were to pass before one of his pupils, Günther Bornkamm, could summon up courage to write his *Jesus of Nazareth*. Even so, Bornkamm's opening sentence, 'No one is any longer in a position to write a life of Jesus',[21] bears the stamp of *Formgeschichte*.

Gone, too, were the days of full expositions of Jesus' message. The British scholar, T. W. Manson, who never subscribed to form criticism, could still produce a major work of this kind in the thirties[22] but his 'old-fashioned' approach was superseded in influential German circles by New Testament theologies. Again, the original impetus came from Bultmann who, typically, dared to allot, out of a total of 620 pages in the 1965 fifth edition of his *Theologie des Neuen Testaments*[23] a mere thirty-four pages (thirty in the 1952 English translation) to the preaching of Jesus on the grounds that it is a *presupposition* of New Testament theology but does not actually belong to it![24]

It will seem from what has been said so far that in persisting in my search for Jesus' authentic religious thought I am running against the tide. But form criticism, for all that it has enriched New Testament study with profound insights and sophisticated analyses, contains some fundamental flaws. In fact, several of Bultmann's more recent followers have themselves recognized the fragility of his historical scepticism and tried to correct it.

But their improvements still leave much to be desired. The system's chief weakness lies, I think, in the absence among its developers and practitioners of any *real* familiarity with the literature, culture, religion and above all spirit, of the post-biblical Judaism from which Jesus and his first disciples sprang. Instead, it is in the Hellenistic world of early Christianity that Bultmann and his pupils are at home.

I need hardly say that I am not in total disagreement with present-day New Testament scholarship, with form criticism, tradition criticism,[25] redaction criticism[26] and the rest. I concede that none of the evangelists were professional historians, not even the Synoptists. I also grant that each had his own theological vantage-point and told his story with a specific end in view. But a theological interest is no more incompatible with a concern for history than is a political or philosophical conviction. As long as this interest is recognized, and as long as the interpreter realizes that it is likely to affect the whole work under scrutiny, he ought with a minimum of critical skill to be able to make allowance for it. In this connection, the fact that we have *three* theologically motivated accounts, and not just *one*, is in a sense fortunate and helpful because those elements which are common to them all are thus easily detectable and the historian is enabled to exercise his judgement on these basic data. Where the life-story of Jesus is concerned, for instance, no serious scholar of today would query the main threads of the narrative: Jesus entered into his public ministry during the mission of repentance preached by John the Baptist; he enjoyed a greater measure of success in Galilee; he clashed with the authorities in Jerusalem; he died there on a cross; and all this took place during the middle years of the prefecture of Pontius Pilate, who governed Judaea between AD 26 and 36.[27]

On the other hand, one of the chief theories of the form critics calls for serious reflection. Is it really, as they assert, self-evident that the composition of the Gospels is due entirely to the didactic-theological requirements of the primitive church? If the evangelists were primarily preoccupied with teaching Christian doctrine, how are we to explain their choice of *biography* as their medium? They cannot have been influenced by tradition; no Jewish convention exists that the sayings of the sages should be transmitted in this way. Anecdotes conveying them abound in rabbinic literature, but nothing by way of any similar biography has been handed down and there is no reason to imagine that one ever existed. The authors of the Qumran scrolls record no life-story of the Teacher of Righteousness, or of any other member of the sect for that matter. They do not even disclose the real names of people, but allude to them by means of cryptograms. So if the church opted for that particular literary form to expound its message, we have to ask ourselves what it can have hoped to gain from it. Liveliness and colour? But to amplify the account of Jesus' life by introducing Palestinian ideas and customs, and by including Semitic linguistic peculiarities and oriental realia of all sorts, will have rendered it largely incomprehensible to non-Jewish Hellenistic readers and have demanded continuous interpretative digressions bound to have been catechetically harmful and counter-productive. Other first-century Christian teachers, in any case – Paul, James or the author of the first church manual, the *Didache* or Doctrine of the Twelve Apostles – saw no advantage in a life-story as the vehicle of theological doctrine, moral exhortation, and disciplinary of liturgical rules, but like the Essenes and the Palestinian rabbis chose to communicate their religious thoughts directly.[28]

Again, if the raison d'être of the Gospels was to provide for the doctrinal needs of the churches, how are we to understand the insertion into them of sayings of Jesus, and attitudes of mind, which actually conflict with essential teachings of primitive Christianity? The evangelists note that Jesus made disparaging remarks about Gentiles.[29] They observe that he was apparently unwilling to allow his followers to announce him as the awaited Messiah.[30] Neither of these matters can have greatly suited the first promulgators of the gospels, whose main task was to convince non-Jews of the truth that 'Jesus is the Christ' (John 20.31; cf. Acts 2.36).

It is consequently difficult to avoid concluding that if the evangelists chose to tell the story of Jesus' life, it was because, whatever else they may have intended, they wished also to recount history, however unprofessionally. And if they included circumstances which were doctrinally embarrassing, it was because they were genuinely believed to be part of the narrative. In that case, Bultmann's dictum about the impossibility of knowing anything about Jesus or his personality, 'because the early Christian sources show no interest in either',[31] becomes a plain misjudgment.

If the extreme, but highly influential, wing of contemporary New Testament criticism is distinguished by its almost all-inclusive historical scepticism, it must in fairness be recognized that when German theorizing marches alongside British (and occasionally American) common sense, the outcome is compromise. In a work entitled *Rediscovering the Teaching of Jesus*, the late Norman Perrin,[32] though a whole-hearted form critic, advanced various criteria by which a scholar may determine whether a Gospel saying or parable is authentic. The first is the principle of *dissimilarity*. If a teaching has no parallel in Judaism or in the primitive church, it most probably originates in Jesus. The second is *coherence*. Material from the earliest layers of gospel tradition may be classified as genuine if it is consistent with a doctrine already established as authentic through the principle of dissimilarity. A third and auxiliary criterion is *multiple attestation*. The discovery of a doctrinal motif in more than one source (e.g., Mark and Q), as well as in a variety of literary contexts (sayings, parables, stories, proclamations, etc.), postulates authenticity.[33] In a later publication Perrin added a fourth principle to these three: *linguistic suitability*.[34] For a saying surviving in a Greek gospel to be associated with Jesus, who did not teach in Greek, it must be susceptible to a Semitic rendering.

Perrin's criteria – which are shared by a number of scholars all over the world – are valid as long as they are accompanied by *caveats*. Dissimilarity is certainly significant; but if it implies an entire absence of antecedents, it will be rarely found. Originality in the field of religion mostly consists in giving a new twist, lending a fresh understanding, to ideas that are in themselves age-old. Also, it should be remembered that today's originality may appear less striking tomorrow, as has been amply shown by the Dead Sea discoveries. Above all, care must be taken never to base an assertion of uniqueness on incomplete knowledge and information. This is a constant danger where New Testament scholars – the majority – have no direct independent access to the vast Hebrew and Aramaic sources of post-biblical Judaism. Their dependence on secondary sources is fraught with hazard.[35] The principle of coherence is self-explanatory. Its specific gravity is less than that of dissimilarity; at the same time it is applicable to a much broader range of cases. Multiple attestation is an external literary manifestation of consistency. For instance, the fact that Jesus' love and kindness towards the outcasts of Jewish society appears in stories, sayings, parables etc., is a safe indication of valid historical evidence.[36] As for linguistic suitability, I would refer in this connection to the second half of *Jesus the Jew*, where Jesus' various titles of prophet, lord, messiah, son of man and son of God, are subjected to a thorough analysis within the appropriate Aramaic-Hebrew philological context with a view to discovering their historical significance.[37] Interestingly, this often turns out to be very different from the meaning attached to the terms by Christian tradition.[38] The most striking finding is that the celebrated epithet 'son of man', on which so much modern christological speculation has been based, does not in fact represent an established concept in post-biblical Judaism and cannot be applied as a title in Aramaic. It cannot, therefore, be accredited to Jesus as such.[39]

To these criteria devised by New Testament exegetes who are as a general rule scholars and churchmen, the independent historian is able to add several of his own. When he deals, for example, with contradictions in the Gospels, he will not try to reconcile them. Bearing in mind that the brevity of Jesus' career will have allowed him no time for his ideas to evolve, it will seem no more than sensible to conclude that if one saying ascribed to Jesus appears to be sharply at variance with another, they cannot both be authentic.[40] His xenophobic utterances and his institution of an apostolic mission to the nations cannot both be accepted as genuine.[41] Nor for that matter can the sympathy with the tax-collector evident in, 'The tax-collectors and the harlots go into the kingdom of God before you' (Matt. 21.31), be judged to tally with the contempt for tax-collectors and Gentiles apparent in the advice, 'If (your brother) refuses to listen even to the church, let him be to you as a Gentile and a tax-collector' (Matt. 8.17). The same man, in such a brief period of teaching, cannot have been responsible for both these remarks.

Most importantly, no objective and critical evaluation of the Gospels can overlook the impact of Jesus' tragic fate on the first chroniclers of his story and on the evangelists themselves. They present him as God's emissary, as God's son, sent to usher in the kingdom of God; yet beyond a tiny area of rural Palestine his word went largely unheeded. From the Judaean leaders he encountered nothing but hostility. And when he was finally brought before the Roman governor and sentenced to die by crucifixion, even his own deserted him, even, so he felt, his heavenly Father himself. '*Eloi*', he cried, '*Eloi, lema shevaqtani?*', 'My God, my God, why have you forsaken me?'[42] Could a failure such as this ever be recognized as the ultimate spiritual teacher, the elect of heaven, lord and Messiah? Without eliminating the scandal of the cross, clearly no.[43] The historian's eye will therefore inevitably look for the hand of early Christian apologists in those parts of the story which first imply, and subsequently try to prove, that contrary to common Jewish expectation,[44] the violent death of the Messiah was divinely fore-ordained. Furthermore, he will apply, *pace* C. H. Dodd, the great British New Testament specialist, the same treatment to the tales of the resurrection transforming disaster into triumph.[45] In Mark, the earliest of the Gospels, he will find merely a simple insinuation of a happy ending, and he will notice that subsequently this implication becomes more and more fully elaborated by the later evangelists. He will observe, moreover, that on this topic also the Gospels display intrinsic contradictions.[46] On the one hand, they assert that Jesus repeatedly foretold his resurrection on the third day following his death. On the other, they describe the total disarray of the apostles and disciples immediately after the crucifixion and their startled perplexity at hearing that Jesus had risen from the grave. The evangelists themselves, in fact, testify to a progressive development, refinement and reinforcement of the evidence concerning the resurrection. In the first version it is based on hearsay: the report is brought by untrustworthy female witnesses whose words strike the apostles as 'an idle tale' in which they do not believe.[47] In the next version the news is confirmed by the trustworthy Peter, or by Peter and another disciple (Luke, John). Elaborated still further, the resurrection testimony becomes evidence at first hand: apparitions of the risen Jesus are seen by the eleven apostles either in Jerusalem (Luke) or on a Galilean mountain (Matt.), and subsequently (Paul) by a crowd of over five hundred brethren, many of whom are said by the apostle to be still alive (in faraway Galilee?) in the mid-fifties of the first century, at the time of writing his first letter to the Corinthians (I Cor. 15.6).

Gospel references to the *parousia*,[48] Christ's glorious return, have also to be viewed in the setting of a career terminating in seeming humiliation and ignominy. The resurrection argument is addressed to believers only, to initiates. There is no suggestion in the New Testament that the risen Jesus was encountered by outsiders. To tell the truth, not even the apostles and disciples seem to have recognized the person who joined them on the road to Emmaus and who entered the room where they were hiding.[49] The majestic second coming, by contrast, was to be the vindication and triumph of Jesus in the eyes of the whole world, the whole of mankind (Matt. 25.31–32). In its earliest stage, this *parousia* tradition expects the day of the Lord to come very soon, even during the lifetime of Jesus' own generation; members of the church in Thessalonica have to be advised to keep strict control of their enthusiasm.[50] But only a little later, Christians are being encouraged to be watchful; the bridegroom's coming may be delayed until midnight (Matt. 25.6; cf. Luke 17.34). And a little later still, they are exhorted to cultivate the great virtue of endurance (II Peter 3). Then, with the *parousia* still not realized the apocalyptic momentum flags, and soon after the completion of the New Testament, the end-time, the *eschaton*, is deferred *sine die*, relegated to the remotest future.[51]

Although I myself think it incompatible with Jesus' essential religious outlook, it can doubtless be argued that the *parousia* speculation originated in his own eschatological and apocalyptic teaching rather than in later Christian apologetics.[52] The apologetic nature of the *parousia* expectation is moreover strongly supported by the eschatology of the Dead Sea Scrolls. In Essenism, the consecutive postponements of the day of the Lord are also attended by exhortations to patience and perseverance. The Habakkuk Commentary reads: 'The final age shall be prolonged and shall exceed all that the Prophets have said; for the mysteries of God are astounding. *If it tarries, wait for it, for it shall surely come and shall not be late* (Hab. 2.3). Interpreted, this concerns the men of truth who keep the Law, whose hands shall not slacken in the service of truth when the final age is prolonged. For all the ages of God reach their appointed end as He determines for them in the mysteries of His wisdom.'[53]

In sum, if we accept that in reporting the life and message of Jesus, the intention of the evangelists was, to some extent at least, to recount history, and if it seems reasonable to assume that the resurrection and *parousia* material is attributable to the doctrinal and apologetic needs of the early church, it becomes as clear *a posteriori* as it has been *a priori* that our understanding of the real Jesus must derive basically from an analysis of the synoptic data relating to his actual ministry and teaching that are unaffected by accretions deriving from the creative imagination of nascent Christianity.[54]

The main force of the New Testament representation of the 'Christ-event' (*Christusereignis*) – to use the jargon of contemporary theologians – still embryonic in the synoptic gospels but fully developed in the letters of Paul, is directed towards providing a history of salvation. It sets out to announce the redemptive function and effect of the suffering, death and resurrection of Jesus. In the Pauline writings, the ordinary details of Jesus' life and teaching receive negligible attention compared with the stress laid on the ultimate purpose of his mission. Indeed, it is sometimes held that since all the New Testament writers without exception stand on a central theological platform, so that the 'dogmatic' approach dominates the Jesus story at every level of its transmission, it is unscholarly to disregard it and to attempt to reach behind the screen of the primitive Christian 'myth'. Anyway, it is asked, is it likely that every single one of the first-century spokesmen misrepresented most of the major issues, and that the twentieth-century historian, after a lapse of some nineteen hundred years, is able to correct their tendentious distortions and draw a more reliable outline of the happenings of their times, offer a more authentic version of a message nearly two thousand years old?

The answer is that on the face of it success would appear unlikely. But it is not impossible. And methodologically, the endeavour is perfectly legitimate. The very fact that the synoptic portrait of Jesus as a person and the synoptic character of his teaching are so manifestly and radically at variance with the figure and message found in the theological canvas of Paul itself guarantees that, notwithstanding all the redactional and editorial manipulation carried out by the primitive church and the evangelists, a concrete basis exists on which to reconstruct history. In addition, the critical student of the gospels will be aware of the cultural cataclysms which took place during Christianity's earliest period. The civilization to which Jesus and those who heard and followed him belonged was Jewish; their provenance and province was Palestinian-Galilean; their language was Aramaic-Hebrew. From the middle of the first century onwards, by contrast, Christianity was transplanted and took root in Graeco-Roman soil, in a Graeco-Hellenistic civilization.[55]

In parenthesis, I am of course acquainted with the recent tendency in New Testament scholarship to seek to efface the differences between Judaism and Hellenism by blurring the frontiers dividing them. But I am firmly convinced of the untenability of Martin Hengel's statement that from 'the middle of the third century BC *all Judaism* must really be designated "Hellenistic Judaism"', and that 'the differentiation between "Palestinian" and "Hellenistic" . . . proves no longer adequate'.[56] Fergus Millar, one of our leading ancient historians, is fully justified in asserting that no reader of inter-testamental Jewish literature, and of the Dead Sea Scrolls in particular, 'will be readily disposed to assent without severe qualifications to the proposition that Palestinian Judaism was as Hellenistic as that of the Diaspora'. 'On the contrary,' he adds, 'what we should emphasize is the uniqueness of the phenomenon of an original and varied non-Greek literary activity developing in a small area only a few miles from the Mediterranean coast.'[57]

Returning to the upheaval caused by the migration of Christianity from a Jewish milieu to pagan Syria, Asia Minor, Egypt, Greece and Rome – there can be little doubt that if in one sense some continuity persisted, in another, the uprooting was so thorough that as a source for the historical understanding of Jesus of Nazareth, the reliability of the Gentile church, together with all the literature composed especially for it, can be ruled out.[58] In many respects, the Hebrew Bible, the Apocrypha, the Pseudepigrapha, the Qumran writings, and the enormous body of rabbinic literature, are better equipped to illumine the original significance of words and deeds recorded in the Gospels.[59]

Another historical consideration remains, involving the question of why the Judaeo-Christians, the first of Jesus' followers, withdrew so relatively fast from the main body of the church. Rarely confronted, this problem is nevertheless of methodological importance because the most likely reason was that the Ebionites became convinced that they were witnessing in the Hellenistic communities a fatal misrepresentation of Jesus, a betrayal of his ideals, and their replacement by alien concepts and aspirations.[60]

Dealing now with a preliminary issue of a different kind – nobody doubts that the Jesus of history was a teacher, but to understand his teaching function properly, together with the lesson itself, we need to consider them against the backcloth of his other activities, in the context of his ministry as a whole. As well as a teacher, Jesus was a physician of the body and the mind. Curing physical ills and disabilities and 'exorcizing' sick spirits, ministering to the diseased in the name of God, his place was in that stream of Judaism inherited from the prophets and exemplified by such figures as Elijah and Elisha which I have termed 'charismatic'.[61] Here, in a genre of popular piety which has endured for centuries, the hero is neither priest nor sage but the *ish ha-elohim*, the man of God. In his excellent paper, 'Popular Religion in Ancient Israel', J. B. Segal writes: 'The "man of God" performed miracles – not grandiose affairs, but acts within the context of everyday life that the people could understand . . . In times of famine he assured the return of food in plenty . . . A small quantity of grain would suffice to feed . . . a hundred men. Elisha not only healed the great Naaman from leprosy, but restored from death a small child. And it was when Elijah had resuscitated her son that the widow of Zarephat knew that he was a "man of God".'[62]

In an age and society in which the combination of sanctity and the miraculous was considered normal, Jesus' talents and activities fitted the image of the holy man. Authority, as in the era of the prophets, frowned on charismatic acts as potential or actual threats to religious order, but it could usually do little to stop them because of the high esteem in which the man of God was held. The rabbis themselves were ambivalent about them. The various manifestations of the miraculous in the Bible could hardly be ignored, and the many *obiter dicta* in Talmud and Midrash demonstrate that even in post-biblical times supernatural occurrences were still recognized. But among the learned, their importance was played down.[63] The childlike confidence of the 'men of deed', the *anshe ma'aseh*, offended the conventional standards of many of the sages.[64]

That Jesus was a renowned exorcist is well attested in the Synoptic Gospels, though this function of his ministry goes unmentioned in the rest of the New Testament. Inheriting the inter-testamental notion of a world ruled by spirits of light and darkness, he rejected the opinion of apocalyptic circles that in the struggle against evil, human beings have only to act as insignificant aids to a heavenly host of angels, powers and dominations. He injected reality into the fight against the devil. When nervous and mental disorders were attributed to demonic possession, he cured them by himself overcoming the evil spirits believed to be inhabiting the minds of the sufferers. And he mended the bodies of men and women sure that illness is the result of sin by loosening Satan's grip on them with a declaration of forgiveness.[65] The same understanding of healing, but divested of its eschatological associations, and without any mention of a mediator, survives in the later Talmudic saying: 'No sick man shall recover from his illness until all his sins have been pardoned' (*bNed.* 41a). But the principal distinguishing feature of Jesus' activity as exorcist and healer was his assumption that his work heralded the coming of the kingdom.[66]

'A prophet mighty in deed and word' (Luke 24.19), is how Jesus is depicted in the Gospels; and in the Greek phraseology of Josephus' renowned *Testimonium Flavianum* the partial authenticity of which is increasingly recognized, as a 'wise man' famous for his *paradoxa erga*, his 'marvellous deeds'.[67] In this guise, as one who converted into reality his convictions and beliefs, Jesus appears to represent a Jewish piety more typical of rural Galilee than of the sophisticated Judaism of the south, and of Jerusalem in particular.[68] I am not alone in emphasizing this. In the paper already referred to, Professor Segal comments: 'It should be remarked that, like Elijah and Elisha, Jesus came from northern Palestine . . . Perhaps . . . most significant is the bond of sympathy between the womenfolk and Jesus, reminiscent of that between women and the "man of God" in North Israel.'[69]

Jesus the teacher cannot properly be understood without taking into simultaneous account Jesus the man of God, Jesus the holy man of Galilee, Jesus the *Hasid*. With this firm statement, I realize that I expose myself to the charge, actually voiced by Seán Freyne in a recent monograph, of partially prejudging the issue.[70] I assure him, and those among you who may share his concern, that I have been watching this carefully, but have never noticed any incompatibility between the *Hasid*-concept and Jesus' teaching. But I am also sure that if I had neglected to bring out this aspect of his character and ministry, Professor Freyne, or someone else, would have been quick to point out that the social and religious setting of the doctrinal message of Jesus the Jew was missing from the synthesis.

By now, I trust that I have made plain the nature and difficulty of the task facing the historian in search of Jesus' gospel, and the various ways in which his approach differs from that of the theologian. I will aim at determining the principal features and motives of his preaching, his thought rather than his specific words. Once the real qualities of his vision of God are identified – and this will be the purpose of the next chapter – we shall be able to reconstruct the spiritual aspirations which that vision inspired. We shall in other words come closer to grasping the piety taught and practised by him. In the third chapter on this theme of 'the Gospel of Jesus the Jew' I shall try to express my understanding of the piety characteristic of Jesus and to compare it with Christian religion as we know it.

3

The Gospel of Jesus the Jew II:
The Father and His Kingdom

In addition to his ministry as healer and exorcist, Jesus also taught.[1] Disciples, sympathizers and even passers-by regularly address him as teacher or master, *rabbi* or *rabbuni* in Aramaic, rendered as *didaskale* or *epistata* in Greek.[2] But what kind of teacher was he? The Semitic title might suggest that he was regarded as a 'scribe',[3] the contemporary equivalent of what later became the office of 'rabbi'. No less an authority than Bultmann categorically asserts that this was so. Jesus, he maintains, 'actually lives as a Jewish rabbi. As such he takes his place as a teacher in the synagogue. As such he gathers around him a circle of pupils. As such he disputes over questions of the Law . . . He disputes along the same lines as Jewish rabbis, uses the same methods of argument, the same turns of speech.'[4]

As so often happens, Bultmann's view has been taken up and repeated so frequently that it has come to be accepted as the established truth. But it is in fact somewhat misleading. The title of rabbi does not seem to have acquired by Jesus' lifetime the meaning attached to it in later ages of a fully trained exponent of scripture and tradition. None of his predecessors or contemporaries, not even the great Hillel or Shammai, or the elder Gamaliel, are referred to as rabbi in the Mishnah or the Talmud.[5] *Rabbi*, signifying literally 'my great man', must be taken here in its broader sense, without prejudging the type and style of either the teacher or his teaching.

On the other hand, since the evangelists so often depict Jesus involved in scholarly controversy and exegetical debate[6] with Pharisees, Sadducees, and lawyers, should we not assume that he too belonged to the intellectual élite, and as he always wins the argument, that he was more learned and possessed greater expertise than his opponents? Perhaps. But again, perhaps not, for our knowledge – which although admittedly imperfect is knowledge all the same – of Galilean culture of the late Second Temple era, and the New Testament evidence itself, support to some considerable extent the opinion that Jesus was an amateur in the field.[7] In the first place, although it was normally the speciality of the Pharisaic scribes to expound and interpret the Bible, not only is there no mention in the gospels of Jesus belonging to their ranks; neither Josephus nor rabbinic literature indicate any noticeable Pharisee presence or impact in Galilee at all prior to AD 70.[8] The village scribes[9] whom Jesus met regularly were men able to draw up contracts, marriage settlements, bills of divorce, and to teach children in the schools, but are not to be confused with the luminaries of Jerusalem Pharisaism. Also, there is no hint in the New Testament of Jesus having received any specialized training – not to mention the fact that rabbinic sources go out of their way to describe the Galileans as being in any case not conspicuous for their erudition.[10]

Moreover, reflecting on the doctrinal sections of the Gospels, particularly the bulk of the literary forms in which Jesus' teaching is expressed – words of wisdom, prophetic warnings, and above all parables – we are bound to notice that they demand no skill in Bible interpretation proper, or particular familiarity with the intricacies of Jewish law.[11] More positively, all three Synoptic evangelists assert at the outset of his preaching career that his style *differed* from that of the scribes. Their prime concern was to invest all religious doctrine with the sanction of tradition as being part of a strictly defined chain of transmission originating – in fact, or by means of exegetical ingenuity – in scripture, and preferably in the Pentateuch.[12] Jesus, by contrast, is said to have taught with *exousia*, with authority, without feeling the need for a formal justification of his words.[13] Some of the most authentic of the controversies in which he was involved, such as the discussion whether his powers of exorcism derived from Beelzebub or 'the finger of God', and another on the true cause of defilement, include no scriptural proof-texts at all.[14]

The proposal advanced by the form critics that many of the scholastic debates and arguments between Jesus and the Pharisees should be post-dated and identified as exchanges between the leaders of the Jerusalem church, the 'Judaizing' circles of Palestinian Christianity, and their Pharisee opponents, appears in consequence very persuasive.[15] Jesus was a charismatic holy man, a Hasid, not only as an exorcist but also as a teacher. He did not sit in a schoolhouse[16] reading and interpreting Holy Writ, or analysing and reconstructing the tradition of the elders. His existence was rather that of an itinerant preacher and healer.[17] And such was the force of his personality that those whom he treated, and to whom he spoke, sensed that his lessons possessed great driving-force and that they were listening to a man of God, a 'prophet mighty in deed and word before God and the people' (Luke 24.19), to repeat the quotation cited in the previous chapter.

Jewish religious teachers did not excel in creating doctrinal systems.[18] The prophets, sages and rabbis associated God with the reality which they knew. They did not go in for abstract speculation. Jesus was cast in the same mould. Analysis of the divine nature and of the divine mysteries was not for him. Not for him was God a transcendent idea, an eternal and boundless absolute, an *ens per se*. God was thought of, and spoken of, by him, not in philosophical or theological terms, but in existential language.

For Jesus, God was King and Father: implicitly King and explicitly Father, both divine forms inherited from scripture. Whether the famous synagogal prayer beginning, 'Our Father, our King', *avinu malkenu*,[19] already existed in the first decades of the Christian era, is uncertain. The Talmud ascribes it to Rabbi Akiba in the early second century (*b.Taan.* 25b), but the phrase itself is included in one of the benedictions preceding the recitation of the *Shema'*, 'Hear O Israel, the Lord our God, the Lord is one!', and according to some liturgical experts may go back to the days of the Temple.[20] These two notions of God as King and Father must in any case have been widely current in Jesus' time.

Let us think first about king and kingdom. Jesus' teaching on the kingdom of God is generally thought to be the heart of his doctrine. To quote a recent writer, 'Jesus' teaching was focused . . . upon what he referred to again and again as the reign of God'.[21] For another modern scholar the kingdom of God is 'the central aspect of the teaching of Jesus . . . All else in his message and ministry serves a function in relation to that proclamation and derives its meaning from it.'[22]

The concept of the kingdom of God has a long history reaching from rabbinic and inter-testamental literature back to the Old Testament. To determine Jesus' precise understanding of it, we must therefore compare the gospel usage with the rest of the Jewish evidence. A number of modern and easily accessible studies of the subject are available,[23] so I will not enter here into the history of the idea but limit myself to outlining the four ways in which it is formulated.[24]

The feature common to them all is that the kingdom of God relates to God's sovereignty itself rather than to the realm over which he governs. When the Jewish nation was a monarchy, divine sovereignty was the counterpart of earthly kingship. The king was designated 'son of God', his representative on earth. Israel believed that it enjoyed a privileged position in the economy of providence and salvation and constituted the *de facto* province over which God was ruler. But it is believed also that his *de jure* kingdom extended far beyond Israel's boundaries and that one day a powerful king would subjugate the wicked Gentiles and compel them to pay homage to the one true God. The psalms are full of such themes. God promises power and conquest to the king of Israel.

Ask of me, and I will make the nations your heritage,
and the ends of the earth your possession . . .
Now, therefore, O kings, be wise . . .
Serve the Lord with fear. (Ps. 2.8–11)

Elsewhere, the divine king is portrayed as a source of awe and dread to the Gentiles.

The Lord reigns; let the people tremble! . . .
The Lord is great . . . over all the peoples.
Let them praise thy great and terrible name! (Ps. 99.1–3)

With its loss of independence in the sixth century BC, Israel looked to a new David to re-establish God's visible and institutional rule over Jews liberated from the foreign empires, and to impose this rule over mankind as a whole. Thus biblical messianism came into being, increasing in strength with the passage of the centuries to reach its apogee during the inter-testamental era. The most powerful expression of royal messianism appears in one of the Psalms of Solomon from the middle of the first pre-Christian century, in the early days of the Roman occupation of Palestine, conquered in 63 BC by Pompey.[25]

Behold, O Lord, and raise up unto them their king, the son of David . . .
And that he may purge Jerusalem from nations
that trample her down to destruction . . .
And he shall have the heathen nations to serve him . . .[26]

The same figure of a victorious and holy king appears in a Qumran composition known as the Benediction of the Prince of the Congregation, a sectarian title for the royal Messiah.[27] It is also mentioned in the synagogal prayer par excellence, the *tefillah*, which has been in daily use since the first century AD, if not earlier:[28]

Cause the shoot of David to shoot forth quickly,
and raise up his horn by thy salvation.[29]

In addition to the notions of king and Messiah, a third concept emerged in Jewish apocalyptic milieux during the same intertestamental period,[30] namely that the kingdom of God was to ensue from the victory on earth of heavenly angelic armies over the hosts of Satan. Israel's final glorious triumph was to be the corollary in this world of God's total dominion over the world of the spirits. Such a kingdom was of course not to be built. It was to irrupt into the world here below, annihilate it, and set itself up in a new heaven on a new earth. The Dead Sea Scroll's Community Rule and War Rule afford a perfect insight into the ideology of the extremist dreamers who looked forward to a kingdom of this kind. For the members of the Qumran sect, the universe was divided into the dominion of the Prince of Light at the head of the spirits of truth and the just among mankind, and that of the Angel of Darkness leading the spirits of iniquity and the wicked among mankind.[31] Their struggle would be without end because the spiritual hosts would equal each other in strength.[32] But the 'great hand of God' was to intervene and the stalemate then be broken.[33] Victory was to fall to Michael the archangel in the realm of the spirits, and Israel was to achieve dominion over 'all flesh'.[34] Apocalyptic visions of this type may or may not include a messianic figure, but even when they do, he is, like Qumran's Prince of the Congregation, a shadowy, and on the whole secondary and unimportant, character.

The fourth concept of the kingdom is quite different, with no associations whatever with violence or war. It was largely an exilic and post-exilic phenomenon, attested already by Deutero- and Trito-Isaiah in the second half of the sixth century BC. The pagans, suddenly realizing that Israel's God is the only Saviour, were all to flock to Jerusalem to offer worship to him and submission to his people.

> The nations shall come to your light . . .
> The wealth of the nations shall come to you . . .
> They shall bring gold and frankincense
> And shall proclaim the praise of the Lord . . . (Isa. 60.1–6).

A pure and sanctified Israel was to draw the Gentiles to God. The manifestation of God's sovereignty over his own was to serve as a magnet to the rest.

The recognition of this sovereignty was viewed by the rabbis of the post-biblical era as manifested through personal obedience to God's Law, i.e., through the acceptance of 'the yoke of the Torah' (*mAb.* 3.5) described also as 'the yoke of the Kingdom of Heaven'. Listing the various uses of the phrase in his renowned monograph, *Die Worte Jesu*,[35] the great Aramaic scholar, Gustaf Dalman, shows that according to rabbinic exegesis of Leviticus 20.26, the assumption of this yoke by the Israelites demands that they should set themselves apart from wrongdoing.[36] The link between submission to God's supreme authority[37] and obedience to the divine precepts is asserted in the Mishnah in connection with the *Shema*ʻ, Judaism's confession of belief in God and his unity: 'A man should take upon himself first the yoke of the kingdom of heaven and thereafter the yoke of the commandments'.[38] Nevertheless, the Bible's concept of the nations' acknowledgment of God's rule coincides with rabbinic thought when it suggests that the Gentile convert, the proselyte, is one who has taken on himself the yoke of the kingdom of heaven.[39]

Now how does Jesus' view of the kingdom of God relate to those already current? The first, which in its time was an actual political-religious reality, would obviously have been irrelevant to him. Throughout his adult life, Judaea was administered directly by Rome, and his own Galilee was governed by a Herodian prince. As far as the second idea is concerned, that of the King-Messiah, there is little evidence in the Gospels of a kingdom of God to be established by force. There was no plan for Jesus to reconquer Jerusalem, or any indication that he intended to challenge the power even of Herod, let alone that of the emperor of Rome.[40] This leaves us with the apocalyptic imagery on the one hand, and on the other, the prophetic and rabbinic conception of a quiet and willing submission to the yoke of God the King.

When the Gospel teaching of the kingdom is considered in its entirety – or more exactly, with the omission of the Matthean passage concerning the last judgement, which in its present form is bound to be secondary[41] – one feature stands out: Jesus' representation of it includes little that is specifically royal. Some parables introduce a monarch as the central figure, but they are few and belong uniquely to the style of Matthew. Thus, 'The kingdom of heaven may be compared to a king who wished to settle accounts with his servants' (Matt. 18.23). And, 'the kingdom of heaven may be compared to a king who gave a marriage feast for his son' (Matt. 22.1). But in neither case is royalty an essential element. The quasi-parallel to this parable in Luke speaks simply of 'a certain man', *anthrōpos tis*, described later more precisely as the 'landowner', *oikodespotēs*, which is intended in its turn to correspond to the Hebrew, *ba'al ha-bayith* (Matt. 14.16, 21). And in the story of the servants required to justify their handling of money entrusted to them, 'king' in Matthew 18 is replaced in Matthew 25.19 by 'master', and in Luke 19.12 by 'nobleman'. Even more interesting, whereas in a Talmudic parable it is a king who hires workers for his vineyard,[42] in the gospel it is once more a landowner: 'For the kingdom of heaven is like a landowner who went out early in the morning to hire labourers for his vineyard' (Matt. 20.1).

In the same way that Jesus, by practising and thereby sanctioning the powers of exorcism and healing, tended to locate in this world the fight of good against evil instead of in a mythical arena outside the world,[43] so he also transforms into reality the 'unreal' ingredients of the inherited imagery of the kingdom. The royal theme belongs to this category. In the kingdom as he envisages it there are no thrones, no courtiers, no heavenly choirs, no clashing hosts with chariots, swords or javelins. In their place we encounter the landscapes, worktools and inhabitants of the Galilean country and its lakeside life. The kingdom of heaven is like a field.[44] The kingdom is like a vineyard in which day-labourers are treated fairly and even generously by their employer.[45] The kingdom is like a tiny seed of mustard which grows into a plant so large that birds are able to nest in its branches.[46] Or again, Jesus associates the kingdom with the fish, the net, the catch (Matt. 13.47ff.) and with the cook who adds leaven to her flour to make dough for her bread (Matt. 13.33; Luke 13.20–21). The kingdom of heaven belongs to the little children, and to those who resemble them, the humble and the trusting (Matt. 18.3–4; Mark 10.13ff. par.). It belongs to the poor; the rich will find it more difficult to enter than the camel to pass through a needle's eye, i.e. they will find it impossible.[47]

But when was this kingdom of Jesus' parables to come about? Fairly soon, as contemporary apocalyptics thought? Very soon? Was it conceived by him as close and already tangible? The Gospel evidence appears inconclusive. Occasionally, the evangelists seem to establish the kingdom in a world to come, in a new age, as when Jesus is depicted as prophesying, 'Truly, I say unto you, I shall not drink again of the fruit of the vine until that day when I drink it anew in the kingdom of God' (Mark 14.25 par.). Elsewhere, the kingdom belongs to the here and now. Like the seed planted in the ground, it is already coming into being. Like the leaven in the dough, it is already at work.

This situating of Jesus' kingdom of God in a context of time has been the subject of much learned, and to my mind futile, controversy.[48] Albert Schweitzer's 'consistent eschatology' (*konsequente Eschatologie*) assigns it to the near future.[49] C. H. Dodd places it in the present time in the form of a 'realized eschatology'.[50] Joachim Jeremias compromises, and with his '*sich realisierende Eschatologie*', eschatology in process of being realized, allots it partly to the present and partly to the future.[51] Many New Testament scholars, furthermore, compound the difficulties facing them by taking it for granted that Jesus, for all his eschatological convictions, looked towards a temporal future. His ethical teaching was to serve as a pattern of life for his disciples during the interval between his first and his second coming: an irrational attitude of the eschatological mind, in the opinion of Rudolf Otto.[52]

One of the methodological principles proposed in the previous chapter is that a doctrine which includes the notion of a *parousia* is likely to reflect church apologetics and not Jesus' own ideas. If he was convinced, as he undoubtedly was, of the imminence of the coming of the kingdom, he would not have exhorted his followers to settle down to wait for the day of the Lord.[53]

But to dismiss the problem thus summarily would be high-handed. Staying with it a little longer, I would therefore remark as a first point that the chief weakness of the Schweitzer–Dodd–Jeremias school of thought is that it applies ordinary time-concepts to Jesus' eschatological outlook. Admittedly, modern scholarship thereby merely follows ancient Jewish and Christian eschatological speculation. In the former, historical periods are distinguished from the beginning to the epoch of consummation. To take one of the best known examples, Daniel divides the age extending from the Babylonian exile to the moment of final salvation into seventy 'weeks of years' (or seventy seven-year periods), and sees his own time as falling within the last of these sabbatical cycles.[54] His principal chronological landmark is the erection in the Jerusalem Temple of the 'abomination of desolation' in the form of a pagan god (Dan. 9.24–27). In early Christian apocalypticism, on the other hand, the history of salvation is represented as evolving in three stages. The first, subdivided into three times fourteen generations, reaches from Abraham to Jesus.[55] The second corresponds to the public life of Christ. And the third leads to the *parousia*, the approach of which is signalled by Daniel's 'abomination of desolation' (Mark 13.14; Matt. 25.15). Paul provides a still more detailed schedule of events heralding the second coming. 'That day will not come', he tells the Thessalonians, 'unless the rebellion comes first, and the man of lawlessness is revealed, the son of perdition, who opposes and exalts himself against every so-called god or object of worship, so that he takes his seat in the temple of God, proclaiming himself to be God . . . And then the lawless one will be revealed, and the Lord Jesus will slay him and destroy him by his appearing and his coming (i.e. *parousia*)' (II Thess. 2.3–4, 8).[56]

Jesus himself holds out no such promise of warnings or portents but says the very reverse: 'The kingdom of God is not coming with signs to be observed' (Luke 17.20). In other words, its hour is unknown; even he does not know it. It is God's secret (Mark 13.32; Matt. 24.36). He and his followers, inspired by faith and unaffected by the spirit of speculation, have entered the eschatological age and now perceive a fundamental difference between their own time and the preceding centuries. From the day when Jesus is moved by the Baptist's call to repentance, time for him is no longer time as we know it but has acquired a quality of finality. 'Repent, for the kingdom of heaven is at hand' (Matt. 4.17; Mark 1.15). The moment of his turning, his *teshuvah*, is the turning-point of his life, as it is of those who afterwards answer his own call to *teshuvah*, to turn back decisively and irrevocably to God. Making their choice, God's kingdom comes, and they enter in. A new era, or rather a new aeon, begins for them, which in Jesus' case manifests itself in powers of healing and powers of communication (sensed by the crowds flocking after him in their effort to storm the kingdom, in the picturesque idiom of the gospel). In the words of Matthew, 'From the days of John the Baptist until now, the kingdom of heaven has suffered violence and men of violence take it by force' (Matt. 11.12), a paradox which becomes more easily understandable in Luke's version: 'The law and the prophets were until John; since then, the kingdom of God is preached, and every one enters it violently' (Luke 16.16).[57]

If my interpretation of Jesus' eschatological mentality is valid, queries concerned with whether the kingdom had come, was on the way, or would come later, must be irrelevant. At issue in New Testament eschatology is the actual movement itself of turning back, of entering into the kingdom. It is in the surrender of the self to God's will that his sovereignty is realized on earth. Does this correspond accurately to Jesus' teaching? The Lord's Prayer, believed to summarize his authentic thought, seems to support such a reconstruction. Both the shorter (Lucan) and the longer (Matthean) recensions of the 'Our Father' give the petition, 'Thy kingdom come', Matthew following on immediately with the paraphrastic explanation: 'Thy will be done on earth as it is in heaven!' (Luke 11.2; Matt. 6.10).[58]

Despite the many references to God's kingdom in the Gospels, there is, as I have said, surprisingly little use of royal imagery in Jesus' language. In particular, he nowhere alludes to, or addresses, God as King, a fact all the more remarkable in that, together with its synonym 'Lord', *adonai*, 'King' occurs frequently in ancient Jewish prayer and continues to do so to this day.[59] Jesus' only mention of God as 'Lord of heaven and earth' appears in a passage of dubious authenticity (Matt. 11.25; Luke 10.21).[60] In all but one of his other recorded prayers, and in his habitual speech, he uses 'Father'.

Father as a divine form has a long biblical and post-biblical history and has been studied extensively by scholars. I have myself dealt with it indirectly in *Jesus the Jew* in connection with the title, 'son of God'.[61] God is represented metaphorically in biblical and apocryphal literature as Father of the chosen people. 'I am a father to Israel and Ephraim is my first-born', declaims Jeremiah (Jer. 3.9). God is invoked as Father by the community: in the words of the Third Isaiah, 'Yet O Lord, thou art our Father ... we are the work of thy hand' (Isa. 64.8). In the inter-testamental period, however, relation with the Father grows to be less of a privilege conferred on Israel as a people, and increasingly dependent on merit. It is those Jews whose hearts are circumcised who receive the divine promise, 'I will be their Father and they shall be my sons, and they shall be called the sons of the living God' (*Jub.* 1.24–25).[62] Kinship with the Father is accounted the privilege of the holy, and of people like the Qumran sectaries who regarded themselves as holy, and of those who suffered and died for their faith. Interpreting Ex. 20.6, 'those who love me and keep my commandments', Rabbi Nathan, a second century AD sage, explains that the supreme proof of devotion to God is total obedience, even to the sacrifice of one's life. The martyr's wounds cause him to be loved by his 'Father who is in heaven'.[63] A parallel version transmitted anonymously in Leviticus Rabbah reads: 'I have done the will of *Abba* who is in heaven' (*Lev. R.* 32.1). But this assurance of filial kinship was of course applied *a fortiori* to the royal Messiah, as is particularly clear from the Qumran explanation of the text, 'I will be his father and he shall be my son' (II Sam. 7.14). Interpreted, so we are told, this alludes to 'the Branch of David who shall arise . . . in Zion (at the end) of time . . .' (*4QFlor.* i, 11–12).[64]

Prayer in ancient Judaism is rich in invocations to God the Father. In the Greek version of Ecclesiasticus, 'Father' is preceded by 'Lord' and followed by 'Ruler' or 'God': 'O Lord, Father and Ruler (or God) of my life' (Ecclus. 23.1, 4). Again, in the Greek text of III Maccabees – a majestic roll-call of titles – 'O sovereign King, Most-High, Almighty God' – ends with 'Father' (III Macc. 6.2–4). The Hebrew Ben Sira imitates the simple biblical style: 'Thou art my Father, for thou art the Hero of my salvation' (Ecclus. (Heb.) 51.10). Similarly, 'Father' appears unaccompanied by other appellations in the Greek Book of Wisdom, where a traveller preparing to set out to sea in a ship, prays: 'It is thy providence, O Father, that is its pilot' (Wisdom 14.3).

Where synagogal prayer is concerned, with its frequent use of 'Our Father', I must confess that it is not possible to prove that even the earliest form extant represents anything actually current during the age of Jesus. It may nevertheless be of interest to recall that, according to the late Joseph Heinemann, author of the influential *Prayer in the Talmud*, while most private and public prayer takes the form of servant–master communication, a number of supplications addressed to 'Our Father, our King' and to 'Our Father who art in heaven', are likely to be 'based on very ancient models', possibly originating in the Temple before AD 70.[65] The Palestinian version of the Eighteen Benedictions, presumed to be the oldest recension of these blessings, includes two petitions invoking the fatherhood of God: 'Grant us, *our Father*, the knowledge (which comes) from thee . . . Forgive us, *our Father*, for we have sinned against thee'.[66]

A word must finally be added relating to the prayer characteristic of the ancient Hasidim.[67] According to the Mishnah, they were accustomed to spend a full hour in recollection before they even began to pray, 'in order

to direct their hearts towards their Father who is in heaven' (*mBer.* 5.1).
And in the years of distress and misery following the destruction of the
Second Temple, the saintly rabbi Eliezer ben Hyrcanus (around AD 100),
and the Hasid, Pinhas ben Yair (second century), comfort themselves
with: 'On whom can we rely now? On our Father who is in heaven' (*mSot.*
9.15; *bSot.* 49b).

Such is the literary and religious background against which I will now
endeavour to reconstruct Jesus' own version of God the Father.

Beginning with his style, we shall concern ourselves in our final lecture
with the implication of the varied *terminology*, 'my Father', 'your Father',
'our Father' and 'the Father'. For the present, we shall concentrate primarily on the *notions* 'Father' and 'heavenly Father', in passages recording
his preaching and instructions, and on the invocation, 'Father!', which
appears in nearly all of Jesus' prayers.[68]

The phrase, 'the Father who is in heaven', *ho patēr ho en (tois) ouranois*,
or 'the heavenly Father', *ho patēr ho ouranios*, appears frequently in
Matthew, once in Mark (Mark 11.25) and not at all in Luke, apart from the
somewhat unusual expression, 'the Father from heaven', *ho patēr ho ex
ouranou* (Luke 11.13). That Matthew's imputation to Jesus of this manner
of addressing God may not always be genuine but his own invention, is
perfectly possible,[69] bearing in mind that to his Judaeo-Christian readers
such an idiom would be quite familiar. The substitution by Mark and Luke
of 'God' for Matthew's 'Father', and 'Father in heaven', is best explained
as an adaptation of Jesus' phraseology for the benefit of non-Jews, to whom
the Semitic nomenclature would have seemed alien. For the same reason,
Matthew's Hebrew-Aramaic 'kingdom of heaven' is replaced by the other
two synoptics with the cosmopolitan 'kingdom of God'.[70]

Jesus' prayers present a different picture. With two exceptions, they use
the short invocation, 'Father', the rendering, we can be reasonably sure, of
Jesus' own Aramaic vocative, *abba*, which is itself preserved once in Mark
(Mark 14.36) and in early Christian prayers cited by Paul (Rom. 8.15; Gal.
4.6).[71]

Much has been written about the significance of the use by Jesus of the
title *abba*, especially by Jeremias and his followers.[72] In the opinion of the
late professor from Göttingen, this *ipsissima vox Jesu* is unparalleled in
Jewish prayer. Compared with that of the ancient Jews, who, as one of
Jeremias's pupils explains, 'maintained the dignity of God, in so far as they
addressed him as Father at all, by scrupulously avoiding the particular
form of the word used by children',[73] it is the 'chatter of a small child'.[74]
Jeremias, that is to say, understood Jesus to have addressed God as 'Dad'
or 'Daddy', but apart from the *a priori* improbability and incongruousness

of the theory, there seems to be no linguistic support for it. Young children speaking Aramaic addressed their parents as *abba* or *imma* but it was not the only context in which *abba* would be employed. By the time of Jesus, the determined form of the noun, *abba* (= 'the father'), signified also 'my father'; '*my* father', though still attested in Qumran and biblical Aramaic,[75] had largely disappeared as an idiom from the Galilean dialect.[76] Again, *abba* could be used in solemn, far from childish, situations such as the fictional altercation between the patriarchs Judah and Joseph reported in the Palestinian Targum, when the furious Judah threatens the governor of Egypt (his unrecognized brother) saying: 'I swear by the life of the head of *abba* (= my father) as you swear by the life of the head of Pharaoh, your master, that if I draw my sword from the scabbard, I will not return it there until the land of Egypt is filled with the slain.'[77]

Jeremias's further thesis that since God is never called *abba* in ancient Jewish prayer, Jesus' usage of the title is unique, is also open to question. It would gain strength if he could point, first, to a representative sample of individual prayers in Aramaic and show that none of them include the vocative *abba*. But as far as I know, no such evidence exists. Second, it would help his argument if he could prove that the invocation was not part of the language of Hasidic piety. Here again, evidence is mostly lacking. To quote David Flusser: 'Jeremias could not find "Abba" used to address God in Talmudic literature; but considering the scarcity of rabbinic material on charismatic prayer, this does not tell us very much.'[78] We have, however, at least one indirect attestation in connection with the rain-maker Hanan, of the first century BC, the grandson of Honi the circle-drawer. Perhaps I should explain at this point that we know that a few holy men were given the honorific title of *abba*, the father.[79] Hanan was one of them, as was his cousin, Hilkiah. During one of the periodic droughts, when Hanan was chased by children in the street shouting, 'Abba, abba, give us rain!' his response was to entreat God to 'render service to those who cannot distinguish between the *abba* who gives rain and the *abba* who does not' (*bTaan.* 23b).[80]

So what do we find when we piece together the main features of God's form as Father as they emerge from the passages judged most likely to transmit Jesus' true teaching? Most of the texts derive, needless to say, from Matthew, but every dominant characteristic finds an echo in other sources also, with or without explicit mention of the word Father, and may be said to satisfy the authenticity criteria of multiple attestation and consistency.

As before, we have to return to the Lord's Prayer for a reliable insight into Jesus' mind. In the first half, he calls on God as Father, implying perhaps an individual supplication, or 'Our Father' suggesting communal prayer, and follows on in the pattern of the ancient hymn of praise, the *Kaddish*, which expresses the wish that God's Name may be sanctified and his sovereignty established.[81] The second half of the Lord's Prayer, in Luke and Matthew, is concerned to ask God to exercise the fatherly functions which are his attributes: to provide for essential needs, to forgive the repentant, to protect from evil. These are topics prominent in the remainder of the gospel material, in the teaching sections as well as in the parables. The Father knows the requirements of all his creatures, human, animal and vegetable, and bestows his paternal care on his 'little ones'.

To those whose instinctive reaction to this image is that it is an idealized dream having little in common with life as we know it, the reply is that Jesus seems to have been fully aware that all is not perfect in this world despite a heavenly Father who is perfect, generous, merciful. The fledgling falls from its nest (Matt. 10.29);[82] the little ones perish; the righteous suffer (Matt. 18.14; 5.10–11 par.). But as I have indicated earlier, Jesus propounded no syntheses. The unity and (illogical) logic of his teaching lies in the domain of subjectivity, in the inspiration and motivation of his religious action.

As I have suggested, he did not intend – and probably possessed no talent for it – to preach on God's nature and being as later theologians have done and continue to do. He tried to carry out his Father's will, to fall in with what he felt the Father demanded of him. And he taught his followers to devote themselves to the same task, irrespective of its outcome. The focus of his concern was not God as such, but himself, his disciples, and the world, in their relation to the Father in heaven and his kingdom.

4

The Gospel of Jesus the Jew III:
Jesus and Christianity

We are so accustomed, and rightly, to make Jesus the object of religion
that we become apt to forget that in our earliest records he is portrayed
not as the object of religion, but as a religious man.

These are not my words. They were written by the renowned New Testament scholar, Thomas Walter Manson.[1] But I could not have found a
quotation better fitted to my theme. Whilst giving it his approval as a
Christian, Manson understood that the church's general approach to
Christ contains an ingredient in conflict with the best historical evidence.[2]
My intention is to explore the gospels for that evidence and to piece it
together so that, re-discerning the character of Jesus the religious man, we
may subsequently contrast the essentials of his piety with the main spiritual thrust of the religion of which he has become the object. But we shall
have first to enquire into the general religious climate of his place and time
if we are to keep his particular contribution to it in perspective.[3]

In this larger setting, the notion of divine sovereignty, as we have seen in
the discussion of the idea of the 'yoke of the kingdom', was associated and
even interchangeable with, the 'yoke of the Law', the Torah.[4] Known in
the Hebrew Bible as the Law of God or the Law of Moses,[5] it regulated
every aspect of private and public existence – agriculture, trading and
commerce, the choice and preparation of food, the intimacies of sexuality,
and even occasionally the materials and styles of Jewish clothing. As a
law-abiding person, Jesus may be presumed to have behaved in respect of
these general rules and common customs like everyone else in Galilee.[6]
Embracing the accepted way of everyday life, he will have conformed
spontaneously to a number of biblical precepts. The Gospels show him
also complying with the laws regulating religious activities proper, partic-
ipating in synagogue worship on the Sabbath (Mark 1.21; 6.2; Luke 4.16
etc.), visiting the Temple of Jerusalem as a pilgrim (Mark 11.15 par.), and
celebrating the Passover (Mark 14.15–16 par.). Some scholars deduce

from the references to the *kraspedon*, the hem or fringes of Jesus' robe, that he must have been a strict observer of the Torah,[7] but he may simply have dressed like his fellow-Galileans. If his own fringes or *ziziyoth* had been unusually long, he would hardly have been described as criticizing others for displaying them too ostentatiously (Matt. 23.5).[8]

More important, though still not particularly meaningful, is the selection Jesus makes of certain biblical commandments as summarizing the individual laws of the Old Testament. There was a general tendency among Jews in the early post-biblical centuries to discover a small number of all-inclusive precepts. The fullest illustration of this trend comes from Rabbi Simlai, a third century AD sage, who explains that all the six hundred and thirteen positive and negative commandments proclaimed by Moses were, according to David, contained in eleven (Ps. 15); according to Isaiah, in six (33.15); according to Micah, in three (to do justice, love mercy and walk humbly with God – Micah 6.8); according to Isaiah again, in two (to observe justice and do righteousness – Isa. 56.1); and according to Amos, in one alone, 'Seek me and live' (Amos 5.4).[9] Philo, Jesus' great Alexandrian Jewish contemporary, maintained that the Decalogue symbolizes all the 'special laws' of the Torah.[10] And when asked what must be done to inherit eternal life, Jesus merely recites from the Ten Commandments, 'Do not kill! Do not commit adultery! Do not steal!' etc. (Mark 10.19 par.)[11] Invited to reduce the many to one, he chooses the first or great commandment in its twofold aspect of love: 'You shall love the Lord your God . . . and your neighbour as yourself' (Mark 12.29–31 par.)[12] At the same time, when there is question of a comprehensive counsel of behaviour, his one-articled code – accredited also, though in a different form, to the great Hillel,[13] who may have been still alive when Jesus was born – explicitly prescribes the single duty, 'Whatever you wish that men should do to you, do so to them,' Matthew adding, 'For this is the Law and the Prophets' (Matt. 7.12; Luke 6.31).[14]

But has it not been asserted through the centuries that Jesus frees man from 'the curse of the Law',[15] that he substitutes for the Law a new dispensation of grace? Yes indeed, but in echo as we shall see of the Diaspora Hellenist, Paul of Tarsus, not of the Galilean. He, as far as one may judge from reliable Gospel evidence, excuses no neglect of the Law as such. Reminiscent of many a rabbinic dictum, his words as reported by Luke, himself a Greek addressing Gentiles, leave no room for doubt: 'It is easier for heaven and earth to pass away than for one tittle of the Law to fall' (Luke 16.17; Matt.5.18).[16]

The controversial sayings attributed to Jesus in the Gospels have to be considered against this faithfulness to the Torah. Some of the arguments turn on the interpretation of customs such as hand-washing before meals (Mark 7.15 par.);[17] others are associated with the Sabbath and its observance.[18] Jewish legal teaching – *halakhah* – was still in a fluid state in his time; the great endeavour of unification and definition resulting in so-called 'orthodoxy' was not made until after AD 70. He is admittedly often represented by New Testament exegetes, mostly on the basis of a gloss appended by Mark to a paradoxical question posed by Jesus, as having rejected the dietary laws.[19] 'Do you not see that nothing that goes from outside into a man can defile him?' Mark gives Jesus to enquire, adding as his own observation, 'Thus he declared all foods clean' (Mark 7.18–19).[20] But on reflection are we not bound to conclude *a priori* that in a Palestinian environment the abolition of all distinction between pure and impure food is almost inconceivable? Besides, what about the historically dependable claim in the Acts of the Apostles that Jesus' immediate followers found the very idea of touching forbidden food horrible and scandalous? (Acts 10.13–16). For them, as appears from Paul's angry criticism of Peter, Barnabas and other 'Judaizers', table-companionship even with Gentile Christians was intolerable and shameful (Gal. 2.11–14). The Marcan comment will have catered for non-Jewish members of the church unprepared to be bothered with such rules.

Again, the Gospels themselves often involve Jesus in polemics over observance of the Sabbath.[21] Here, the main point to remember is that in Judaism the saving of life overrides the Sabbath laws.[22] During the bloody Hadrianic persecution, a hundred years after the time of Jesus, the rabbis recognized it as taking precedence over *all* laws with the exception of idolatry, incest and murder. The text from Leviticus 18.5, 'You shall keep my statutes . . . by which a man shall live', was interpreted to mean that observance of the Torah should not lead to death.[23] In the case of Jesus' Sabbath debates, where the subject at issue is almost always the healing of the sick, the principle emerging from them appears to be that every cure, great or small, is life-saving.[24] The restoration to health of a man with a paralysed hand is as serious as deliverance from death and as cogent a justification for infringing the Sabbath (Matt. 12.9–14; Luke 14.1–6)[25] – if, that is to say, such justification is necessary where the cure is performed by word of mouth and without any accompanying 'work' such as carrying or administering medicines.

Jesus, I would add, not only submits personally to the legal obligations incumbent on a Jew; he more than once expressly urges obedience to the purely ritual and cultic precepts in sayings all the more historically credible in that they are peripheral to the gospel narrative and actually run counter to the essential antinomianism of Gentile Christianity. After curing several lepers, he orders them to report to the priests and to perform the ceremony prescribed by Moses (Mark 1.44 par.; Luke 17.14; cf. Lev. 14.1–32). He approves of sending gifts to the Temple (Matt. 5.33) and of the tithing laws, which will of course have been far from popular among the Galilean rural communities (Matt. 23.23; Luke 11.42). He is even depicted, though I doubt the authenticity of the actual statement, as giving support to the theory, if not the practice, of Pharisee legal teaching.[26]

Where the Law is concerned, the chief distinction of Jesus' piety lies in his extraordinary emphasis on the real inner religious significance of the commandments. Needless to say, he was not the only Jewish teacher to insist on symbolism, inwardness and sincerity. Philo and Josephus did the same.[27] So did many of the rabbis,[28] and the Qumran sectaries.[29] But I believe it is true to say that interiority, purity of intention, played a greater part in Jesus' thought, possibly because of his stress on eschatological finality which we discussed in the previous chapter, but also because of his natural bias towards the individual and personal rather than the collective.[30] He tends in any case to lay a heavy, and sometimes almost exaggerated, accent on the primary causes and ultimate aim of the religious or irreligious act. Murder has its roots in anger;[31] adultery in the lustful gaze.[32] His followers must therefore avoid the lesser faults as scrupulously as they would shun the greater. Similarly, he clearly regards the ritual impurity contracted through transgressing the dietary laws as insignificant compared with the uncleanness of 'fornication, theft, murder, adultery . . . envy, slander, pride, foolishness' (Mark 7.14–23; Matt. 15.10–20). Jesus' teaching is that it is excretion that defiles, not ingestion, and that nothing defiles more foully than the excretion of the wicked heart with its evil thoughts.

Exactly the same principle underlies Jesus' attitude to almsgiving, prayer and fasting. They stand or fall as religious acts in proportion to the integrity with which they are performed. Charitable gifts must be made in secret, without witnesses. Prayer is to be offered in private, not aloud in the streets or in the synagogue. Fasting is to be undertaken with a smiling face, before God alone.[33] Jesus' religious deed was done, in other words, in accordance with Jewish religious Law and laws, but was invested with an added dimension of effectiveness and power, not through elaboration of casuistical detail, but through his genial perception of the Law's inmost significance, its original purpose: namely, to serve as a vehicle for authentic lived relation with God the Father, God the King.[34]

Before examining the concrete manifestations of this God/man-father/ son relation as it is attested in the Synoptic Gospels, brief mention must be made of a few fragmentary statements somewhat theoretical in their attitude *vis-à-vis* God. They may all ultimately derive from the primitive church, but more probably are in part representative of Jesus' thought, and in part ecclesiastical formulations.

The first is the celebrated thanksgiving recorded in Matthew and Luke: 'All things have been delivered to me by my Father; and no one knows who the son is except the Father, or who the Father is, except the son, and anyone to whom the son chooses to reveal him' (Matt. 11.27; Luke 10.22).[35] Whether the idea of revelation contained in this text reflects a Hellenistic milieu, as Bultmann has suggested,[36] or an Aramaic wisdom-school,[37] or whether it is akin to the sort of knowledge-speculation found in the Dead Sea Scrolls,[38] is secondary and almost immaterial compared with the fundamental concept, expressed by the evangelists with great perspicuity, of an ideal reciprocity between Father and son. This reciprocity, it must be stressed, is not equality. It is a remarkable fact that the Father's superiority remains impregnable even in face of the church's editorial intervention. The *panta*, all things, revealed to Jesus by the Father do not include that most crucial knowledge, a knowledge of the end-time. Of that day and hour, it is said, 'no one knows, not even the angels in heaven, nor the son, but only the Father' (Mark 13.32; Matt. 24.36).[39]

This passage, despite the dubious authenticity of the eschatological discourse into which it is inserted, is the more likely to be genuine in that it conflicts with later church doctrine that Christ was endowed with perfect wisdom. Similarly, when the two ambitious apostles, James and John, wish to secure for themselves the best places in the kingdom, they are told: 'To sit at my right hand and at my left is not mine to grant, but it is for those for whom it has been prepared by my Father' (Matt. 20.23; Mark 10.40).[40]

As I have said, these apparently dogmatic statements about God must not be allowed to mislead. It was not Jesus' habit to theorize about the divine. His preoccupation was with enacting to perfection, in his own person, the role of son of his Father in heaven, and with teaching his followers to live likewise. 'Ask', he instructs them, 'and it shall be given you; seek and you shall find; knock and it shall be opened to you.' Would any of them, entreated by their children for bread, give them a stone? Or a snake instead of some fish? 'If you, then, who are evil, know how to give good gifts to your children, how much more will your Father who is in heaven give good things to those who ask him?' (Matt. 7.7–11; Luke 11.9–13).[41] And even this occasional 'asking' is not enough; God's children have to implore their Father daily for the day's needs (Matt. 6.11; Luke 11.3).[42] They must *pester* him like little children until he grants them their desire. Adopting another metaphor, they must be like the man who woke his friend in the middle of the night and importuned him until he arose from his bed and lent him three loaves of bread so that he could feed an unexpected visitor (Luke 11.5–8).[43]

The total simplicity and confidence required of the child of God as Jesus represents him is the biblical *emunah* (faith/trust), the virtue which, according to Martin Buber, Jesus and the prophets possessed in common.[44] It may also point to an inheritance from ancient Hasidism, where the same spirit prevailed. The first-century BC charismatic, Honi (or Onias the Righteous, as Flavius Josephus names him),[45] is famous for his petulant threat that he would not step outside the circle which he had drawn around himself until God showed mercy to his children and ended the long season of drought. Honi's behaviour is said to have provoked Simeon ben Shetah, the leading Pharisee of that time, to comment resentfully: 'If you were not Honi, I would excommunicate you. But what can I do with you, for in spite of your importunity, God does what you want?' (*mTaan.* 3.8).[46] The rabbis were sticklers for correct behaviour and disapproved of temerity such as Honi's; but they were compelled to confess that it sometimes worked. '*Huzpa*', impertinence, 'has its usefulness even towards heaven,' reads the Talmud (*bSanh.* 105a).[47] It is *emunah* that Jesus teaches when he recommends that the child of God should lay aside material and temporal anxieties and commit itself wholly to the care of the Father in heaven. 'Do not be anxious about your life', the Galilean urges; 'what you shall eat . . ., nor about your body, what you shall put on . . . Look at the birds of the air: they neither sow nor reap nor gather into barns, and yet your heavenly Father feeds them. Are you not of more value than they? . . . And why are you anxious about your clothing? Consider the lilies of the field, how they grow; they neither toil, nor spin; yet I tell you, even Solomon in all his glory was not arrayed like one of these . . . Therefore do not be anxious, saying, "What shall we eat?" or "What shall we drink?" or "What shall we wear?" . . . Your heavenly Father knows that you need them all.'[48] And Jesus asks further: 'Are not two small birds sold for an *assarion* [or five for two *assaria*, according to Luke] and not one of them shall fall to the ground without your Father's will . . . Fear not therefore; you are of more value than many sparrows' (Matt. 10.29–31; Luke 12.6–7).

As might be expected, the counterpart of the sort of unconditional surrender to divine providence demanded of his followers by Jesus is a condemnation and rejection of man-made plans and projects, long-term and short. The futility of trying to depend on, and provide for, the future, is illustrated in the parable of the rich landowner who, with a good harvest in view, plans to pull down his barns and replace them with larger ones with the idea of ensuring much food, drink and merriment for years to come. But Jesus exclaims, 'Fool! Tonight your soul is required of you; and the things you have prepared, whose will they be?' (Luke 12.16–20)[49] Even where the immediate future is concerned, his thought extends no further than to the requirements of the day, to the '*daily* bread' (Matt. 6.11; Luke 11.13). Directly and explicitly, his counsel in the Sermon on the Mount is, 'Do not be anxious about tomorrow, for tomorrow will be anxious for itself. Let the day's own trouble be sufficient for the day' (Matt. 6.34).[50] Jesus was a man for whom the present, the here and now, was of unique and infinite importance.

It may be this exclusive concentration on the religious task immediately facing him, inspired by an 'enthusiasm (born) of eschatological presence', to borrow again from Martin Buber,[51] that accounts for Jesus' total lack of interest in the economic and political realities of his age. He was not a social reformer or nationalistic revolutionary, notwithstanding recent claims to the contrary.[52] Nor, provocative though it may appear to say so, did the urgency of his religious vision allow any place for founding, organizing and endowing with permanency an ecclesiastical body of any sort.[53] It was rather the extinction of the *parousia* hope, cultivated in self-contained primitive Christian communities, that conferred durability on a fabric intended by the apostles and the first disciples to last for no longer than a brief span.

In parenthesis, I would once again point out that foresight, farsightedness, make better sense in the context of an expectation of a second coming, or where the spirit of eschatological presence has died away, than in the thought of Jesus.[54] The parable of the 'wise' virgins – supposedly wise, but to my mind cunning and selfish – reflects an insistence on the part of the church to be constantly ready; it contributes nothing to an active participation in the work for the kingdom of God. The young women, foreseeing that the bridegroom may be late, bring with them a good supply of oil for their lamps. But they refuse to share it with their 'foolish' friends. They send them off to find dealers at midnight. And by the time they return, the gate is closed. When they ask to be admitted, no one complies (Matt. 25.1–13). Did Matthew or his later editor not realize that this parable is a travesty of Jesus' teachings on generosity and confident prayer contained in the same Gospel?[55]

Compared with the kingdom and its coming and the affairs of the heavenly Father, everything temporal is of secondary importance. All that matters is action, *now*. There must be no procrastination, no dawdling: 'The kingdom of God is at hand' (Mark 1.15; Matt. 4.17). The disciple must follow the teacher's call, at once. He must not ask for permission to bid farewell to his family; no man 'who puts his hand to the plough and looks back is fit for the kingdom of God' (Luke 9.61–62).[56] He must not return to bury his father (Matt. 8.21–22; Luke 9.59–60). 'Leave the dead to bury their dead', is the paradoxical command.[57] Solemn family ties must take second place to the bond uniting those who do God's will. As Jesus remarks of his waiting relations, 'Who are my mother and my brothers? ... Whoever does the will of God is my brother, and sister and mother' (Mark 3.33–34).

Two important parables adumbrate the single-minded devotion to the cause of the Father which Jesus promoted and the prompt and decisive action which he required of those who seek to enter the kingdom. In the first, where it is compared to a treasure discovered in a field, the finder covers it over and 'then in joy he goes and sells all he has and buys that field' (Matt. 13.44).[58] In the second, where it is compared to a pearl of great value, a merchant of pearls, noticing it, 'went and sold all that he had and bought it' (Matt. 13.45–46). In both parables, the lesson is identical. When the truth is encountered, a choice has to be made, a decision, and it must be acted on immediately, whole-heartedly. And a price must be paid, one amounting to all that one has.[59]

Now that we know something of the workings of Jesus' mind, of the pressures to which he subjected it, and of the values on which he laid the greatest stress, one fundamental question forms itself: what in the last resort was the principle that he adopted, and himself embodied, in his endeavours to live to perfection as a son of God? The reply must be that it was the principle, well attested in Judaism, biblical and post-biblical, of the *imitatio dei*, the imitation of God. 'You shall be holy, for I the Lord, your God, am holy' (Lev. 19.2).

Rabbinic thought is rich in interpretation of this theme that the lover and worshipper of God models himself on him.[60] Confronted with the verse, 'This is my God, and I will praise him,' *zeh 'eli we'anwehu* (Ex. 15.2), the second-century sage, Abba Shaul, reads instead, *zeh 'eli 'ani wa-hu*, 'This is my God, I and He,' expounding the last clause as, 'O be like Him! As He is merciful and gracious, you also must be merciful and gracious.'[61] Similarly, but entering into more detail, an anonymous exegete comments apropos of the words of Deuteronomy 10.12, 'that you may walk in His ways': 'These are the ways of God, "The Lord, a God merciful and gracious ..." (Ex. 34.6). "All who are called by the name of the Lord shall be delivered" (Joel 3.5 (ET 2.32)). How can a man be called by the name of God? As God is called merciful, you too must be merciful. The Holy One blessed be He is called gracious, so you too must be gracious ... and give presents freely. God is called righteous ... so you too must be righteous. God is called *hasid* (loving, devoted) ... so you too must be *hasid*' (*Sifre* on

Deut. 11.22(49)). But one of the most succinct renderings of this doctrine of the *imitatio dei* is given in an Aramaic paraphrase of Leviticus: 'My people, children of Israel, as your Father is merciful in heaven, so you must be merciful on earth' (*Targum Ps.-Jonathan* on Lev. 22.28).[62]

Jesus proclaims the same basic teachings: 'Be merciful as your Father is merciful' (Luke 6.36). 'Be perfect as your heavenly Father is perfect' (Matt. 5.48), but, as I have indicated earlier, injects them with his own extra dimension of integrity and inwardness. Perfect filial behaviour *vis-à-vis* the Father must show itself not simply in mercy and love towards others, but in a mercy and love that expects no return. 'You received without paying, give without payment', he says (Matt. 10.8; cf. II Cor. 11.7). On another occasion, he speaks more forcefully still. 'When you give a dinner or a banquet, do not invite your friends or your brothers or your kinsmen or rich neighbours, lest they also invite you in return, and you be repaid. But when you give a feast, invite the poor, the maimed, the lame and the blind, and you will be blessed, because they cannot repay you' (Luke 14.12–14).[63]

This is his usual custom: to opt for a maximum of exaggeration in order to underline what he is attempting to convey. No teaching exemplifies this better than the command to his disciples to love their enemies.[64] The saying has been the source of much misunderstanding and misinterpretation for there is no denying that to love persons motivated by hatred of oneself, or who subject one to abuse and persecution, must seem unnatural and humanly impossible. But Jesus' words are no more to be taken literally than in that other text requiring the would-be follower to hate his father, mother, wife, children, brothers and sisters (Luke 14.26),[65] or than his instruction to his disciples, 'To him who strikes you on the cheek, offer the other also' (Luke 6.29; Matt. 5.39).[66] The independent Passion narrative of the Fourth Gospel in no ways bears out this last piece of advice. When an over-zealous policeman slaps his face, Jesus does not turn the other cheek but protests with dignity, 'If I have spoken wrongly, bear witness to the wrong, but if I have spoken rightly, why do you strike me'? (John 18.24). The commandment to love one's enemies is as it were an overstatement intended to impress on his hearers that the perfect manifestation of love is to offer it quite freely, gratis. 'Love your enemies, do good to those who hate you, bless those who curse you, pray for those who abuse you . . . If you love those who love you, what credit is that to you . . .? And if you lend to those from whom you expect to receive, what credit is that to you . . .? But love your enemies, and do good and lend, expecting nothing in return . . . and you shall be sons of the Most High' (Luke 6.27–35; Matt. 5.39–45) – 'sons of your Father who is in heaven' (Matt. 5.45).

Jesus' religiousness, the piety peculiar to Jesus the religious man, is marked by a tendency to give more than is asked for, to probe deeper than expected, to risk more than is safe. The 'neighbours' he is to love as himself often turn out to be the outcasts of society, whose company he does not merely accept (Luke 15.1) but positively seeks. Unlike the pious of his day, and of later times, he enters their houses and eats with them (Mark 2.15 par.). He even – scandal of scandals – allows a woman sinner, a prostitute, to dry his feet with her hair, kiss them and anoint him (Luke 7.37–38). He treats them as friends; hence the sarcastic nickname conferred on him by his critics – 'friend of tax-collectors and sinners' (Matt. 11.19; Luke 7.34).[67] But his behaviour should cause no surprise. He is simply imitating in his personal conduct what he understands to be the conduct of the Father towards those of his children who return to relation with him from a state of irrelation. 'There will be', he maintains, 'more joy in heaven over one sinner who repents than over ninety-nine just' (Luke 15.7).

Turning now to Christian religion and religiousness as distinct from the religiousness and religion of Jesus, I am aware that for the vast majority of Christians – and many Jews for that matter – the very statement that Jesus and Christianity are to be differentiated from one another will come as a shock, a total surprise.[68] Present-day Christians are in the main wholly innocent of the gulf dividing their aims and beliefs from his. Even the learned C. H. Dodd assumed, as is apparent from the title of his last highly influential little book, that Jesus actually established Christianity.[69]

Permit me now to reduce to its essentials my exposition of the gospel of Jesus the Jew and to set alongside it a basic sketch of Christianity almost exclusively with the help of the doctrine on which it rests: the teaching of Paul, the true creator in the opinion of many non-Christian historians of the institutional, ecclesiastical religious body, professing a creed centred on the death and resurrection of the Messiah, known as Christianity.[70]

The first marked dissimilarity lies in the Jewishness of Jesus, his environment, his way of life, his purpose. It is a Jewishness that sometimes amounts to downright chauvinism, as is manifest in the unflattering epithets which the blunt Galilean lets fly against non-Jews. 'Dogs', he observes of them, 'dogs' not fit to eat the bread belonging to the children (Mark 7.27; Matt. 15.26)[71] or to be given a 'holy thing' (Matt. 7.6);[72] 'swine', on which his apostles are not to waste the pearls of their teaching (Matt. 7.6).[73] Do not trouble yourselves with them, he explicitly enjoins on another occasion. 'Go nowhere among the Gentiles . . . but rather to the lost sheep of the house of Israel' (Matt. 10.5–6; 15.24).[74] However did the evangelists manage to record such sayings as these, and at the same time attribute to Jesus the view that the Gentiles were soon to displace 'the sons of the kingdom', the Jews, as the elect of God? (Matt. 8.11–12; Luke 13.28–29).[75]

I would suggest that once Paul was acknowledged 'apostle to the Gentiles' (Acts 9.15; Rom. 11.13) and a specifically Gentile mission sanctioned by the church leadership came into being (Acts 15), the original bias of Jesus' ministry suffered a radical transformation. Gentiles in substantial numbers joined the ranks of the church and, following the model of proselytization in Judaism (flourishing in those days), it did its best to comply with the needs of the new situation and to adjust itself to altered circumstances. Moreover, Paul's pronouncement that the Christian communities now formed the 'Israel of God' (Gal. 6.16)[76] will have neutralized the sting of the insults so oddly preserved in the gospel text. The Gentile followers of Jesus, advised to consider themselves henceforth as 'neither Jew nor Greek' (Gal. 3.28), will have been persuaded that it was not they who were the target of their Lord's contempt.

It is possible, incidentally, to argue that an element of universalism is not absent from the inner logic of Jesus' teaching. It may be detected for example in the commandment to love one's enemies, which implies that they are fellow-creatures under the one God to whom charity must be shown, in imitation of the Father of all, who cares for all (Matt. 5.43–48; Luke 6.27–28, 32–36).

Another enormous change arising from the transplantation of the Christian movement into Gentile soil, one that affected its very nature, was that, despite Jesus' injunctions to the contrary, the Torah, the source of his inspiration and the discipline ruling his religious life, was declared by the church to be not merely optional but revoked, abolished, superseded. The Law which he had understood with such simplicity and profundity, and carried out with such integrity in accordance with what he saw to be its inmost truth, was judged by Paul to be in practice an instrument of sin and death. 'Christ', he declared 'is the end of the Law' (Rom. 10.4).[77]

Nevertheless, if Jesus and Christianity seem to stand worlds apart on this issue, neither Paul nor the later church pushed antinomianism so far as to apply it to the ethical sphere. There is no denying that the heart of Jesus' message, with its stress on interiority and supererogation, was heard by the early church and has remained intrinsic to the ideal of individual Christian piety: an ideal on which organized public ecclesiastical piety in its various manifestations has acted as a brake and corrective.

Whereby we arrive at one more radical distinction. The life-blood of Jesus' mission was, as I have explained, eschatological urgency.[78] He believed and taught that the kingdom of God was actually, at that time, in the process of coming into being, and that it would be fully established in the immediate future. As we know, this did not happen. The eagerness and excitement then transferred itself to hope in a second advent of Christ. But once again, it did not happen. He did not come. The resulting emptiness needing therefore to be made good, a corporate body took shape as a quasi-permanent substitute kingdom which was to serve as a repository of religion until the glorious return of Christ the King at the end of days.

And what happened to Jesus' imitation of God within the framework of this institutional church? Primitive Christianity was certainly conscious of it and promulgated it as a rule to be followed. 'Be imitators of God as beloved children', Paul writes to the Ephesians (Eph. 5.1). And yet it was this same Paul who was responsible for giving the unprecedented twist to the *imitatio dei* which opened up a great divide between Judaism and Christianity: 'Be imitators of me as I am of Christ' (I Cor. 11.1). With these words, Paul, deviating from the Jewish imitation of God, introduced inter-mediaries between the imitator and his ultimate divine model. First of all imitate me: who am an imitator of Jesus: who imitated God. Thus originated the trend, still conspicuous in the more ancient forms of Christianity, to multiply mediators and intercessors between the faithful and God: Jesus, Paul, Mary the mother of Jesus, the martyrs, the saints.

This question of intermediaries brings us in effect to the crux of the problem: that the example of Jesus' *hasiduth*, his *theocentric* devoutness, has been overlaid by the ramifications of Paul's *christo-centric* spirituality. His opinion of human nature, unlike that of Jesus, was deeply pessimistic. In his view, man is sinful, incapable of obeying God, potentially damned, and lost without the saving grace of Christ's atoning death.[79] Christ's sacrificial blood is essential to the cleansing of his sins. Except for the redemption obtained by Christ's passion and resurrection, he can never draw close to God. God 'sent forth his son . . . born under the law, to redeem those who were under the law, so that we might receive adoption as sons' (Gal. 4.4–5).[80] With increasing vehemence, in other words, the religiosity of primitive Christianity became trained on the Mediator in place of God. Prayers continued to be addressed to the Father, but more and more frequently to 'the Father of our Lord Jesus Christ' (Rom. 15.6; II Cor. 1.3; 11.31 etc.). Little by little, the Christ of Pauline theology and his Gentile church took over from the holy man of Galilee. Subject to God, but already enthroned at his side (I Cor. 15.28; Rom. 8.34; Eph. 1.20; Col. 3.1 etc.), he then – no doubt in response to the needs and hopes of non-Jewish Christianity – imperceptibly grew to be the 'image of God' (II Cor. 4.4), the 'effulgence of God's glory and the stamp of his nature' (Heb. 1.3), and finally, the equal of God.[81] 'I bid you', writes Ignatius bishop of

Antioch to Polycarp bishop of Smyrna, in the first decade of the second century, 'I bid you farewell always in our God Jesus Christ' (*Epistle to Polycarp*, ch. 8).

And the real Jesus? For there was a real Jesus, without any doubt.

Over the space of months, or perhaps even of two or three years, this Jesus of flesh and blood was seen and heard around the countryside of Galilee and in Jerusalem, an uncompromising, single-minded lover of God and his fellow-beings, convinced that by means of his example and teaching he could infect them with his own passionate sense of relation with the Father in heaven. And he did so. The magnetism of this real Jesus was such that not even the shame and humiliation of the cross, and not even the collapse of his ministry, could extinguish the faith of the men and women of his company. But it is a long time now since he was thought of. Very many ages have passed since the simple Jewish person of the Gospels stepped back and gave way to the rich and majestic figure of the church's Christ.

Yet it occurs to the historian, as he reaches the end of his presentation of the gospel of Jesus the Jew, that the world may not have heard the last of the holy Galilean. In this so-called post-Christian era, when Christ as a divine form seems to ever-increasing numbers not to correspond, either to the age's notion of reality, or to the exigencies of the contemporary human predicament, is it not possible that Jesus the healer, teacher and helper may yet be invited to emerge from the shadows of his long exile? And not by Christians alone? If, above all, his lesson on reciprocal, loving and direct relation with the Father in heaven is recalled and found universally valid, may not the sons of God on earth stand a better chance of ensuring that the ideal of human brotherhood becomes something more than a pipe-dream?

5

Jewish Studies and New Testament
Interpretation

In the mid-1970s, a biblical expert of international repute described an applicant for a university post as one 'among the few New Testament scholars who can take seriously and walk sure-footedly in the Semitic material to the importance of which we all pay lip-service'. This phrase contains a dreadful admission. Apparently the majority of present-day New Testament specialists are unable to 'take seriously and walk sure-footedly in' the languages and literature which form the Jewish background to the New Testament, even though they concede the usefulness to their subject of 'Semitic material', and 'pay lip-service' to its importance.

This is a strange situation, and to clarify it I will have to devote a good deal of this chapter to a historical survey of the attitude of New Testament interpreters to Jewish religious literature written between 200 BC and AD 400 thought capable of throwing light on the text of the Gospels and on other documents of the Christian canon. Today the connection between these two literary corpuses is accepted without demur. It is, I am sure, no surprise to you, as it was to many readers of the great German biblical scholar Julius Wellhausen, at the beginning of the twentieth century, to hear that Jesus was not a Christian but a Jew;[1] that with the exception of Luke, all the known New Testament writers, and all the contemporary followers of Jesus, were Jews; and that consequently the exploration of the Jewish world must be relevant, to say the very least, to the study of the New Testament.

In the past, Christian tradition developed a different view. From the conflict recorded in the Gospels between Jesus and some of his fellow-countrymen, and from the ultimate failure of the apostles' preaching among Palestinian Jews, it began, from the end of the first century AD onwards, to portray Jesus as an opponent of Judaism. The Gentile church, already divorced from Israel, saw, in all the Jews stood for, something fundamentally hostile to Christianity. In such circumstances of heated controversy, it simply never occurred to anyone that familiarity with Judaism could assist the Christian exegete of the New Testament.[2] On the contrary, any recognition of Judaism as not being totally alien to Christianity would have appeared to most church fathers as gross disloyalty to their faith.

This is not to imply that the church in late antiquity was unaware that the Jews were especially expert in biblical matters, but it saw this knowledge as limited to questions pertaining to the Old Testament. In fact, two of the greatest Christian scripture interpreters, Origen of Alexandria in the first half of the third century, and Jerome in the late fourth to early fifth century, are known to have studied with Jews and consulted them on problematic issues.[3] (Jerome even complains that one of his Hebrew masters, a rabbi from Lydda, was charging an exorbitant fee for his lessons on Job![4]) But as far as the New Testament was concerned, the acceptable Jewish contribution seems to have been confined to points of antiquarian interest. Commenting on the mention in Matt. 23.5 that the Pharisees wore broad phylacteries, Jerome explains that these were leather strips attached to the forehead and inscribed with the words of the Ten Commandments, a custom no longer practised in Palestine in his own time, but still prevalent among the Babylonian teachers.[5]

Throughout the whole patristic period, and even more so during the Middle Ages, Jewish–Christian relations in the field of Bible studies continued to be marked by polemics and apologetics. On the one hand, Christian teachers, largely ignorant of the Hebrew language, but helped especially in Spain by educated Jewish converts, insisted in their writings, as well as in public debate, that not only the Old Testament, but even the post-biblical writings of the synagogue, prove the divine truth of the church's teaching. The Jews, they maintained, were simply obdurate. On the other hand, learned medieval rabbis found no great difficulty in picking holes in the Christian argument or in demonstrating that Hebrew scriptural proof-texts were wrongly interpreted in the Latin Vulgate used by their opponents, who also misunderstood the sayings of the Talmud or failed to place a particular excerpt into its proper context. Needless to say, the style of the exchanges was neither detached, objective, nor for that matter edifying.[6] Look at the titles. *Pugio fidei*, 'Dagger of Faith'. The work of a thirteenth-century Dominican, this seeks to destroy Judaism.[7] In the opposite camp, Jewish polemicists of the Middle Ages, equally aggressive, set out to defend Judaism through *Milhamot ha-Shem*, 'The Wars of the Lord', or *Magen wa-Romah*, 'Shield and Spear'.[8] The best known collection of anti-Christian Jewish literature (edited, need I add, by a

Christian) bears the title *Tela ignea Satanae*, 'The Fiery Darts of Satan'⁹ –
and *not*, as a renowned Jewish historian translates it, 'Satan's Fiery Tail'.[10]
A quasi-'scientific' use of post-biblical Judaica in New Testament interpretation did not appear until the middle of the seventeenth century. Its
birthplace was England.

One of the earliest publications of this sort came
from the pen of a Yorkshire clergyman and Cambridge MA, Christopher
Cartwright (1602–58), whose *Mellificium Hebraicum*, 'Hebrew Honey-
making', was printed in London in 1660. It consists of five books, the
second and third of which contain various New Testament passages
followed by copious extracts from post-biblical Jewish documents. But
this work was outshone by that of John Lightfoot (1603–75), *Horae
Hebraicae et Talmudicae*, published in Leipzig between 1658 and 1674
(with posthumously edited supplements in 1678). Like Cartwright, Lightfoot, who was Master of St Catherine's College, Cambridge, selected New
Testament texts and attempted to expound them with the help of rabbinic
quotations. This is how he outlines his project in the preface to his section
on the Gospel of Matthew:

> . . . I have . . . concluded without the slightest hesitation that the best
> method to unravel the meaning of the many obscure passages of the
> New Testament is through research into the significance of the sayings
> in question in the ordinary dialect and way of thinking of the Jews . . .
> And this can be investigated only by means of consulting the authors of
> the Talmud.

These words, written in Latin three hundred and twenty years ago, sound
extraordinarily modern and would be largely approved today. Their
message is this: Study Rabbinics and you will acquire competence in New
Testament exegesis! In a very learned manner, Lightfoot showed how this
should be done, producing Talmudic parallels to the four Gospels, the
Acts of the Apostles, Romans and I Corinthians. But death prevented him
in 1675 from completing his task. It was achieved a few decades later by
Christian Schoettgen. (Perhaps I should mention that this kind of scholarship left these islands in the eighteenth century and migrated to the conti-
nent, to Holland and mainly to Germany.) Schoettgen issued in turn
another Latin volume, *Horae Hebraicae et Talmudicae* (Dresden–Leipzig
1733), the title borrowed from Lightfoot, but offering a commentary to the
whole New Testament (*in universum Novum Testamentum*).

By the middle of the eighteenth century, a further step was made
towards integrating Judaism into New Testament exegesis on a high
scientific level. Johann Jacob Wettstein (1693–1754), a native of Basle and
professor in Amsterdam, published in 1751/2 a new critical edition of the

Greek New Testament, containing more textual variants than any of the previous editions, but also a commentary from ancient literature, including that of the rabbis.[11] This meant that a student of the Greek Testament now had before him a rich collection of Talmudic illustrations, and was no longer obliged to turn to the separate specialist treatises of Lightfoot and Schoettgen. Throughout the second half of the eighteenth, and most of the nineteenth century, Wettstein exercised a profound influence on New Testament exegesis. Indeed, as recently as 1913, a somewhat naive Oxford divine described the work in the following terms: 'So valuable is the amount of illustrative material . . . that those who know the commentary best would not hesitate to place it first among all that ever one man has produced.'[12] And a witty American expert, George Foot Moore, remarked that the rabbinic quotations printed by Wettstein 'passed into a secondary tradition which in the course of repetition has forgotten its origins'.[13]

The nineteenth century yielded no similar compendia, but that golden age of biblical criticism saw great progress in two other domains. First, the so-called Pseudepigrapha, i.e., Jewish writings produced during the intertestamental period, influential in their time but not raised to the dignity of Holy Scripture, were ranked with rabbinic literature as auxiliaries for New Testament interpretation. Also, the full text, surviving only in Ethiopic, of two outstanding compositions belonging to this category, the Book of Enoch and the Book of Jubilees, were first published in 1838 and 1859, respectively.[14] But where the nineteenth century excelled above all, was in offering the scholarly world major syntheses in the form of comprehensive handbooks. Let me single out Emil Schürer's *Jewish History* from the age of the Maccabees in the second century BC to the second Jewish war against Rome under Hadrian in AD 132–35.[15] This tremendous undertaking gives a masterly account of the political events, institutions and literature, though only a very limited sketch of the Jewish religion, during the centuries crucial to an understanding of the New Testament. The other significant manual, in my short-list of two, is Ferdinand Weber's *Jewish Theology*, the first modern attempt at an orderly presentation of the rabbis' unsystematic utterances on belief and practice.[16] These works, instead of offering incidental assistance to the New Testament exegete, were intended to serve as constant guides and were warmly welcomed and used with enthusiasm.

The first half of the twentieth century contributed three further reference works to help the New Testament scholars in their occasional forays among the maze of post-biblical Jewish writings. Two appeared in full, and the third in part, before the end of the Second World War. (I consider 1945

as the closing year of that *ancien régime* which started in the first century
AD.) The first of these monuments is the collected and annotated edition of
the Pseudepigrapha, in German by Emil Kautzsch,[17] and in English by
R. H. Charles.[18] The other two indispensable companions of the New
Testament interpreter opened to him the contents of *Spätjudentum*, or
early post-biblical Judaism. All he needed was familiarity with Greek, a
smattering of Hebrew, and a full knowledge of German.[19]

In 1906, the Lutheran pastor, Paul Billerbeck, with the nominal co-
operation of the Protestant orientalist and theologian, Hermann Strack,
embarked on compiling a large-scale *Commentary to the New Testament
from Talmud and Midrash*. It was published in four fat volumes between
1922 and 1928.[20] This *Kommentar* is a modernized and much enlarged
Lightfoot, set out in the order of the books of the New Testament,
and supplies, wherever Billerbeck judges necessary, illustrative parallels
mainly from the Mishnah, Tosefta, Talmud and Midrash – but also from
the Pseudepigrapha. Unlike Lightfoot, Billerbeck tries to provide in his
presentation of the evidence a semblance of historicity, adding, when possible, supposed dates to the names of the (presumed) rabbinic authors.
There are substantial excursuses on special topics, but the literary sources
are nowhere subjected to any critical analysis.

Shortly after the completion of Billerbeck's *Commentary*, Gerhard
Kittel, heading a German team of contributors, launched the famous
Theological Dictionary of the New Testament.[21] Here, selected words of
doctrinal significance from the Greek New Testament are interpreted in
the light of all relevant literatures – biblical, Hellenistic and post-biblical
Jewish.

Not surprisingly, perhaps, New Testament scholars of the first half of the
twentieth century, furnished with Billerbeck and Kittel, happily believed
themselves to be fully equipped for a 'scientific-wissenschaftlich' exegesis of
the gospels. Indeed their euphoria persisted until fairly recently, a well-
known British author not hesitating in 1964 quite seriously to state:

> In this bright post-Strack-Billerbeck epoch, we are all rabbinic experts,
> though at second hand.[22]

What this writer and his predecessors have failed to realize is not merely
the fundamental insufficiency of second-hand knowledge in creative
scholarship; they have overlooked a fault intrinsic to most of the studies in
Judaica mentioned so far. Religious writings disclose their meaning only to
those who approach them in a spirit of sympathy. Such has not normally
been the case, apropos of rabbinic literature, among New Testament
specialists.

As I have said, Christian anti-Judaism is age-old. St John Chrysostom compared the Jewish synagogue to a brothel, a *porneion* (*Hom.* I, PG XLVIII, 847). And St Jerome described Jewish prayers as 'grunnitus suis et clamor asinorum' – the grunting of a pig and the braying of donkeys (*In Amos* 5.23 PL XXV, 1054). But even our learned post-Renaissance Hebraists whose purpose was no longer polemical but scholarly, nevertheless still felt obliged to make numerous excuses to their pious readers for the unwholesome rubbish they were being offered. John Lightfoot, that man of admirable insight, hastened to accompany his persuasive statement on the value and necessity of the Talmud to New Testament research with the following warning:

> Intending readers of these volumes may be frightened away by the ill-repute of their authors who are very badly spoken of by all . . . These Jewish writings stink (*foetant Judaica haec scripta*) . . . They suffer from some kind of exceptional bad fate which makes them cause displeasure even unread. They are censured by those who have read them, but even more so by those who have not . . . Their readers are tormented, tortured and tired . . . by the stupendous futility . . . of the topics. They so abound in nonsense as though they wished not to be read . . . (However, although) the Jews give themselves nothing but nonsense, destruction and poison to drink, . . . the Christians with their skill and industry can convert these into useful servants of their studies.

Lightfoot's continuator, Schoettgen, advances an odd justification for his use of 'wicked' Jewish works in interpreting the gospels: they are no more pernicious than heathen classics, yet these are often quoted by Christian Bible experts!

Crude reasoning such as this was to some extent refined, but not altogether eliminated, by nineteenth-century scholarly criticism of scripture. German Liberal Protestantism – represented, say, by Wellhausen – promoted a sort of academic anti-Judaism which, in an oversimplified way, may be summed up thus. Authentic Judaism – i.e., all that a nineteenth-century enlightened Christian found acceptable in the Old Testament – was propounded by the prophets before the Babylonian exile. After the return of the Jews to Palestine, came the law which completely suffocated the free impulses of a living religion.[23] The substance of Wellhausen's historical thesis was taken over by Ferdinand Weber in a very influential manual to which I have alluded earlier, his *Jewish Theology*, first published in 1880. In his preface we read:

With the return of Ezra . . . the influence of the prophetic word retreated
. . . indeed, the Law became the only religious principle. It generated
. . . a peculiar Jewish theology, which is distinguished from the teaching
of the Old Testament . . .; in fact, it is opposed to it.[24]

Weber's theological 'insight' was borrowed by Schürer in his notorious
chapter, 'Life under the Law',[25] and also, be it noted, by Billerbeck, who
has passed it on to subsequent generations. Very often the choice of the
illustrative material in the famous *Commentary to the New Testament from
Talmud and Midrash* is governed by Weber's understanding of Judaism. In
fact, there is an all-pervading tendentiousness in this great opus which
renders its handling delicate and even dangerous. A recent writer remarks
that it

may retain some usefulness . . . with several provisions; that the user be
able to look up the passages and read them in context, that he disregard
as much as possible Billerbeck's own summaries and syntheses, and that
he be able . . . to find passages on the topic not cited by Billerbeck.[26]

In brief, what this author seems to imply is that Billerbeck's *Commentary to the New Testament*, intended for non-specialists in Judaica, is helpful only to experts in post-biblical Jewish literature – to those who need it
the least, that is to say.

And what about Kittel's *Theological Dictionary*, the other sacrosanct
work, which together with Billerbeck is considered by critical scholars of
the New Testament, who as a rule show limited respect for the integrity,
authenticity and historicity of the gospels themselves, as a gospel truth
above criticism![27] As far as the use of the Jewish sources is concerned,
many of the articles edited by Kittel depend on Billerbeck, and consequently stand, and quite often fall, with the latter. But this is not all. In
assessing the *Dictionary*, the personal history of Gerhard Kittel should not
be ignored: and it does not inspire confidence. In the same year that the
first fascicles of the *Theologisches Wörterbuch* were published – produced
by a team chosen by Kittel – the editor-in-chief also issued a little book of
his own: *Die Judenfrage*, 'The Jewish Question'. The year was 1933, and it
was, as you may have guessed, an antisemitic tract.

Perhaps you will allow me to digress slightly at this point in order to
make sure that my comments on Kittel will not be misinterpreted. Some
civilized German theologians found his behaviour scandalous. Karl
Ludwig Schmidt, a renowned New Testament scholar and editor of the
monthly, *Theologische Blätter*, was courageous enough to publish in the
August 1933 number an open letter to Gerhard Kittel by the great Jewish

author, biblical scholar and religious thinker, Martin Buber.[28] This in its
turn provoked the following magnificent response to Buber on the part of
another leading German New Testament specialist, Ernst Lohmeyer.

I have just read your open letter to Gerhard Kittel and am impelled to
tell you that, for me, every one of your words is as though spoken from
my own heart. But what impels me is not only this sentiment of spiritual
solidarity . . . but to be frank, something like shame that fellow theologians should think and write as they do, that the Lutheran church
should remain silent as she does, and like a ship without captain should
herself be blown off course by the political storm of an after all fugitive
present. This letter is meant to show you that not all those in the theological faculties, and also not all New Testament scholars, share Kittel's
ideas.[29]

Kittel himself, a learned man, split between love and hatred for Judaism
(he sent a copy of his odious booklet to Buber as a present), continued both
to edit the *Dictionary* and to pursue his political activities. He wrote for the
official Nazi publication, *Forschungen zur Judenfrage* (Researches into the
Jewish Question)[30] and compromised himself so profoundly that in 1945
he was deprived of his university chair and was subject to a kind of house
arrest in the Benedictine abbey of Beuron. He died in 1948, aged fifty-nine.
Some of the other contributors to the *Dictionary* also suffered, I believe,
temporary set-backs in the post-war process of de-Nazification in
Germany.

What I have said about Kittel does not mean that the early instalments
of the *Theologisches Wörterbuch* contain noticeably antisemitic utterances,
or that they are devoid of valuable articles; nevertheless it is not unreasonable to question whether a work issued by such an editor in Hitler's Third
Reich is to be relied on for an unbiased presentation of the Jewish
sources.[31]

After this disproportionately long introduction, we may now glance at the
post-war scene. The recent developments in our domain are attributable
to two main causes. The first is the impact on the Christian world of the
horror of the Holocaust. Let me simply quote the words of dedication
with which two outstanding books open. Both are devoted to the New
Testament and written by Jews. Jules Isaac, the well-known French histo
rian and founder of Amitiés judéo-chrétiennes, or 'Jewish Christian
Friendships', published shortly after the end of the Second World War a
passionate and powerful criticism of Christian scholarly and ecclesiastical
attitudes to Judaism.[32] His dedication runs:

A ma femme, à ma fille martyres
tuées par les nazis d'Hitler
tuées simplement parce qu'elles s'appelaient ISAAC.

And who can remain unmoved by the inscription on the first page of *On the Trial of Jesus*, that splendid work of scholarship composed with loving devotion in the midst of grim poverty in London by the Jewish refugee from Czechoslovakia, Paul Winter?

> To the dead in Auschwitz, Izbica, Majdanck, Treblinka, among whom are those who were dearest to me.[33]

In the shadow of the chimneys of the death-camps, anti-Judaism, even academic anti-Judaism, has become not only unfashionable but obscene. For the moment at least, it has largely disappeared, and we have now a more open, positive and constructive approach by New Testament scholars towards post-biblical Judaism.

A second powerful influence on recent developments has been the discovery of the Dead Sea Scrolls in the vicinity of Qumran in eleven caves between 1947 and 1956. These compositions have not only revived interest in the Jewish background to the New Testament, but in a real, and not journalistic, sense revolutionized it.[34]

The Dead Sea discoveries created much excitement and sensation because they yielded for the first time in history Hebrew and Aramaic manuscripts belonging to the era prior to the destruction of Jerusalem in AD 70. They mark an enormous step forward in our understanding of the history of the biblical text and of Jewish ideas and customs in the intertestamental era. They were hailed as epoch-making because, among other reasons, deriving as they do from the period between the second century BC and the first century AD, they are potentially able to add to our knowledge of Jesus and the origins of Christianity. Some of the initial views expressed in this respect in the early 1950s were extreme. A French orientalist of international stature claimed to have uncovered in the Scrolls a pre-Christian Christianity, with a suffering and executed Messiah who rose from the dead and returned in glory to take revenge on an ungodly Jerusalem.[35] A Jewish scholar from Cambridge went even further. He identified the Habakkuk Commentary and other Qumran writings as Judaeo-Christian documents in which the leader referred to as the Teacher of Righteousness is none other than Jesus himself.[36] But these were, as I have said, extreme views and their impact was short-lived. The majority of world scholarship, students of every nationality, some of them religious,

Christian or Jewish, some agnostic, applied themselves with energy and perseverance to piecing together, deciphering, translating and evaluating the Scrolls. A considerable amount of work aimed also at determining the relationship between them and the books of the New Testament. The results are of major significance.[37] In the field of terminology, Qumran parallels to New Testament phrases prove that the evangelists and the letter-writers used idioms which were current in their time, and that the full meaning of a passing reference to, for example, 'the sons of light' in Luke, John or Paul can be established only when the expression is seen against the rich imagery of a universal struggle between Light and Darkness, between the Prince of Light and the Angel of Darkness, between the Spirits of Light and the Spirits of Darkness, and their earthly allies the Pious and the Wicked.

Certain key New Testament concepts take on new substance. For instance, Messiah as a generic term can apply in the Scrolls to at least two, and possibly three, different persons and functions. The Messiah of Israel, or Branch of David, is the victorious King of the last days. But he is subordinate to the Messiah of Aaron, or the High Priest of the end of time. And both of these are preceded or accompanied by a messianic Prophet or prophetic Messiah who conveys God's final message to the elect.[38]

Moreover, the formation and organization of the Christian community are no longer phenomena *sui generis* but strictly paralleled at Qumran. The Teacher of Righteousness of the Scrolls was, like Jesus, believed to have served as transmitter and interpreter of the divine mysteries, of God's definitive revelation. Like Jesus, he was surrounded by faithful disciples who continued to adhere to, and practise, his doctrines after his death and preached perseverance when the 'final age' and the establishment of the kingdom of heaven were delayed beyond all expectation. Like Jesus' followers, they organized themselves into a separate, self-contained body of the chosen, some of them living like the Jerusalem church out of a common purse and shunning private ownership of property. In fact, it is a comparison of the groups that brings into relief the distinctive marks of each. For example, whilst Jesus addressed himself only to the 'lost sheep of the house of Israel', his disciples decided, not without argument and hesitation, to admit non-Jews into their midst without obliging them to pass through Judaism, and this soon led to a largely, and later exclusively, Gentile church. The Qumran sectaries, by contrast, closed the doors of their community to all except Jews, or possibly also full converts to the religion of Israel.

At this point, a methodological question must be raised. Should the Jewish background to the New Testament be viewed in our post-Qumran era as roughly identical with the Dead Sea Scrolls? Some scholars would answer yes. The Scrolls, they would point out, together with some insignificant inscriptions are the only Jewish writings surviving in their original Hebrew and Aramaic chronologically parallel to the New Testament. In particular, when linguistic aspects are involved, only they can serve as terms of comparison: Jewish traditional literature, the compilation of the rabbis, belongs to the subsequent centuries and its relevance is dubious.[39] There is some truth in this point of view, but on the whole it is a sophism. If we can choose between an evidence that is contemporaneous with the gospels, and another that is more recent, we must obviously prefer the former. But since the Qumran material is tiny compared with Mishnah, Talmud and the rest, and is more often than not fragmentary, many facets of the New Testament would remain deprived of a Jewish background if recourse to rabbinic literature were precluded. But few serious scholars would deny today that rabbinic writings, though compiled between AD 200 and 500, include a large quantity of traditions traceable to the first century AD and that with a minimum amount of critical skill, it is often possible to distinguish among them between the old and the more recent.

Thus instead of restricting the boundaries of the Jewish background to the New Testament, the Dead Sea Scrolls have enlarged them: they are additional to the pre-existing material. As a matter of fact, serious students of the Qumran texts have quickly realized that they cannot be treated as autonomous, but need to be inserted into the larger body of Jewish literature: Bible, Apocrypha, Pseudepigrapha, Dead Sea sectarian writings, the great Hellenistic Jewish authors Philo and Josephus, rabbinic compositions, including the Aramaic paraphrases of the Old Testament. The latter, called Targums, very largely reflect the ordinary understanding of scripture by the ordinary Jew in late antiquity. In fact, apart from the Scrolls, the study of these Targums forms today one of the liveliest branches of Jewish studies.[40] In 1956, the year in which the last of the Dead Sea Scrolls were found, a singularly important copy of the whole Palestinian Aramaic version was also identified, not in an exotic hide-out like Qumran, but in Rome, where it had rested unrecognized for centuries because a careless cataloguer of the Vatican Library had recorded it under an erroneous description.[41]

In short, it has become obvious to many – in theory at least! – that expertise in the Jewish background to the New Testament is not an optional extra, but that, on the contrary, no adequate understanding of Christian sources is conceivable without it.

So far the issue of New Testament interpretation has been considered from the viewpoint of its own practitioners. It is now time to ask how it is seen by a historian of first-century Judaism. For him the problem is twofold, and requires a twofold basic re-orientation of approach.

First, for theological reasons the New Testament has always been considered by its exegetes as a subject to which all others must be subservient. If the Jewish background – seemingly distinct from the New Testament – is to be studied, it is in the hope that it may throw light on the gospels. It may help to solve New Testament puzzles. It is on this account that the questions are to be asked. The background must speak only when spoken to.

A historian cannot share these attitudes. For him, the New Testament, however marvellous and influential, is but a fraction of the literary legacy of first-century Judaism. In fact, I believe it not improper to suggest that for a *historical* understanding, the age-old distinction between the New Testament and its Jewish background should be abolished and the former looked at deliberately as part of a larger whole. This would mean that the New Testament's monopoly of always formulating the queries would come to an end. Questions should be asked in the light of the total evidence, and answers sought from the various Jewish groups represented by, say, some of the Pseudepigrapha, Josephus and Philo, the Dead Sea Scrolls, the New Testament and rabbinic literature. It is only by comparing these answers with one another, and with Old Testament data, that they can be understood, singly and together, in perspective.

Allow me to illustrate this by means of the problem of divorce in inter-testamental Judaism.[42] The Bible includes no detailed legislation on this important topic: Deuteronomy 24 simply envisages the special case of the remarriage of a man and his former wife, who has in the meantime been married to another man and divorced by him or left a widow. Such a union is forbidden, but in setting out this case, the grounds for divorce are laid down in the vaguest terms by the legislator: a bill of divorce may be given by the husband if the wife 'finds no favour in his eyes because he has found in her (literally) the nakedness of a thing (something indecent)'.

First-century Judaism in general interpreted the divorce rules very elastically. Josephus, describing the Jewish law for Gentile readers speaks of divorce 'for whatever cause', adding that 'with mortals many such may arise (*Ant.* iv, 253). Alluding to his own marital difficulties, he remarks casually that he dismissed his wife because he was 'displeased with her behaviour' (*Vita* 426). The influential Pharisaic school of Hillel likewise argued that even a spoilt dinner was sufficient reason for severing the marriage bond. By contrast, the more demanding rival school of Shammai allowed divorce only if the husband found 'unchastity' in his wife (*mGittin*

9.10). Now let us look at the question put to Jesus in Matt. 19.3. 'Is it lawful to divorce one's wife for any cause?' echoes the current Hillelite view. His answer, 'No, except for fornication', accords with the doctrine of the school of Shammai. But in another New Testament account, in Mark 10, Jesus, when asked in absolute terms whether divorce is permissible, gives a negative reply, allowing for no exception: a man or a woman who initiates divorce and follows it with a second marriage commits adultery. Thus the proper formulation of the conflict between the Jesus of Matthew and the Jesus of Mark, and the possible resolution of the problem of historicity, are more likely to arise from a reconstruction of the entire puzzle in which Matthew and Mark represent two small pieces, rather than the other way round. Incidentally, a woman could not formally divorce her husband in Jewish law; consequently, to be tenable, the Marcan version requires a flexible interpretation, which *ipso facto* weakens its claim for historicity.[43]

In sum, the insertion of the New Testament in a larger canvas provides it with added clarity and fuller meaning. It is a critically sound method, and to my mind the *only* acceptable one.

In addition to realizing that the New Testament is historically part of the greater body of first-century Jewish literature, the exegete must also bear in mind, if he is to comprehend them correctly, that the books of the New Testament belong in a sense to the genre of translation. I do not imply by this that some parts of the New Testament were first composed in Aramaic (or Hebrew), though this may have been the case, and subsequently rendered into Greek, the only surviving form of the text and justifiably designated as original. What I mean is that both Jesus and his immediate disciples were native Semitic speakers. Consequently, if anything genuinely and directly traceable to them remains in the Greek New Testament, apart from *Ephphatha, Talitha kum, Abba, Eloi eloi lamma sabachtani, Maranatha* – the few obvious Aramaic relics – it must have an underlying Aramaic or Hebrew original. Moreover, terminology is not the only area requiring critical analysis: in a broader sense, one must also remember that the religious culture permeating the Greek New Testament is not Greek/Hellenistic but Hebrew/Jewish. Together, these two factors, the terminological and the cultural, prompt a large number of crucial questions in regard to verbal and conceptual equivalents. Let me give you two examples.

The Hebrew word *Torah* (doctrine, instruction) was translated into Greek before the Christian era as *nomos*, law. Hellenistic Jews nevertheless appear to have been aware of the Hebrew connotations of their *nomos*, and Aramaic speakers, perhaps to avoid the pitfalls created by the choice of the

Greek term, preferred to render *Torah* as *Orayta*, teaching, enlighten-ment.[44] It is only by stressing the Greek, without paying attention to the Semitic, significance of the term, that one can with Paul and Hellenistic Christianity construe the law, with its condemnation and death, as the opposite of Christ the Saviour. With *Torah* equated to *nomos*, the Law, Christianity inherited from Hellenistic Judaism an incorrect translation of a key-concept. And by developing its Greek associations alone, the church finished by distorting the Hebrew/Jewish meaning of the Judaeo-Hellenistic *nomos*.

My second example is the phrase, 'son of God'.[45] To a Greek speaker in Alexandria, Antioch or Athens at the turn of the eras, the concept *huios theou*, son of God, would have brought to mind either one of the many offspring of the Olympian deities, or possibly a deified Egyptian-Ptolemaic king, or the divine emperor of Rome, descendant of the apotheosized Julius Caesar. But to a Jew, the corresponding Hebrew or Aramaic phrase would have applied to none of these. For him, son of God could refer, in an ascending order, to any of the children of Israel; or to a good Jew; or to a charismatic holy Jew; or to the king of Israel; or in particular to the royal Messiah; and finally, in a different sense, to an angelic or heavenly being. In other words, 'son of God' was always understood metaphorically in Jewish circles. In Jewish sources, its use never implies participation by the person so-named in the divine nature. It may in consequence safely be assumed that if the medium in which Christian theology developed had been Hebrew and not Greek, it would not have produced an incarnation doctrine as this is traditionally understood.[46]

To conclude, I would like to return to my opening quotation. The candidate recommended by my anonymous referee was said to be 'among the few New Testament scholars who can take seriously, and walk sure-footedly in the Semitic material to the importance of which we all pay lip-service'. If there is truth in what I have tried to convey to you in the fore-going pages, the exceptional knowledge ascribed to our nameless candidate must be downgraded and become the ordinary qualification required of any competent student of the New Testament. In fact, it will be a mini-mum qualification. A good New Testament scholar will have to endeavour to become a citizen of that larger world to which his discipline belongs (and that means not only the Jewish, but also the Hellenistic world), so that he will be able to understand the arguments advanced by the experts in the various provinces of that world, but also, to think out new and pertinent questions and initiate fresh research likely to be beneficial to New Testa-ment study.

Is this an unattainable reverie? Its fulfilment is admittedly impossible within the framework of our present academic curricula. The New Testament is taught in most British universities as part of an undergraduate programme in theology, a programme in which it occupies an important, but not disproportionately large, part. If we also bear in mind that the classical linguistic instruction in our schools is no longer what it used to be, it is hardly reasonable to expect that at the end of three short years, our theological faculties and departments should turn out New Testament students properly qualified to embark on research. In the circumstances, only graduate training can provide a solution to the problem.

Here it may be claimed with truth that the University of Oxford has taken up an avant-garde position. Since 1977–78, the Faculty of Oriental Studies has been offering a course leading to a Master's degree (MPhil) in Jewish Studies in the Graeco-Roman period. Students admitted to it have to acquire specialized knowledge in the history, literature, religion and culture of the Jews from the second century BC to the fifth century AD, and to familiarize themselves with Jewish literature of that period in Hebrew, Aramaic and Greek.[47] The programme has been devised for graduates of all kinds who wish to become expert in Jewish studies in late antiquity, but those with a particular interest in the New Testament are specifically catered for. If similar courses are established in other centres as well, a new era will open in New Testament research.

One thing is in any case sure. We shall not get the revival of scholarship that we look for until interpreters of the Christian gospels learn to immerse themselves in the native religion of Jesus the *Jew*, and in the general climate of thought of the world and age in which he lived.

6

Jewish Literature and New Testament
Exegesis: Reflections on Methodology

The present study follows an endeavour to lay down a few guiding-lines,
within the context of history, for the use of Jewish documents in New
Testament interpretation.[1] Here an attempt is made, for the first time as
far as I am aware, to provide a methodological outline, incomplete though
it may be, of this intricate and complex branch of scholarship.

To start with, two commonplaces have to be taken into account. Firstly,
it is accepted that the New Testament is in some way connected, not
only with the Hebrew Scriptures (which it often cites), but also with post-
biblical Judaism. It is consequently assumed that the literary relics of
ancient Israel may from the viewpoint of language and content prove useful to New Testament exegesis. Secondly, the earliest surviving form of
the New Testament is Greek. Yet although a good deal of it was actually
composed in that language, neither Jesus himself nor his original milieu
belonged in any real sense (*pace* Hengel) to Hellenistic Judaism,[2] so any
valid approximation of his genuine message must entail a linguistic and
religious-cultural 're-translation' from the Greek into Aramaic/Hebrew
concepts and thought-forms.[3]

Is such a reconversion possible, and if so by what means?[4]

Apart from the exceptional cases of Origen and Jerome, who applied the
expertise acquired from Jewish consultants and teachers in expounding
difficult New Testament passages,[5] it was not until the seventeenth century that the technical issue of interpretation with the help of Judaic
sources was confronted. In the preface to his section on the Gospel of
Matthew, John Lightfoot wrote these remarkable lines in *Horae Hebraicae
et Talmudicae* first published in 1658:

> I have also concluded without the slightest doubt that the best and most
> genuine method to unravel the obscure passages of the New Testament
> (of which there are many) is through research into the significance of the

phrases and sayings in question according to the ordinary dialect and way of thinking of that (Jewish) nation, those who uttered them as well as those who listened to the speakers. For it is of no consequence what we can make of those locutions with the help of the anvil of our expressions, but what they meant to them in their common speech. And this can only be investigated by consulting the authors of the Talmud, who both employ the common idiom of the Jews and treat and open up all things Jewish.[6]

Between the seventeenth and the twentieth centuries, however, methodological progress was practically nil. In vain, for instance, does one search the *Kommentar zum Neuen Testament aus Talmud und Midrasch* by Hermann Strack and Paul Billerbeck,[7] or Gerhard Kittel's *Theologisches Wörterbuch zum Neuen Testament*,[8] for a reference to the system they intend to employ. In their *Vorwort* to vol. I of the *Kommentar* dated 1922, Strack and Billerbeck proclaim simply:

> By bodily descent, the Lord belonged to the Jewish people and most of the New Testament writers were Jews ... So the Judaism of their time must be known if their utterances are to be understood correctly (p. VI).

Some help, they say, may be obtained from the Apocrypha and Pseudepigrapha but the authors themselves concentrate mainly on Talmud and Midrash with a view to presenting objectively the beliefs, outlook and life of the Jews in the first century AD. Their only acknowledgment of the existence of an historical dimension in this enterprise consists in the assertion that whenever possible they give the name and date of the authority quoted (p. VI).

This skeletal manifesto of the *Kommentar* fails to point out one of the major difficulties facing the New Testament interpreter, namely that his recorded comparative material is substantially younger than his documents. On page I vol. I of Strack–Billerbeck, citations are borrowed from R. Eleazar (*c.* AD 270), Rav Yehudah (died 299), Samuel (died 254) and R. Pinhas bar Hama (*c.* 360). But not a word is said by way of explaining whether or how these third and fourth century traditions are relevant to the exegesis of Matt. 1.1, which no doubt dates to the end of the first century. The use of the rabbinic data testifies moreover to a kind of historical fundamentalism; every attribution is believed, and every citation is seen to represent the truth. Nowhere is there any sign of awareness that rabbinic ideas themselves evolved. In fact, quite frequently the more developed form of a tradition is preferred to another closer in time to the New Testament!

Kittel has even less to reveal concerning his employment of Jewish texts. *TDNT* being a dictionary and not a commentary, it looks for its relationship to previous works of the same kind rather than for links with the sources of another literary culture attested in a different language. G. Friedrich, editor of the later volumes, reports in 'Prehistory of TDNT', that J. Kögel, the reviser of H. Cremer's *Biblisch-theologisches Wörterbuch der neutestamentlichen Gräzität*,[9] was of the opinion that 'the rabbinic element in his new edition was too brief'.[10] To fill the lacuna, he recruited as a collaborator G. Kittel who, on Kögel's death, inherited the whole project. The preface to vol. I, which appeared in 1933, announces that all the contributions have been sent for annotation from the standpoint of rabbinics to Kittel, and to two other young Judaica specialists of sixty years ago, the late K. G. Kuhn and K. H. Rengstorf. But as far as the use of post-biblical Judaism is concerned, the early volumes of *TDNT*, or rather *TWNT*, chiefly depend on Strack and Billerbeck.

From the 1930s onward, one area of post-biblical Jewish literature largely neglected by Billerbeck, the Aramaic paraphrases of scripture, received fresh attention.[11] Interest in the Palestinian Targums to the Pentateuch was aroused by P. Kahle when he published in 1930 the fragments retrieved from the Cairo Genizah,[12] and was subsequently revived by A. Díez Macho's re-discovery of Codex Neofiti I in the Vatican Library in 1956.[13] The most influential work to result from these finds was the monograph, *An Aramaic Approach to the Gospels and Acts* by M. Black.[14] The Targumic exegesis of the New Testament has the advantage, compared with other branches of rabbinic literature, of being entirely based on Palestinian – i.e. Galilean – Aramaic texts which were probably subjected to a less thorough updating than the Mishnah, Tosefta, Talmud and halakhic Midrashim. It nevertheless suffers from the same methodological weakness as Talmudic-Midrashic New Testament interpretation inasmuch that in its redacted form (even when we discount obviously late additions such as allusions to Byzantium or to Islam), no Palestinian Targum is likely to predate AD 200.

The most revolutionary change in the position of the New Testament exegete concerned with Jewish comparative data occurred in 1947 with the discovery of the Dead Sea Scrolls. Not only did he now find himself equipped with non-biblical Qumran documents written mostly in Hebrew and Aramaic, and in a broad sense contemporaneous with Christian beginnings, but they derive in addition from a sectarian setting more or less similar to that of the early church. Also, practically all of the literature is religious, including a fair amount of Bible interpretation.

In many respects it would be hard to invent a literary corpus more suitable for the study of the New Testament than these scrolls[15] and not surprisingly there is a growing tendency in contemporary New Testament study to restrict comparison exclusively to them. Indeed, apart from the (unacknowledged) advantage of eliminating the arduous work of consulting rabbinic sources, pan-Qumranism has much in its favour: chronology, language, eschatologico-apocalyptic background, similarity in religious aspirations, etc. On the other hand, does recognition of the importance of the Qumran documents (and of epigraphical material of the same period) signify that contributions from Mishnah, Talmud, Midrash and Targum are now to be regarded as negligible, as deprived of any validity? Professor J. A. Fitzmyer seems to think it does.[16]

It should in fairness be stressed that he argues primarily from a linguistic stand, claiming that Qumran Aramaic (and the Aramaic of first-century AD tomb and ossuary inscriptions) – or more abstractly Middle Aramaic evidence – 'must be the latest Aramaic that should be used for philological comparison of the Aramaic substratum of the Gospels and Acts'.[17] Elsewhere, he emphasizes that Qumran Aramaic yields 'privileged data that take precedence over the material derived from the classic targumim and midrashim'.[18] In practice, however, Fitzmyer does not stay with philology. In addition to Aramaic words and phrases preserved in the New Testament and to Aramaisms in, and mistranslations from Aramaic into, New Testament Greek, he deals with literary forms in prose and poetry, Jewish literary traditions in the New Testament and in Aramaic sources, and even with Jewish practices and beliefs emerging from the Qumran Aramaic texts.[19]

In abstracto, Fitzmyer's thesis is defensible. If we could lay hands on comparative material belonging to the appropriate period, in the appropriate type of language, representing the appropriate literature, and extant in sufficient quantity, it would be unnecessary to consult documents of a later age for interpretative purposes of any description.[20] But we are not so fortunate. An unintentional and hence particularly significant outcome of Fitzmyer's *Manual of Palestinian Aramaic Texts*[21] has been, in effect, to highlight the limitations of the available evidence from the intertestamental epoch. Despite inclusion of a substantial number of tiny fragments producing no meaningful sequences of words, the sample is small, the literary genres quite limited and the vocabulary meagre. Aramaic speakers of New Testament times used many more words than those attested in the extant literary and inscriptional remains. It is with these facts in mind that we have to judge Fitzmyer's programme: 'Discussions of the language of Jesus in recent decades have been legion, and much of that discussion has been based on texts that are of questionable relevance. Our purpose in gathering Palestinian Aramaic texts of the period . . . is to try to illustrate what should be the background of that discussion.'[22]

In fact, the policy thus outlined, even if executed blamelessly, cannot avoid running into serious difficulties because of the scarcity of comparative material recognized by Professor Fitzmyer as admissible. This basic flaw is compounded by his handling of the evidence in the few cases where he provides his own illustrations. Examining Aramaic words preserved in the New Testament, he notes that *korban* is still explained by M. Black as 'a form of solemn prohibition found . . . in the Talmud',[23] and that the overtones of the Talmudic usage have always embarrassed the New Testament commentator appealing to them in connection with Mark 7.11 ('any support that you might have had from me is *korban*', i.e., a gift made to God). Fitzmyer then reminds the reader of two recently found Aramaic inscriptions from Palestine, one of which, an ossuary epigraph published by J. T. Milik, reads: 'All that a man may find to his profit in this ossuary is a *korban* to God from him who is inside.' Here, the 'dedicatory sense' of the term is apparent, whereas in the rabbinic occurrences (as understood by Fitzmyer) it is not. He therefore concludes that 'such evidence . . . renders unnecessary the references to later Jewish material from sources such as the Talmud'.[24]

Besides stressing the need also to take into consideration Josephus' mention of *qorban* = *dōron theou* as an oath form,[25] I should also point out that Fitzmyer's statement amounts to a concatenation of factual errors allied to a possible general misconception. *Ned.* 3.2 quoted by him, refers to the Mishnah and *not* to the Talmud. The text is in Hebrew and *not* in Aramaic. Moreover, the example is not only ill-chosen as far as the substance is concerned; it may also be philologically unsuitable, for the New Testament word, a quasi-liturgical exclamation, can just as well reproduce a Hebrew as an Aramaic original.[26] In this connection it should be noted that Fitzmyer's second so-called Aramaic inscription containing the single word *qrbn* can just as easily be Hebrew.[27] Finally, it can hardly be questioned that the Mishnaic formulae (paralleled in substance though not terminologically in the Damascus Rule 16.14–15, where the notion of *herem* appears) provide a much more apt illustration for Mark 7.11 since they imply that through *qorban* a deprivation was inflicted on the members of a person's family, a nuance missing from the ossuary inscription.

Equally unlucky is the treatment of *mamōnas*. We are informed that what he calls its 'alleged' Aramaic background 'has been illustrated by appeals to the Babylonian Talmud (*bBer.* 61b), a Palestinian Targum (Gen. 34.43) . . ., and to passages in the Palestinian Talmud'.[28] Against these, the American scholar cites the Hebrew Ecclesiasticus 31.8, various

Qumran texts also in Hebrew,[29] and the Punic usage mentioned by Augustine (the latter dating to Talmudic times, rather odd *qua* evidence in the circumstances). Fitzmyer then asserts: 'Here is an instance where we may have to cease appealing to Aramaic for the explanation of the Greek *mamōna* and resort merely to a common Semitic background of the word.'[30] This reasoning strikes a sensitive linguist as peculiar. The availability of contemporaneous Hebrew, and more recent Punic, attestations of a term are seen to be sufficient grounds for discarding later Aramaic parallels to interpret a New Testament noun displaying a distinct Aramaic ending! But of course the whole argument is ill-founded for by the time it was published (1975), *(m)am(on)ah* had already been encountered in the Aramaic Job Targum (Job 27.17) from 11Q (1971).[31] Fitzmyer himself lists it in the Glossary of his *Manual* (1978).[32] Yet he still advises us in 1979 to 'cease appealing to Aramaic'.

Among New Testament Aramaisms, Fitzmyer could hardly overlook *ho huios tou anthrōpou*, in his words, 'a Greek phrase that is often said to carry an Aramaic nuance'. He was bound to repeat his by now familiar thesis that the noun *nash/a*, written without the initial aleph, being of late provenance, 'one should . . . be wary of citing texts in which (the shortened) form of the expression occurs as if they were contemporary with the NT material'.[33] Without wishing to launch once more into the 'son of man' debate,[34] I note signs of some *rapprochement* in his position. He now admits (or readmits) that the case for the circumlocutional use of 'son of man' has been made out at least once, and that Matt. 16.13 ('Who do men say the son of man is?') compared with Mark 8.27 ('Who do men say that I am?') suggests that the substitution of ' "Son of Man" for "I" . . . reflects current Palestinian Aramaic usage'.[35] In the absence of first-century positive evidence supporting my case, he nevertheless feels entitled to hesitate over 'some of the interpretations' proposed by me.[36] Yet at the same time, he does not flinch from the possibility that the Targumic idiom was influenced by the New Testament![37]

Glancing finally at a conjectural mistranslation from Aramaic into Greek as adduced by Fitzmyer apropos of Matt. 7.6, 'Do not give dogs what is holy // and do not throw pearls before swine', he recalls that it has long since been proposed that the Greek interpreter misread *qᵉdasha*, ring, as *qudsha*, holiness = *to hagion*, and thus spoiled the parallelism between ring and pearls. In the past, the hypothesis was based – Professor Fitzmyer tells us – on 'late Syriac and other texts', but now the 11Q Job Targum (on 42.11) supplies the word in the sense of a ring: 'And each man gave him a sheep and each a gold ring (*qᵉdash had di dᵉhab*)'.[38] I am not sure who it was who appealed to late Syriac texts but am somewhat surprised that

Fitzmyer seems to have failed to notice that the reading of 11Qtg Job is almost literally identical with that of the *traditional* Targum of Job, where the second half of 42.11 reads: *we-'ʿnash qʿdasha didʿhaba ḥad.*[39] In sum, taking into account the patchiness of the new evidence and the imperfections apparent in its application to the study of the New Testament, I believe we may be forgiven for considering the general problem not solved by Fitzmyer but on the contrary still wide open.

The one area where Qumran Aramaic could play a decisive role would be the study of first-century literary Aramaic documents, which apart from *Megillath Taʿanith* (not regarded by Fitzmyer as really relevant)[40] and the lost Aramaic draft of Josephus' *War* (*BJ* i. 3, 6), consist only in the Qumran texts themselves, since it is reasonable to suppose that much of the Aramaic reflected in the Greek gospels belongs to the spoken, if not colloquial, form of the language. Trying now to piece together a methodology, borrowing where appropriate from the theories already outlined, but setting the data into a broader and more refined framework, the first question requiring an answer concerns the purpose of the enterprise. What do we hope to achieve by bringing inter-testamental and rabbinic Jewish writings to bear on the understanding of the New Testament?

In the case of the gospels and the early chapters of Acts, there is clearly no hope of retrieving their Semitic original beyond transliterated words and phrases and a few obvious Aramaisms in New Testament Greek (e.g., 'to bind and to loose', *'ᵃsar* and *shʿrē*).[41] As for the famous *ipsissima verba*, a quest for these presupposes a degree of reliability in gospel tradition that modern research simply cannot justify. Sayings attributed to Jesus in the New Testament (and to the rabbis in the Mishnah and the Talmud), are often edited and sometimes even freely supplied. But is it possible nevertheless to grasp at the very least something of a master's teaching? I would suggest that we can manage to perceive his ideas, the *ipsissimus sensus*, even without the actual words in which they were formulated. Where the gospels are concerned, the required preliminaries are the various kinds of criticism: form-, source-, tradition- and redaction-criticism. Subsequently, study of the Greek New Testament can be assisted powerfully by means of appropriate Hebrew/Aramaic parallels. Thus if on the basis of internal gospel evidence it is assumed that Jesus' teaching implies not the abolition but the continuity of the Torah (Matt. 5.17; Luke 16.16–17), the Aramaic/Hebrew idiom, *lʿbattala/lʿbattēl lʿqayyama/lʿqayyēm*, cannot be without value in interpreting the Greek *katalusai* and *plērosai*.[42]

The sectors likely to benefit most from comparison with Jewish sources are those of religious concepts and motifs such as Messiah, Lord, son of God, holy man/miracle-worker, exorcist/healer, etc. With the proviso that an acceptable method of evaluation is agreed on, the juxtaposition of the New Testament and Jewish parallels is sure to lead to the discovery of how the original audience or readership understood the words, phrases or themes in question. This matter is discussed at length in *Jesus the Jew*, especially in its second half.[43]

Another branch of comparative study is concerned with Aramaic/Hebrew literary units attested in the New Testament, such as proverbs, Bible interpretation, parables and the like. Here again, if and when the preliminary issue of admissibility is settled, the Semitic material can pinpoint common traits and underline distinctive peculiarities. A certain amount of important work has already been done in this field, to mention only Rudolf Bultmann's analysis of proverbial sayings among the *logia*,[44] or Joachim Jeremias' study of the parables,[45] but it goes without saying that in both domains much remains to be done. In particular, attention should be further concentrated on the special thrust characteristic of common themes. For example, in the parable of the Prodigal Son (Luke 15.18–24), the initiative in the return/*teshuvah* lies with the repentant and trustful son, whereas in the oft-quoted rabbinic parallel attributed to R. Meir (*Dt.R.* 2.3 on Deut. 4.30)[46] the son is too overcome by shame to make such a move and it is the father who prompts the homecoming.

Following this endeavour to outline the purpose of the venture and to offer topics for comparative study, we have now to cope with the thornier task of determining the procedure to be adopted. Here it seems reasonable to argue that if the aim is historical, the method must be similarly historical. In other words, in place of the traditional handling of rabbinic documents, i.e., without regard for the effect on them of evolutionary factors, an eye must constantly be kept on development.

Where, of course, evidence is available from inter-testamental sources such as the Septuagint, Apocrypha and Pseudepigrapha, Qumran, Philo and Josephus, this comparative process can go ahead without further ado. It has to be asserted at this juncture, against occasional ill-conceived criticism,[47] that although Josephus and some of the Pseudepigrapha, e.g., IV Maccabees or Ps.-Philo, may date to decades slightly later than some parts of the New Testament, their use as *inter*-testamental documents remains legitimate inasmuch as they are, in general, not creative works but mostly represent pre-existent religious ideas. Where in any case such straightforward comparative material is at hand, the historico-exegetical work may proceed without glancing backward and forward in time, as Qumran parallels can show. For example, the portrayal of the apostles as princes seated on twelve thrones, and of the church as composed of twelve tribes,[48] echoes the claim encountered in the same form at Qumran. In both, a dissident community models itself on, and identifies itself as, the true Israel.[49] Again, eschatologico-apocalyptic disenchantment (delay of the *parousia*, postponement of the end-time) inspired the leaders of the Essenes and of the Christian church to preach hope and rank perseverance as the most essential virtue of the moment.[50] In a polemical context, the common gospel theme of healing = forgiveness of sins, though depicted as scandalizing lawyers and Pharisees – an attitude manifest in rabbinic tradition, too – finds near perfect support in the Qumran Prayer of Nabonidus in which the Babylonian king speaks of a Jewish exorcist who forgave his sins and thereby cured him of a long illness.[51]

Whilst, as I have already maintained, study of a New Testament passage in the light of inter-testamental parallels leads in many cases to a clarification of its historical significance, it can happen that time after time sources more recent than these contain ideas that improve our understanding of the original sense of a text . . . provided once more that an acceptable methodology is devised to justify the use of such non-contemporaneous material. It is enough to recall rabbinic speculation on the Binding of Isaac and its impact on the explication of the death of Jesus as a sacrifice in the Epistle to the Hebrews and elsewhere;[52] or, as will appear later, the Mishnaic, Talmudic and Midrashic views on divorce in relation to the New Testament, and specifically to the Matthean teaching on that subject.

However, the real crux comes when a New Testament saying, concept or motif figures distinctly in Targum, Midrash or Talmud, but entirely lacks (for the time being at least) pre-rabbinic corroboration. Consider Jesus' quintessential summary of true piety: 'Be merciful as your Father is merciful' (Luke 6.36); 'Be perfect as your heavenly Father is perfect' (Matt. 5.48). The Gospel *logion* closely resembles the paraphrase in Targum Ps.-Jonathan of Lev. 22.28: 'My people, children of Israel, as your Father is merciful in heaven, so you must be merciful on earth.' But this Targum is merely part of a much broader rabbinic doctrine on the imitation of God.[53] The second-century Tanna, Abba Shaul, bases this teaching on an artifically construed esoterical pun on Exodus 15.2, 'This is my God and I will praise him', which is read as, 'This is my God, I and He', and expounded as, 'Be like Him: as He is merciful and gracious, you also must be merciful and gracious'.[54]

The fullest version of the rabbinic teaching appears in the Babylonian Talmud attributed to the third-century Palestinian sage, Hama bar Hanina, interpreting Deuteronomy 13.5 (*bSot.* 14a), and also in Targum Ps.-Jonathan on Deuteronomy 34.6. The latter runs:

Blessed be the name of the Lord of the World who has taught us his right ways. He has taught us to clothe the naked as he clothed Adam and Eve. He has taught us to join the bridegroom to the bride as he joined Eve to Adam. He has taught us to visit the sick as he revealed himself in his Word to Abraham after his circumcision. He has taught us to comfort the mourners as he revealed himself to Jacob on his return from Padan in the place where his mother had died. He has taught us to feed the poor as he caused bread to descend from heaven for the children of Israel. He has taught us to bury the dead through Moses to whom he revealed himself in his Word and with him companies of ministering angels.

This Talmudic-Targumic form of the doctrine has its Christianized adaptation in Matthew 25.31–46, where the 'King' in the eschatological judgement commands the 'sheep' on his right hand to 'Come, enter and possess the kingdom. For when I was hungry you gave me food; when thirsty, you gave me to drink; when I was a stranger you took me home; when naked, you clothed me; when I was ill you came to help; when in prison, you visited me.'

What is the relationship between these two sets of texts? I see four possibilities that may be represented by the following models (NT = New Testament: R = Rabbinic literature; JT = Jewish tradition):

1. The similarities are purely coincidental.

Bearing in mind the amount of overlap and the variety of attestation, such a diagnosis is highly unlikely.

2. The rabbinic doctrine is inspired by, or borrowed from, the New Testament.

Chronologically, this is obviously possible but to render such a conjecture viable we must be able to demonstrate that the rabbis of the Tannaitic and Amoraic age were not only aware of the New Testament teachings but actually willing to learn from them: which is asking a lot.

3. The New Testament depends on Targum and Midrash.

NT ◀— R

That the New Testament should utilize current Jewish themes is both possible and likely, but actual dependence presupposes that R existed in the first century. This too is very problematic; though the Qumran Genesis Apocryphon, with its Midrashic accretions, shows that such material was extant in written form before ad 70.

4. The New Testament and the rabbinic doctrine both derive from a common source, viz., Jewish traditional teaching.

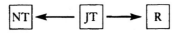

Here we have a theory that is certainly possible and even probable. It could also bring about a much improved understanding of the New Testament. It would nevertheless be difficult to conceal its methodological lameness. It could doubtless be shown that the procedure works and a convincing case could even be made out to demonstrate that the presupposition is reasonable. But the fact remains that such a process would hinge on a presumption, and for the unconverted – e.g., Professor Fitzmyer and his uncritical followers – that would come very close to begging the question.

All the same, it has to be reiterated that the system seems to work. So can it be that we are trying to answer a wrongly formulated question?[55] What if the whole argument were reversed, and instead of interpreting Matthew and Luke with the help of Tannaitic sayings from Mekhilta and Sifre, Amoraic exegesis preserved in the name of a third-century master in the Babylonian Talmud and anonymous and undated Targum excerpts, an attempt were made to trace the Targumic tradition to its origin via the Talmud (say AD 500 in its final redaction, third to fourth century for the formulation of the tradition in question), the Tannaitic Midrash (second to third century) and the New Testament (first century)? Assuming that the basic New Testament divested of its patently Hellenistic accretions is recognized as a witness of first-century Jewish religious thought, a view few serious scholars will contest, does not this suggested procedure seem methodologically sound and valid? And if so, why have we been plagued for so long with a twisted problem?

The answer lies at the heart of the age-old Jewish–Christian conflict. On the one hand, New Testament specialists, as a rule scholars and churchmen in one, almost inevitably attach to the New Testament an image which must appear distorted to the historian. The writings in which the Christian faith originates possess for them centrality, finality and ultimacy. These experts see all else – in historical terms, the whole of Judaism and Hellenism – as gravitating round the New Testament. To adopt another metaphor, for them the New Testament is the mistress, and Jewish documents, especially of the post-biblical variety, mere ancillaries at best. On the Jewish side, by contrast, the New Testament has for religious-polemical reasons been largely ignored and its Jewishness tacitly denied. Even during the last hundred years or so, recourse to it for historico-exegetical purposes has been uncommon, not only because of a lingering subconscious dislike among rabbinic scholars for all things Christian, but also, and perhaps mainly, because of their unfamiliarity with Greek and with the technical issues raised by the academic study of the New Testament.

Divested, however, of its denominational garb, the matter takes on another colour. The New Testament then ceases to be insignificant for Jews or autonomous and in every sense primary for Christians. Jesus and the movement that arose in his wake are recognized as belonging to first-century Jewish history. Furthermore, a good deal of the New Testament appears as reflecting a brief moment in the age-long religious development of Israel that starts with the Bible and continues via the Apocrypha, Pseudepigrapha, Qumran, Philo, the New Testament, Josephus, Pseudo-Philo, the Mishnah, Tosefta, Targum, Midrash, Talmud – and so on and so forth. For Jews, the study of rabbinic literature benefits greatly inasmuch as the New Testament is able to fulfil the exceedingly important function of providing a chronologically well-defined segment of tradition applicable as a yardstick in dealing with undated material.

But what happens to the complex of New Testament interpretation? How does the new perspective affect the scholarly approach to it? Negatively, one outcome is that there is no longer any call for works in which the New Testament occupies the centre of the stage. There is no need for a *Kommentar zum Neuen Testament aus Talmud und Midrasch* or, I regret to say, for *Compendia Rerum Iudaicarum ad Novum Testamentum*.[56] There is no need either for rabbinic theologies where insufficient attention is paid to pre-rabbinic sources, including the New Testament. Positively, what is required is an effort to examine the movement of Jewish religious-theological thought as a whole, and while so doing, to determine the place, significance and distinctiveness of its constituent parts. In other words, instead of looking at the New Testament as an independent unit set against a background of Judaism, we have to see it as part of a larger environment of Jewish religious and cultural history.

Unless I am wholly mistaken, the procedure proposed in this chapter avoids or overcomes the chronological difficulty that has bedevilled until now the utilization of rabbinic literature in the exegesis of the New Testament. If the latter is envisaged, not as standing apart from Judaism and above it, but as organically bound up with it, the stages of religious thought preceding it and following it are not merely relevant but essential to an historical understanding and evaluation of its message, including its originality and peculiarity. This may be illustrated by comparing the two approaches. To interpret the New Testament teaching on divorce,[57] and in particular the Matthean exception clause in Matt.5.32, *parektos logou porneias* ('except for fornication'), Strack and Billerbeck assemble an impressive array of illuminating rabbinic parallels, starting with *mGittin* 9.10, and follow with citations from Sifre on Deuteronomy, *bGittin*, *yGittin*, etc.[58] Needless to say, all these texts post-date the Gospel. In contrast to this, the procedure suggested here examines Jewish attitudes to divorce in the Bible, at Qumran, in Josephus, in the New Testament and in rabbinic literature in such a way that, inserted into a broader canvas, the links between the various units, and also their individuality and bias, stand out in relief and acquire fuller meaning. The effect furthermore is reciprocal in that the New Testament authenticates the second-century echoes in the Mishnah of the alleged first-century controversy between the Houses of Hillel and Shammai. In parenthesis, it should be noted also that in commenting on the *apostasion* (bill of divorce) in Matt. 5.31, the rabbinic data listed by Strack and Billerbeck should not be superseded, as Professor Fitzmyer would no doubt have it, but preceded and supplemented by the well-preserved Aramaic *get* found at Murabba'at.[59]

What in practical terms would be entailed in any serious attempt to substitute a strictly historical treatment of the New Testament for the 'theology' currently in vogue?

Clearly, a critical assessment of the development of Jewish religious ideas from Apocrypha to Talmud would be a long-term undertaking of monumental proportions. But there is no reason why two preliminary tasks, and one intermediary operation, should not be embarked on at once. As a first step, a small group of experts in inter-testamental, New Testament and rabbinic studies could initiate a survey with a view to drawing up a list of (*a*) 'Jewish' problems amenable to explication with the help of the New Testament, and (*b*) New Testament issues needing clarification from 'Jewish' sources. The intermediary project would involve the composition of a Schürer-type *religious* history of the Jews from the Maccabees to AD 500[60] that fully incorporates the New Testament data. Equipped with a detailed index, its aim would be to serve as a reliable guide to the diverse streams of post-biblical Judaism in all their manifestations and reciprocal influences.

Who is willing to take up the challenge?

7

The Present State of the 'Son of Man' Debate

A few days after my arrival in Oxford as newly elected Reader in Jewish Studies, the late Dr F. L. Cross was kind enough to accept my last-minute offer to read a paper before an international New Testament Congress. The lecture, 'The use of *barnash/bar nasha* in Jewish Aramaic', was delivered in this same hall in September 1965, before appearing in print in 1967.[1] In it, I set out to enquire into the meanings of the Semitic expression underlying the famous Gospel phrase, and advanced various conclusions. My task here is to expose the present state of the 'son of man' debate which followed in the wake of 1965 communication.

The issue in a nutshell is this. The expression occurring in the Gospels, *ho huios tou anthrōpou*, is not a genuine Greek idiom. In recent years, it has been described as 'unusual in Greek';[2] 'a rather inelegant barbarism';[3] or 'a literal rendering of the determinative [Aramaic] bar *('e)nasha* which is ambiguous in Greek'.[4] It is in fact generally, though not universally, thought that the Semitic model from which the Greek derives is Aramaic.[5] Hebrew is in disfavour because, with one possible exception, it never uses the definite article with *ben adam*.[6]

Prior to 1965, there had been two waves of philological research. The first, from the turn of the century, comprises the works of Arnold Meyer,[7] Hans Lietzmann,[8] Gustaf Dalman[9] and Paul Fiebig.[10] The next wave, which dates to the years immediately following the end of the Second World War, has as its most important participants J. Y. Campbell,[11] John Bowman,[12] Matthew Black,[13] and Erik Sjöberg.[14] On a number of linguistic points, there was agreement among the protagonists, but on two major matters, the circumlocutional and the titular use of the expression, opinions remained divided.[15]

My own thinking on the subject began with an observation which seemed so self-evident as to constitute a truism: 'Since "the *son of man*" is not a Greek phrase, but Aramaic, if it is to make sense at all, it must be Aramaic sense.'[16] So before we try to determine the meaning of *ho huios tou anthrōpou* in the Gospels, it is imperative to find out in what sense, or senses, *bar ('e)nasha* was actually used in real, extant Jewish Aramaic texts. In 1963 and 1964, I therefore completed a survey which, although by no means an exhaustive investigation, was based on a much larger sample than the previous studies. Among its four main results, the first two confirms the theses propounded by Meyer and Lietzmann that (1) *bar nash(a)* is a regular expression for 'man' in general; and (2) that *bar nash* often serves as an indefinite pronoun. The third, and perhaps most novel of the conclusions actually illustrates the circumlocutional use of *bar nasha*, instead of merely postulating it on the basis of a similar Aramaic idiom, *hahu gabra* ('that man'). In fact, I adduced ten examples of direct speech – monologue or dialogue – in which the speaker appears to refer to himself, not as 'I', but as 'the son of man' in the third person, in contexts implying awe, reserve or modesty. The fourth conclusion stresses that in none of the passages scrutinized, not even in the Jewish messianic exegesis of Daniel 7, does the expression *bar nasha* figure as a title.[17] It may even be inferred that Aramaic linguistic usage renders the expression unsuitable to describe an eschatological office because occasionally *bar nash* is employed with the pejorative nuance of a crafty, unscrupulous fellow.[18]

Predictably, the last two theses have aroused mixed reactions, and these form the third wave of the philologically based 'son of man' debate. This may conveniently be outlined with the help of the following three questions:

1. Has a periphrastic use of *bar nash(a)* been convincingly demonstrated, and is the evidence applicable to the New Testament?

2. Is it still tenable that a Jewish 'son of man' concept and title existed during the life-time of Jesus?

3. Can the new linguistic analysis of the Aramaic phrase contribute positively to the interpretation of the New Testament?

I

The first reactions to the new circumlocution theory queried the demonstrative force of the proof-texts marshalled to support it in the 1965 lecture and the 1967 publication. F. H. Borsch[19] and C. Colpe[20] emphasized that my examples are primarily generic statements though they may include the speaker. None of them is a clear-cut substitute for 'I'. Both authors expressed their views as early as 1967, as did also Joachim Jeremias in an argument formulated in greater detail. According to him, whereas the phrase *hahu gabra*, the model on which my theory is constructed, means 'I and no one else', and points exclusively to the speaker, *bar nasha* has an indefinite nuance: 'man, therefore I, too'. It is, consequently, not a circumlocution for the first person personal pronoun.[21]

This objection, I submit, fails on two counts. Firstly, the critics in question do not seem to appreciate that a circumlocution is not just a synonym, but by definition, roundabout and evasive speech. It is expected to entail ambiguity. In genteel English, people speak of 'passing away' rather than of dying, and no one would dream of asking a veterinary surgeon to 'kill' his pet, but to 'put it to sleep'. Aramaic speakers to obtain the same blurred effect, rendered slightly ambiguous, not the predicate, but the subject. They found it easier to say, 'That man' (or 'The son of man') is going to die, than, '*I* am going to die'. Likewise, 'The son of man' will be approved or rewarded by God, sounded in their ears less boastful than if the same assertion were expressed in the first person singular.

As for Jeremias' distinction between the unequivocal *hahu gabra* (standing for 'I and no one else') and the ambiguous *bar nasha* (meaning 'anybody, and that includes me') is forced because *hahu gabra* is not necessarily unequivocal. In the well-known legendary conversation between Yohanan ben Zakkai and Vespasian, the rabbi, who had just escaped from a besieged Jerusalem, salutes the Roman commander, in Latin, with *Vive Domine Imperator*! Vespasian exclaims in Aramaic: 'You have greeted me with a royal greeting although I am no king. When the king (Nero) hears about it, he will kill *hahu gabra*' (*Lam. R.* 1.5(31)). But 'that man' here can refer to *either* speaker. It may apply to Yohanan, as in the parallel Talmud passage where Vespasian tells him that he has brought upon *himself* capital guilt: 'I am no king, and yet you have called me king' (*bGit.* 56a). But *hahu gabra* may equally designate Vespasian, who in another account is reported as expostulating: 'You have killed me! Why have you greeted me with a royal greeting although I am no king? When the king hears of this, he will despatch someone to kill *me*.'[22]

This apparent misunderstanding of the aim of circumlocutional talk may explain why John Bowker, although in general sympathy with the Aramaic approach advocated by this writer, is unable to follow the argument all the way.[23] For him, a circumlocution must be crystal-clear. 'The case for circumlocution would be immeasurably stronger', he writes, 'if the text read: "The disciple of *bar nasha* is as dear to *me* as *my* son" [instead of the extant wording in the third person: "as dear to him as his son"].'[24] In my view, such a formula would spoil the original purpose of the idiom. R. Hiyya's wish was *tactfully* to appoint his pupil, R. Levi, as his heir. The veiled saying was obviously understood since Levi is said to have received his master's valuables.

Though this is a slight digression, it may be worth noting that oral equivocations of the *hahu gabra / bar nasha* type tend again and again to be resolved when they reach the written stage. For instance, when in the Midrash Rabbah Jacob asks Esau: 'Do you want money or a burial-place?', Esau replies: 'Does *hahu gabra* want a burial place? Give *me* the money and keep the burial-place for yourself.' (*Gen. R.* 100.5). The same phenomenon – a periphrasis rendered explicit by a subsequent direct reference to the speaker – appears in Mark 2.10: 'To convince you that *the son of man* has the right on earth to forgive sins . . . *I* say to you . . .'. Elsewhere we may find the ambiguous form in one text, and the straight equivalent in a variant, or a synoptic parallel. 'Not even a bird is caught without the will of heaven' – comments Simeon ben Yohai – 'how much less the soul of *bar nasha*'! But another manuscript reads: 'how much less *my* soul!' (*Gen. R.* 79.6). It is impossible not to be reminded here of Matt. 16.13, 'Who do men say *the son of man* is?' and compare it with Jesus' question in the Marcan wording, 'Who do men say that *I* am?' (Mark 8.27; cf. Luke 9.18).

Returning to the philological issue, I should mention at this juncture P. M. Casey's interesting contribution, 'The Son of Man Problem'.[25] In an attempt to reconcile my thesis and the comments made by Colpe and Jeremias, Casey suggests that an Aramaic speaker would choose *bar nasha* as a self-designation when applying a general statement to himself. Thus in declaring that '*The son of man* is going the way appointed for him in the scriptures' (Mark 14.22), Jesus 'announces that he is about to die, as all men do, by divine decree'.[26] Since in the main, Casey argues in what seems to me the right direction, it would be ungracious to quibble over inessentials. Nevertheless, his re-formulation would be more impressive if he were able to provide additional illustrations of how 'general statements are used in Aramaic' – over and above my *bar nasha* quotations – and if he could also justify the need for a special turn of phrase to express the obvious.

In sum, I still venture to maintain that the very nature of the indirect reference to the self requires an element of uncertainty. And if it is correct to apply this linguistic pattern to the New Testament, the thesis advanced by Bultmann and his school, that the 'coming Son of Man' alluded to by Jesus was someone other than himself,[27] provides a nearly perfect example of how sophisticated modern scholars can be taken in by a clever Aramaic *double entendre*.

Joseph A. Fitzmyer's criticism is of a very different kind.[28] For him, it is almost immaterial whether I have made out a case for the circumlocutional use of 'the son of man'. In 1968, he thought the argument 'convincing';[29] six years later he declared that *bar nasha* is 'never found as a circumlocution for "I".'[30] Whatever the merits of my case for the texts examined, it has no relevance to the New Testament because these texts do not belong to works written in the first century AD. Worse still, all my quotations contain the form *bar nash* or *bar nasha*, whereas the noun 'man' in biblical or Qumran Aramaic is spelt with an *aleph: 'enash* or *'enôsh*. Shortening of this sort, he observes, is a sign of lateness, and in 'philological comparisons of the Aramaic substratum of the Gospels . . . it is quite illegitimate to appeal to later texts'.[31]

The methodological principle stated by Fitzmyer is incontestably valid . . . when it is applicable. It would indeed be wrong to rely on sources more recent – or for that matter, older – than the New Testament when the proper kind of contemporaneous documents are available in sufficient quantity. But in the 'son of man' question this is patently not the case. Let us consider then the odd situation that ensues if Fitzmyer is taken as our guide. We all agree that the Greek *ho huios tou anthrōpou* is an Aramaism used in the first century AD. Yet the gospel interpreter is condemned to a stalemate. His first-century comparative material is extremely scarce; moreover, it does not represent the appropriate genre, style, vocabulary and dialect. On the other hand, for mere chronological reasons, he is ordered to forego a wealth of possible clues which appear, indeed are, significant and helpful. Nevertheless, speaking quite objectively, if we accept that the phrase reflected in *ho huios tou anthrōpou* was originally coined in Aramaic by Galileans, is it not sensible, indeed obligatory, to investigate the relics of the Galilean dialect, closest in time to the Gospels, the Palestinian Talmud and similar Galilean rabbinic sources, especially when there is good reason to think that their dialectal peculiarities pre-date the period of their codification? Is this plain logic as I will attempt to show, or is it a 'Vermes' flight to *obscurum per obscurius*' as Fitzmyer puts it?[32]

To begin with, is the spelling *nash(a)* with no initial *aleph* (which may have been silent even when written as in Syriac) a definite indication of lateness? Two arguments militate in favour of a negative answer. Firstly, Galileans were notorious for their mispronunciation (or non-pronunciation) of gutturals.[33] Secondly, the Gospels themselves attest the neglect of the initial *aleph*: they refer to men called *Lazarus*.[34] Now the form *nasha* instead of *'enasha* parallels exactly the change represented by *Lazar* instead of *El'azar*. And the Gospel spelling of Lazarus is not a freak occurrence: the Palestinian Talmud regularly substitutes *Lazar* for *El'azar* and *Li'ezer* for *Eli'ezer*.

This observation, expressed lightheartedly in *Jesus the Jew*,[35] provoked the following riposte: 'The difference between the first century Hebrew spellings of the name(s) . . ., and those that he finds in the Palestinian Talmud of several centuries later is just what one would expect! But in all this the real question that he has not faced is whether one can argue from proper names to common nouns; the former are notoriously liable to shortening . . .'.[36]

I believe both halves of Fitzmyer's reply are incorrect. Firstly, is it true that the shortened form of the names *El'azar/Eli'ezer* as *Lazar/Li'ezer* is several centuries more recent than the age of the New Testament? For even if we disregard first-century Greek transcriptions as *Lazar(os)* not only in the Gospels, but also in a passage of Josephus[37] and a fragmentary ossuary inscription from Jerusalem,[38] is it exact that the Palestinian Talmud is our oldest source? The truncated spelling of the two names is displayed in some of the best manuscripts of the Mishnah, another Galilean composition preceding the Talmud by a couple of centuries, namely in the manuscripts from Cambridge and Parma and the Kaufmann codex from Budapest.[39] Furthermore, there are several ossuary inscriptions from Jerusalem and its environs which spell both names without the *aleph*. Need I remind you that most of these Jerusalem ossuaries date to the first century or earlier, and that none of them is likely to be post-Hadrianic?[40] We encounter a woman, *Shallon bath Li'ezer*[41] and two men, one called simply *L'azar*[42] and another, *Eli'ezer ben Lazar*, the latter figures in a bilingual inscription and is accompanied by the Greek *Eliezros Eleazarou*.[43] So, although the classical spelling with the *aleph* is attested more frequently in first-century documents,[44] there is sufficient evidence to permit us to trace the beginnings of the abbreviating tendency to the age of Jesus.

Secondly, is the dropping of the opening *aleph* in a proper name such a special case that it may not be taken as a model for a common noun of the *'enasha/nasha* type? This question may be disposed of quite promptly. As is evident from Dalman's Grammar,[45] the trend implied was general in the Galilean Aramaic dialect. But examples appear already in the Qumran and Murabba'at documents, where the verb *'amar* (to say) is spelled without the *aleph* on three occasions,[46] and the phrase, 'in the face of', is written once as *banpe* instead of *be'anpe*.[47] The editor of this last text, J. T. Milik, commented in 1961: 'omission de l'aleph comme souvent en judéo-palestinien'.[48]

Here I will rest my case. The arguments in favour of a circumlocutional use of *bar nash/bar nasha qua* indirect reference to the speaker appear able to stand up to all the criticisms formulated until now.

II

The second controversial finding announced in the 1965 lecture, namely the absence of a titular use of *bar nasha* in Aramaic, flatly contradicted the *opinio communis* of that time. Most New Testament interpreters took the opposite view for granted. Some twenty years ago, Oscar Cullmann wrote: 'We come to the following conclusion concerning the Jewish concept of the Son of Man . . . He is a heavenly being, now hidden, who will appear only at the end of time . . . We find this exclusively eschatological figure in Daniel, the Book of Enoch, and IV Ezra.'[49] 'The intimate connexion of the synoptic presentation of the Son of Man with that of Jewish apocalyptic literature can no longer be contested', echoed H. E. Tödt.[50] In a similar vein, Ferdinand Hahn asserted: 'It is . . . overwhelmingly probable that already in pre-Christian Judaism a titular use had established itself which was adopted by Jesus and the primitive community.'[51]

Yet the philologically-based denial of such an eschatologico-messianic title almost immediately found allies among literary critics. In his book, *Rediscovering the Teaching of Jesus*, published in 1967, the late Norman Perrin discarded in no uncertain terms the so-called 'Son of Man concept',[52] and in March 1968, Ragnar Leivestad read a paper, which appeared in the same year under the self-explanatory title, 'Der apokalyptische Menschensohn: ein theologisches Phantom'.[53] In a revised English version, issued in 1972 with an equally provocative title, 'Exit the Apocalyptic Son of Man',[54] Leivestad writes: 'I am quite convinced that the apocalyptic Son of Man title is a modern invention. A Jewish Son of Man title was completely unknown to Jesus and the primitive church.'[55] In a style less blunt, and with gentle irony, my much lamented friend Paul Winter remarked in, of all places, the *Deutsche Literaturzeitung*: 'If Perrin's interpretation of the Son of Man sayings in the Synoptic Gospels is correct . . . then the place of origin of the [Son of Man] myth is not to be sought in Iran, or in Judea or even in Ugarit, but in the German universities.'[56]

This wind of change was greatly assisted by the absence of the Book of Parables, the main alleged source of the 'son of man' concept, from the Qumran Aramaic manuscripts of Enoch, although in the late 1960s, reputable scholars admittedly queried the validity of such a deduction. In 1967, Morna Hooker still preferred to date the Parables to between 63 BC and AD 70, and declared the Qumran evidence impressive but indecisive.[57] A year later, J. A. Fitzmyer expressly attributed to 'sheer chance'[58] the silence of the scrolls. However, when it emerged from J. T. Milik's publications that Book II, or the Parables, was not merely lacking in the Enoch material represented by eleven fragmentary manuscripts from Cave 4, but was replaced there by the Book of Giants, the chance theory in regard to the missing Parables became highly improbable.[59] I should mention in addition Edward Ullendorff's authoritative statement to the effect that 'the Ethiopic evidence has little or nothing to contribute [to the "son of man" question] and that it remains essentially an Aramaic . . . issue.'[60]

My own examination of the relevant sections of Daniel, IV Ezra and I Enoch, published in *Jesus the Jew*, has persuaded me that no titular use of the phrase, 'the son of man', can be substantiated in any of these works.[61] In other words, the date of the Parables is not an essential ingredient of the thesis. It may be noted in parenthesis that no argument compels us to adopt Milik's theory that the Parables were composed by a Christian in Greek, or his extravagant dating of them to AD 270.[62] This composition belongs most likely to the last quarter of the first century AD, or perhaps to the first to second century as Matthew Black suggests.[63]

Several publications of the 1975 to 1977 vintage on this subject seem to adumbrate a new kind of consensus. Barnabas Lindars honestly declares: 'It has now become embarrassingly obvious that the Son of Man was not a current title in Judaism at all.'[64] Maurice Casey's study, 'The Use of the Term "Son of Man" in the Similitudes of Enoch' is just as negative: 'The way is left open to us to deny a special "Son of Man" concept in Judaism.'[65] In the Supplementary Volume to the *Interpreter's Dictionary of the Bible* Norman Perrin re-asserts that the notion presupposed by many New Testament scholars is without support in ancient Judaism,[66] and John Bowker concurs: 'Even if the problem of date (of the Parables) were solved, the apocalyptic use is insufficient to establish that there was a widely known figure in Judaism known as "the son of man".'[67] Even J. P. Brown who at the end of last year appears to have been curiously unaware of the philological debate or of any contribution to the problem after 1972, presupposes, in a paper devoted to the theory that 'son of man' is an ironical self-description, that there was no concept of a coming 'Son of Man' available to Jesus.[68]

The important corollary is this. If the present trend continues and the academic myth of a pre-Christian Jewish 'son of man' concept finishes by being definitively discredited, the bottom will have fallen out of most current exegeses of *ho huios tou anthrōpou*. And this, in turn, will demand a complete re-interpretation of all the New Testament passages.

III

The debate is still in progress and the battle is not yet won. Only New Testament Semitists have reacted so far. In a voluminous *Festschrift* of 489 pages entitled *Jesus und der Menschensohn*, the philological issue is bypassed by all its contributors.[69]

Nevertheless, there are also a few hopeful signs. Of course, it is not for me to appraise *Jesus the Jew*, in which, to use our Aramaism, 'the son of man' endeavours to expound the Gospel passages in the light of the circumlocutional theory, and claims that the association between *ho huios tou anthrōpou* and Dan. 7.13 constitutes a secondary midrashic stage of development, more understandable in Greek than in Aramaic.[70]

I always remember with emotion and pleasure that admirable octogenarian, C. H. Dodd, who did not hesitate in 1970 to re-adjust a life-time of exegesis so that it accorded with freshly assimilated information concerning the Aramaic usage of 'son of man'.[71] Also in 1970, Jürgen Roloff explicitly appealed to the Aramaic self-reference theory in interpreting the gospel.[72] Barnabas Lindars, although he still entitles his recent paper, 'Re-enter the Apocalyptic Son of Man', bids in fact goodbye to that concept. He whole-heartedly embraces the 'self-reference' theory which enables the speaker 'to make his point with greater delicacy than would be possible otherwise',[73] and notes also its particular relevance to the passion predictions in the Gospels.[74] In the end, he proposes to replace the apocalyptic 'son of man' notion by that of an agent of God in the final judgement, and asserts that not only did the New Testament writers identify Jesus as this agent, but he himself was conscious of fulfilling such a function.[75] Be this as it may, it is beyond question that from a philologico-historical viewpoint Lindars' study marks a definite step in the right direction.

John Bowker, though adopting a very different conclusion, strives also to take his inspiration from Semitic data. He sees in the biblical use of 'son of man' a pointer to human subjection to death as well as, in Dan. 7, to divine justification. Acknowledging his dependence, at least partially, on the self-reference theory, he thinks his own formulation suits better the Marcan portrayal of Jesus who 'talked of himself as a man subject (unequivocally) to death, and yet also as one who will be vindicated'.[76]

But this identification of 'the son of man' as a mortal but divinely vindicated individual brings us back to the old 'title-and-concept' situation, with the particular disadvantage that it is derived from the Hebrew where no determined form of the singular *ben adam* is certain to exist. The hypothesis will have, moreover, to face all the classic difficulties: why is 'the son of man' phrase placed only on the lips of Jesus, and why is he never addressed or described as *ho huios tou anthrōpou?*[77]

I have left to the end what seems to be perhaps the most encouraging result of the 'son of man' debate. A few weeks ago in Madrid Luis Alonso Schökel drew my attention to the new Spanish Bible's treatment of the phrase 'the son of man'. 'El Hijo del hombre' has completely disappeared from the *Nueva Biblia Española* of 1975.[78] In Dan. 7.13, *bar 'enash* has become 'una figura humana', and in the New Testament *ho huios tou anthrōpou* is rendered as 'hombre' in all the passages where it is thought to be used in a generic sense. But when Jesus employs it as a self-reference, it is translated as 'este Hombre' ('this man').[79] In the Spanish, that is to say, we have the Aramaic underlying the Greek; or as Jerome would have put it, the words of the gospel interpreted 'secundum Chaldaicam veritatem'.[80]

8

The Jesus Notice of Josephus Re-examined

Scholarly attitudes to the famous Testimonium Flavianum (*Ant.* xviii 63–64) have fluctuated a great deal during the last hundred years. A few writers, chief among them F. C. Burkitt[1] and Adolf von Harnack,[2] have maintained that the passage is essentially authentic. A larger number, including such renowned scholars as Bernhard Niese,[3] Emil Schürer,[4] Eduard Norden,[5] Jean Juster,[6] Eduard Meyer,[7] and Solomon Zeitlin,[8] have recognized it to be an interpolation. Finally, Théodore Reinach[9] and an increasing number of recent authors (André Pelletier,[10] L. H. Feldman,[11] Paul Winter,[12] A.-M. Dubarle,[13] Ernst Bammel,[14] Otto Betz,[15] and G. H. Twelvetree,[16] among others) hold the Testimonium to be partly genuine and partly rewritten. The basic arguments in favour of the respective theories (and the corresponding objections raised against the conflicting theses) are by now well established, as may be seen in Feldman's note appended to the passage in the Loeb edition. The three arguments may be summarized as follows.

A. The presence of the notice in all the manuscripts of *Antiquities*, and its literal reproduction at the beginning of the fourth century by Eusebius in *Historia ecclesiastica* i 11 and *Demonstratio evangelica* iii 5, 105, are seen by the upholders of authenticity as weighty proof in favour of the Josephan origin of the paragraph.

B. By contrast, the protagonists of the interpolation theory emphasize that the Testimonium contains blatant Christian statements (e.g. 'He was the Christ') which cannot be attributed to the Jew Josephus. In fact, Origen explicitly asserts that Josephus did not believe that Jesus was the Messiah.[17] Hence they assign the whole section to a Christian forger. Zeitlin goes so far as to identify him as the historian Eusebius.[18]

C. The case of those who consider our text as partly genuine and partly interpolated rests on a twofold reasoning. The fact that Origen denies that Josephus believed in the messianic status of Jesus indirectly proves that the version of the *Antiquities* known to the Alexandrian master in the middle of

the third century included something about Jesus. Furthermore, and more
directly, the characterization of Jesus preserved in the surviving notice is
atypical of third- or fourth-century church terminology and consequently
it would be an error to ascribe it to a Christian editor living at that time.
The present paper will not be concerned with all the problems arising
from the Testimonium Flavianum, but only with a re-examination of that
part of *Ant.* xviii 63 where Jesus is described as a 'wise man' (*sophos anēr*)
and a 'performer of astonishing deeds' (*paradoxōn ergōn poiētēs*). I will
attempt to show firstly that these two phrases are consonant with the style
of Josephus; secondly, that they are unlikely to be Christian fabrications;
and thirdly that, on the contrary, the second epithet echoes a primitive
popular representation of Jesus which is attested with contradictory doctrinal emphases both in the New Testament and in rabbinic literature. The
conclusions will be necessarily preliminary and will require confirmation
in the light of a full investigation of the Jesus passage.

A few textual remarks first.

The Greek witnesses, i.e. the Josephus manuscripts, the Eusebius
quotations already mentioned and the Byzantine sources,[19] reproduce,
apart from very minor stylistic variations, exactly the same wording. As
regards the versions, *sophos anēr* is rendered in Latin as *vir sapiens* (Jerome,
De viris illustribus xiii). The Syriac and Arabic translations are also strictly
literal.[20] In the case of *paradoxōn ergōn poiētēs*, the Latin and the Syriac
show slight variations (*mirabilium patrator operum* and 'doer of glorious
deeds'[21]), whereas Agapius substitutes for the specific Greek formula a less
colourful sentence: 'and his conduct was good'.[22]

(1) The form of the description of Jesus as *sophos anēr* and *paradoxōn
ergōn poiētēs*, when compared with the presentation of other personalities,
biblical and post-biblical, strikes me as genuinely Josephan. King Solomon
is referred to as 'a wise man possessing every virtue' (*andri sophō kai pasan
aretēn echonti*) (*Ant.* viii 53). The prophet Elisha was 'a man renowned for
righteousness' (*anēr epi dikaiosunē diaboētos*) who performed *paradoxa erga*
(*Ant.* ix 182). Daniel, in turn, is portrayed as 'a wise man and skilful in
discovering things beyond man's power' (*sophos anēr kai deinos heurein ta
amēchana*) (*Ant.* x 237). A little later he appears as 'a good and just man'
(*anēr agathos kai dikaios*) (*Ant.* x 246). Ezra is said to have been 'a just
man who enjoyed the good opinion of the masses' (*dikaios anēr kai doxēs
apolauōn agathēs para tō plēthei*) (*Ant.* xi 121). Among post-biblical personalities, Honi-Onias is called 'a just man and beloved of God' (*dikaios anēr
kai theophilēs*) (*Ant.* xiv 22), and Samaias 'a just man' (*dikaios anēr*) (*Ant.*
xiv 172). John the Baptist is introduced as 'a good man' (*agathos anēr*) who

'exhorted the Jews to lead righteous lives, to practise justice towards their fellows and piety towards God' (*Ant.* xviii 117). As for the leading Pharisee at the time of the outbreak of the first revolution, Simeon ben Gamaliel, he is presented as 'a man highly gifted with intelligence and judgement' (*anēr plērēs suneseōs kai logismou*) (*Vita* 192).[23]

Of these, Solomon and Daniel are the obvious parallels to Jesus *qua* wise men. Both were celebrated as masters of wisdom. Hence it is not surprising to find that the epithet 'teacher' (*didaskalos*) follows closely the phrases under consideration in the Testimonium. The more peculiar designation, 'performer of astonishing deeds', has also been anticipated in substance in the Elisha passage which has already been mentioned and to which I will return later.

In brief, there seems to be no stylistic or historical argument that might be marshalled against the authenticity of the two phrases in question. In fact, the clause that follows 'wise man', viz. 'if indeed one might call him a man' (*eige andra auton legein chrē*), which is generally recognized as an interpolation, seems to support – as Paul Winter has aptly pointed out – the originality of *sophos anēr*, an idiom which in the mind of a later Christian editor required further qualifications.[24]

(2) In addition to appearing *prima facie* to be Josephan, closer analysis of *sophos anēr* and *paradoxōn ergōn poiētēs* points to the improbability of their later Christian provenance. To begin with, the title 'wise man' has no New Testament roots, and in the absence of such an authoritative backing it is, I think, totally unfit to express the kind of elevated theological notion that a forger would have intended to introduce into Josephus' text. It would have been meaningless to *invent* a testimony that did not support the belief of the interpolator. But not only does it fail to convey the idea of the divine Christ of the church; it actually conflicts in a sense with New Testament terminology. Jesus is admittedly twice identified by Paul in I Cor. 1.24 and 30 with the abstract 'wisdom of God', but the adjective *sophos* as applied to men in the same chapter (vv. 18–31) carries a pejorative connotation. Furthermore, on the only occasion where the Gospels put this word into the mouth of Jesus, 'the wise' are unfavourably compared to 'babes' (*nēpioi*) (Matt. 11:25; Luke 10:21). In the few instances where the term *sophos* is employed positively, it relates to Christian teachers, but never to Jesus himself.[25]

In spite of its potentially richer significance, the formula 'performer of astonishing deeds' has largely escaped the attention of the students of the Testimonium Flavianum. Those few who have bothered to comment on it have arrived at contradictory conclusions. Thus at the end of the

nineteenth century, Theodore Reinach suggested that the phrase concealed a 'nuance de mépris' and insinuated that Jesus was a 'thaumaturge
professionnel'.[26] On the other hand, A. Pelletier argues that *paradoxos* is
'une épithète le plus souvent laudative'.[27] The term requires, therefore, a
fuller examination in Jewish–Hellenistic usage.

In the LXX, the verb *paradoxazein* renders the Hiph. of *plh*, to distinguish, to set apart,[28] whereas in the Greek Sirach (10.13), 'the Lord
brought upon them extraordinary afflictions' (*paredoxasen . . . tas epagōgas*)
translates freely the extant Hebrew (*wyb' . . . ng'h*). In two passages without Hebrew equivalent, *paradoxazein* refers to an astounding deed of God
(II Macc. 3.30; III Macc. 2.9). *paradoxa erga* occurs only once in Sir. 43.25
(*npl'wt*) in Hebrew) in an allusion to extraordinary creatures seen by sailors
at sea. Elsewhere, the Greek adjective indicates something *abnormal*, like
fire continuing to burn in water (Wisd. 16.17), which is a regular meaning
of the word in non-Jewish Hellenistic texts.[29]

In Philo's language, also, the concept combines divine action with an
unexpected, hence for humans astonishing, result.[30] To take a striking
example, according to Philo God promulgated the Decalogue 'by a voice
which – most paradoxical thing [*to paradoxotaton*] – was visible'.[31] Such
paradoxa of abnormal, praeternatural or supernatural character, amazing
though they may appear to men, are but 'child's play' (*paignia*) for God.[32]

A similar manner of speech is attested in Josephus too, but his language
seems to be more varied. As in non-Jewish Greek and in Wisdom, a 'paradox' may be for him a rare natural phenomenon like the gigantic size of
Goliath with all his four and a half cubits, or six feet eight inches (*Ant.* vi
171). It may be a most uncommon, though perhaps not unique, occurrence
such as the division of the Red Sea (but did not something similar happen
to Alexander the Great at the Pamphylian Sea?), an occurrence attributable either to the divine will or to an accident (*kata tautomaton*) (*Ant.* ii
347–48).[33] It may be presented positively as the work of God, like manna,
a divine and paradoxical nourishment (*Ant.* iii 30), or the equally 'paradoxical' spectacle of the burning bush which, though alight, still remained
green and laden with fruit (*Ant.* ii 266–67).

More important still from the point of view of his Jesus passage,
Josephus characterizes some of the actions performed by men of God as
'paradoxical'. The water gushing from the rock after Moses has struck it
with his staff is described as a paradox astounding the thirsty Jews in the
wilderness (*Ant.* iii 37–38). Similarly, the many miracles of the prophet
Elisha were *paradoxa erga* for which he was remembered by the Hebrews
(*Ant.* ix 182).

This summary survey of the various uses of the adjective *paradoxos* shows that this term is not the most obvious choice for a Christian inter-polator intent on manufacturing a testimony for apologetic purposes. The only justification for the use of the phrase would be established Christian terminology, but such is surely not the case. *paradoxa* is a *hapax legomenon* in the New Testament, employed in Luke (5.26) by uncommitted ob-servers witnessing the healing of a paralytic by Jesus. Filled with fear, they are said to have exclaimed: 'We have seen astonishing things today!' (*eidomen paradoxa sēmeron*).[34] Instead of *paradoxa erga*, a Christian forger would have selected a New Testament term such as 'mighty deeds' (*dunameis*) or 'signs' (*sēmeia*).

(3) If the phrase *paradoxōn ergōn poiētēs* did not originate with a Christian editor, is it possible to determine in what sense Josephus employed it? Our survey of the use of this word in Hellenistic–Jewish writings has made plain that the concept may reflect what we understand by 'miraculous'; but to assert, as some recent writers have done, that *paradoxōn* is the 'common term' in Hellenistic Judaism for miracle is something of an exaggeration.[35] As a matter of fact, students of Josephus seem to agree that the word best expressing his notion of 'miracle' is *sēmeion*, sign. This is especially true when the issue concerns an extraordi-nary deed achieved by a man of God. The miracle-sign – Otto Betz explains – is an unnatural (supernatural) occurrence that authenticates its author as a messenger of God, and generates faith in the witnesses in regard to the mission of the wonder-worker.[36] To emphasize this meaning, Josephus tells us that when Moses recounted to the Israelites the marvel-lous events at the burning bush, they remained unmoved, but when he miraculously showed them the signs themselves, they immediately believed in him (*Ant.* ii 280). As for the prophet Isaiah, he was – according to Josephus – explicitly required by King Hezekiah to perform 'a sign and a wonder' (*sēmeion ti kai terastion*) in order to demonstrate that he was God's envoy (*Ant.* x 28). Needless to say, the 'paradoxical deeds' of Jesus are not referred to as 'signs' by Josephus. By contrast, the twelfth-century Michael Glykas (*PG* clviii, 444) instinctively substitutes *megalōn sēmeiōn ergatēs* for the original idiom.

The next step in this investigation concerns the source of a 'paradoxical deed' performed by a man. To take Moses once more as our example, the marvels accomplished by him in the presence of Pharaoh are described by Josephus in words attributed to Moses himself as proceeding from God's power (*dunamis*) (*Ant.* ii 284–86). Likewise the *thaumasta . . . kai paradoxa erga* of Elisha are said to have been produced 'through prophecy' (*dia tēs prophēteias*) (*Ant.* ix 182). Note that in both instances, by alluding to the supernatural character of the 'paradox' without expressing any reservation,[37] Josephus implicitly indicates his own faith in the miracles.

The Jesus notice, though verbally closely related to the Elisha passage, lacks a positive evaluation by Josephus. His is a fairly sympathetic but ultimately detached description: he reports traditions concerning Jesus, but he is personally not committed to them. André Pelletier has arrived at a very similar conclusion. Josephus – he writes – 'ne se prononce pas, comme il le faisait pour Elisée, sur le pouvoir en vertu duquel Jésus accomplissait ses miracles. Cette réserve répond bien à ce qu'on attend de lui.'[38]

As for the relationship between this notice and the New Testament, Jesus' portrayal as a miracle-worker – we are told by Anthony Harvey – is 'basic to the whole gospel tradition'.[39] This statement is true in substance, but once more demands a more careful formulation, because the author of the quotation would be the first to remind us that the epithet 'performer of paradoxical deeds' does not represent in full the 'gospel tradition' about Jesus.

What these three words recall in fact is not the doctrinally evolved image of Jesus adopted by the Gentile church, or even that emerging from the Fourth Gospel (which is more or less contemporaneous with *Antiquities*), but what seems to be the earliest pre-Pauline Judaeo-Christian portrait. On the first Pentecost, Peter apparently declared:

> Men of Israel, hear these words, Jesus of Nazareth, a man attested to you by God with mighty works and wonders and signs [*dunamesi kai terasi kai sēmeiois*], which God did [*epoiēsen*] through him in your midst . . . (Acts 2.22).

Also, the two disciples travelling to Emmaus in the company of a stranger (who turns out to be the risen Christ) sum up Jesus of Nazareth for his benefit as

> a man (who was a) prophet mighty in deed and word [*anēr prophētēs dunatos en ergō kai logō*] before God and all the people (Luke 24.19).

In fact, this mention of *anēr prophētēs* recalls one of the basic Gospel traditions which, on account of his miraculous powers, depicts Jesus during his lifetime as a prophet. Reacting to the antipathetic behaviour towards him of the inhabitants of Nazareth, Mark and Matthew credit him with the famous saying which, *pace* Bultmann,[40] I consider to be genuine:

> A prophet is not without honour, except in his own country, and among his own kin and in his own house. And he could do no mighty work there

[*ekei poiēsai oudemian dunamin*], except that he laid his hands upon a few sick people and healed them.[41]

Again, in the story of the raising of the dead youth at Nain, the awe-stricken bystanders recognize in the miracle the presence of a 'great prophet' (*prophētēs megas*) (Luke 7.16).

As I have observed earlier, the representation of Jesus as a wonder-worker or prophet belongs to the most primitive stage of Gospel tradition. Widespread though it may have been, it was soon superseded in Christian circles by titles reflecting a higher status: eschatological prophet, Messiah, son of God, etc. Nevertheless, it is reasonable to suppose – and later rabbinic criticism of Jesus confirms this supposition – that on the popular level the notion of miracle-worker/exorcist continued to circulate in Jewish Palestine, all the more so since charismatic activity of this type was – or is said to have been – practised among Jewish Christians of the early generations.[42] Before formulating a final assessment of the meaning of the passage under study in the Testimonium Flavianum, therefore I would like to draw attention to the elasticity, and even equivocality, of both concepts 'performer of paradoxical deeds' and 'prophet'.

It is scarcely necessary to stress that in the last resort the representation of an extraordinary event is entirely dependent on the stand, positive, negative or neutral, taken by its chronicler. Thus Josephus ascribes the signs produced by Moses to God's providence and power (*theou pronoia kai dunamis*), but the (identical) counter-miracles performed by the Egyptian priests and wise men are for him acts of magic (*mageia*) (*Ant.* ii 286). Not surprisingly, in Pharaoh's judgement, by contrast, Moses' acts are mere tricks, arising from 'wizardry and magic' (*teratourgia kai mageia*) (*Ant.* ii 284).

Josephus likewise shows his hand when he attributes Elisha's *paradoxa erga* to 'prophecy', i.e. to prophetic power. The same committed stance is revealed in Luke's description of Jesus as *anēr prophētēs dunatos en ergō*. Yet, apropos of the same phenomena, Celsus, quoted by Origen, manages to cast doubt in a single succinct phrase on the reality of Jesus' miracles, and to attribute these apparent paradoxes to the much despised sorcery:

It was by magic [*goēteia*] that he was able to perform the *paradoxa* which he appeared to have done.[43]

Indeed, we need not go beyond the Gospels themselves to discover the same dual attitude. In the famous Beelzebub controversy,[44] the exorcisms of Jesus are explained by his opponents, Jerusalem scribes (Mark), Pharisees (Matt.) or certain men in the crowd (Luke), as achieved through the power of the prince of the demons, Jesus himself being said to be possessed by an unclean spirit (Mark 3.30).[45] Vehemently rejecting this allegation, Jesus asserts that it is with the spirit (*en pneumati*) (Matt. 12:28) or the finger (*en daktulō*) (Luke 11:20) of God that he expels demons.

Yet, as is well known, the pejorative interpretation did not fade away: in Talmudic times it became one of the foundations of the hostile rabbinic portrait of Jesus the magician. In a famous baraitha we read:

> They hanged Yeshu on the eve of Passover. For forty days a herald went before him (proclaiming): 'He is going out to be stoned because he practised sorcery and he seduced and led astray Israel.' (*bSanh.* 43b)

When these two charges are examined, they turn out to be the pejorative representation of the two characteristics of Josephus' Jesus portrait. For 'seducer'/'false prophet' and 'sorcerer' are the negative equivalents of 'wise man' and 'miracle-worker'.

All this seems to imply that Josephus deliberately chose words reflecting a not unsympathetic neutral stand. When he wishes to indicate his disagreement with certain claims, he has no difficulty in doing so. He reports, for example, that both Theudas and 'the Egyptian' announced themselves as prophets (*prophētēs einai*), but he makes clear that they were 'impostors' (*goētes*) (*Ant.* xx 97, 169). And when he refers to Judas the Galilean as teacher, he does not call him *sophos anēr*, but uses the equivocal *sophistēs* (*BJ* ii 118, 433).

It is possible therefore that by describing Jesus as 'wise man' and 'performer of paradoxical deeds', Josephus achieved what few if any of his successors, ancient or modern, have done, namely that by neither approving nor disapproving of him, he managed to sketch a portrait of the Galilean master that is in a true sense *sine ira et studio*.[46]

9

A Summary of the Law by Flavius Josephus

The central importance of the Torah in the inter-Testamental and Mishnaic–Talmudic periods is widely attested. The Qumran sectaries held it to be the charter of their covenant. The Tannaim and the Amoraim supplemented, interpreted and systematized it. Jesus declared the Law permanently enduring, and the legacy of Moses inspired much of the work of Philo of Alexandria, especially *De Decalogo, De Specialibus Legibus*, and one of the surviving sections of his *Hypothetica*.

Flavius Josephus was likewise preoccupied with a fresh presentation of this corpus. In the latter part of his career he planned to devote to it a major autonomous treatise which he mentions several times *en passant* and for which he had already a title, *On Customs and Causes (Peri ethōn kai aitiōn)*,[1] and a fairly elaborate scheme:

> It is also my intention [he writes] to compose a work in four books on the opinions that we Jews hold concerning God and his essence as well as concerning the laws, that is, why according to them we are permitted to do some things while we are forbidden to do others.[2]

The title, 'On Customs and *Causes*', the outline just quoted, and the extant legal works of Josephus show clearly that his interest lay not in detailing what was licit or illicit but in providing a religious explanation and moral justification of the Jewish way of life.

Prior to this major, apparently unfinished, project, Josephus twice tried his hand at composing summaries of the Torah. Books iii and iv of his *Antiquities* represent the first and best known of his accounts. In iii 90–286, he starts with a discussion of the Ten Commandments and goes on to describe the Mosaic institution of the Tabernacle, the priesthood, the sacrifices, the laws relating to purity, diet and marriage, and finally the sabbatical and jubilee years. The constitution (*politeia*) of the Jewish people is presented in iv 196–292 with sections concerning the Temple, festivals, prayer, law courts, the king, duties towards the poor, marriage, the rebellious son, and various humanitarian precepts. This peace-time constitution is followed by an appendix (iv 293–301) regulating Jewish warfare.

Although, as is well known, Josephus enriches his retelling of the Law with extraneous data mostly taken from the halakhah and haggadah current in his days, he claims in no uncertain manner that he reproduces the Bible, 'neither adding to it, nor omitting from it'.[3] The most likely meaning of this is that his rewording of Scripture does not change its sense and is, in consequence, wholly trustworthy.[4]

A second, and considerably shorter summary of the Torah appears in *Contra Apionem* ii 164–219, or when less strictly defined, ii 145–219. It is introduced as Josephus' answer to the distortions of the code of Moses published by Apollonius Molon.[5] These 'false accusations' are positively refuted through a demonstration that the Mosaic Law, faithfully practised by the Jews, has nothing in common with Apollonius' description of Judaism (145–50). Though unquestionably the more recent of the two compositions, this does not seem to depend on *Antiquities* in any sense and is definitely not an abridgement of it. Not only does it have its own structure; as will be shown presently, it even departs here and there from the stand taken by Josephus in his earlier work.

The sketch contained in *Contra Apionem* provides an introduction (164–89) followed by an actual outline of the Mosaic Law (190–219). In common with *Antiquities* (iv 196, 292), the Torah is characterized as a body of customs and statutes representing the constitution of the Jewish *theocracy*, a term apparently coined by Josephus (165). Theocracy, unlike the monarchic, oligarchic or democratic organization of other nations, assigns ultimate rule and authority to God. Also, in contrast to Greek educational systems that impart moral instruction through the teaching of precepts (like the Athenians) or by subjecting pupils to practical training (like the Lacedaemonians and Cretans), Moses combines both methods. He specifies the observances of daily life (such as the food the Jew is permitted to eat, the people with whom he may associate and the periods during which he is to abstain from work). Yet he simultaneously ensures that the rules proclaimed are not merely learnt but put into practice (173–74). Indeed, the weekly reading of the Torah on the sabbath (or as Josephus puts it, 'when all other work is forsaken') is devised to procure complete familiarity with its contents (175). Their thorough training in the commandments explains, according to him, the uniformity of ideas and conduct among all the Jews. Each of them, even their women (about whom Josephus has otherwise little good to say) knows that all their activities must be inspired by piety (*eusebeia*), the source of which is the Law (180–81). Moreover, attachment to the ancient statutes is the essence of wisdom (*phronēsis*) and virtue (*aretē*), 'the only wisdom, the only virtue, consists in refraining from every action, from every thought that is contrary to the laws originally laid down' (183).

This Mosaic constitution (*politeuma*) is not only the oldest in the world, but also the finest imaginable, because it makes God the ruler of all and recognizes the priests, under the hegemony of the high priest, as the administrators of the most important matters, viz., divine worship, supervision of the Law, the conduct of trials, and the punishment of convicted criminals (186–87).

Two points in this introductory section of Josephus deserve brief consideration.

Firstly, his lack of concern with topics such as ritual cleanness and uncleanness, dietary laws, sabbath observances, liturgical rules relating to festivals etc., is quite remarkable, especially when seen against the singular emphasis laid on these matters in rabbinic literature. Purity, strictly linked to Temple worship, reappears in the main body of the summary; but the rest receives no further attention. Indeed, even in the longer section devoted to ritual cleanness in *Antiquities* (iii 258ff.), the issue of food laws is given very superficial treatment, though this is coupled with the promise of a fuller discussion in *On Customs and Causes*, in which he planned to furnish the reasons that had motivated Moses in his decisions (259). The implication seems to be that for Josephus the dietary, purity and sacrificial rules, at least in their concrete wording, were not divine but Mosaic institutions (iii 273). He tells us, in fact, that the Decalogue alone was formulated and proclaimed by God directly, 'to the end that the excellence of the spoken words might not be impaired by human tongue in being feebly transmitted' (iii 89).

Secondly, Josephus refers to Torah reading on the sabbath (175), a custom attested by the New Testament as current both in Palestine and in the Diaspora;[6] by Philo, describing the hebdomadal gatherings of the Jews[7] and also the Essene assemblies;[8] and by rabbinic literature in general.[9] Yet the Bible is silent on this subject and mentions only a septennial recitation of the Torah (Deut. 31.10). Only the latter institution is mentioned in *Antiquities* (iv 209) yet, according to the next paragraph, its purpose is the memorization of the precepts: 'These laws should be so graven on their hearts . . . that they can never be effaced' (210). Clearly, a weekly reading as presented in *Contra Apionem*, rather than a recitation once every sabbatical year, serves better the didactic aim in question.[10]

The Constitution

Although the main body of the summary purports to provide a sketch of 'the commandments and prohibitions' (190), it is not a simplified list of the biblical legislation, but a carefully structured exposition beginning with a section on God (190–92), followed by outlines of man's relation to the Creator (193–205) and to fellow creatures (206–14).

The subheadings of the second section are: Temple and priesthood (193–94), sacrifices (195–97) and purifications associated with sacrifice (198). This last point leads to a consideration of three types of uncleanness. The first impurity derives from sexual acts: in this connection, Josephus gives a précis of Jewish marriage laws (199–203). The second is linked to childbirth: here a few tangential observations are appended concerning the upbringing and schooling of children (204). The third kind of uncleanness results from contact with a corpse, a subject providing Josephus with an opportunity to formulate moral advice regarding funeral ceremonies (205).

The third section, dealing with human relationships, describes duties towards parents (206), attitudes towards friends (207–08) and a more detailed exposition of Jewish behaviour towards Gentiles (209–14).

The summary ends with two brief appendices, the first alluding to the punishment awaiting the wicked in this world (215–17), and the second, to the reward in the future life reserved for faithful observers of the Law (218–19).

It is time now to examine more closely Josephus' Torah.

I

The first of the three sections, on the doctrine of God, is based on the Decalogue. However, unlike Philo who expressly arranges his presentation of the special laws around the Ten Commandments,[11] Josephus does not refer to them directly. Instead, he advances rational grounds to justify the scheme he adopts. He must start with God, he tells us, because he is 'the beginning, the middle and the end ... of all' (*archē kai mesa kai telos ... tōn pantōn* (190)). This idea that God is the beginning and the end of all things is paralleled in Revelation 1:8, 'I am the alpha and the omega', to which some manuscripts and the Vulgate add *archē kai telos – principium et finis*, but the next clause, like Josephus' definition, is tripartite: 'who is, who was and who is to come'. Likewise, a third century AD Amoraic saying attributed to Resh Laqish interprets the divine name *'Emeth*: "*'Aleph* is the beginning of letters, *taw* is the end, and *mem* is in the middle'.[12] In other words, Josephus' reasoning appears to rest on traditional foundation.[13]

Continuing implicitly with the Decalogue, Josephus offers two arguments in support of the Mosaic doctrine prohibiting any figurative representation of the deity. The first asserts that no matter is sufficiently precious and no skill sufficiently excellent to reproduce the divine image even had we knowledge of it, but since no one has seen God, it is impious to invent a likeness for him (191). Secondly, because God is the sole creator of all things producing them without hands and without helpers, he must be worshipped by the practice of virtue alone (192). By emphasizing the essentially spiritual character of *therapeia*, Josephus hints in advance at the symbolical significance and value of the institutions and rites that are the subject of the next section.

II

Turning to the cult, Josephus stresses that it is founded on the principle of unity: there being only one God, there can be but one Temple (193). He makes the same point in *Antiquities:* there exists one holy city, one temple and one altar because God is one, as is also the Hebrew race (iv 200–01). (The multiplicity of sanctuaries in the biblical past is conveniently ignored.) Also, it is a logical inference from the theocratic nature of the government instituted by Moses that the specific group of persons chosen to be the worshippers of God par excellence (viz., the priests headed by the high priest, himself to be obeyed as God) should be entrusted in addition with the teaching, administration and enforcement of the laws. Here, Josephus propounds a doctrine of priestly hegemony the first clear formulation of which is traceable to Hecataeus of Abdera (c. 300 BC)[14] and which is still manifest in the writings of the Qumran sect.[15]

There are curious omissions in this latter statement by Josephus. Thus, for reasons of his own, he is silent on the non-priestly judiciary. Yet not only was he aware of their existence (in *Antiquities* (iv 214–15) he tells of groups of seven just men, attended by two Levites, in charge of the administration of cities, and in iv 287 he explicitly describes them as 'seven judges'). He even claims to have established such magistrates in the Galilean towns during the first revolution, as well as a court of seventy – no doubt in imitation of the Jerusalem Sanhedrin (outlined in iv 218) – under his own presidency, to deal with important matters and capital cases (*War* ii 570 71). Moreover, he leaves unmentioned the Mosaic legislation relating to the king. In this respect he may have been motivated by political considerations: the merest hint at the institution of the monarchy must have carried ominous connotations at the end of the first century. In fact, when reference to it is inescapable, as in *Antiquities* iv 223–24, he portrays it as a downward step from the ideal aristocracy of direct rule by God. Moses did not propose, but as it were suffered, the institution: if the Israelites were to decide to have a monarch, he was to be of Jewish race and prepared to accept guidance in all matters from the high priest and his council.[16] In connection with the Temple cult, Josephus underlines Jewish sobriety during sacrificial banquets and the precedence of the common good (*koinōnia*) over personal interests (195–96), and he reminds his readers that the purpose of the prayer accompanying a sacrifice is not to urge God to grant good things (he does so spontaneously), but to enable the worshipper to receive and keep them (197). In this paragraph on the Temple and the priesthood, one particular feature gives food for thought. It is generally admitted that *Contra Apionem* is the last of Josephus' surviving works, dating to the very end of the first, and possibly to the opening years of the second, century AD. Yet he alludes to the sanctuary and its sacrifices as continuing realities. The Mishnah is therefore not the only post-70 Jewish document to express the hope of a quick restoration or to portray a utopian world with an enduring sacrificial worship as though the destruction of Jerusalem had never happened.[17] The issue of ritual purification is also directly associated by him with the Temple: 'It is in view of the sacrifices that the Law has prescribed purifications after funeral, after childbirth, after sexual intercourse and many other occasions' (198). As has been indicated earlier, the three paradigmatic cases are used, not to discuss causes of uncleanness and the means by which it can be removed, but to outline ethico-legal matters.

Apropos of marriage laws, which are listed in conjunction with sexual impurity, Josephus maintains firmly that the purpose of marital union is procreation (199), thereby echoing the common Jewish teaching based on the divine commandment, 'Be fruitful and multiply' (Gen. 1.28). The same view is voiced in the Mishnah,[18] in Josephus' own description of married Essenes (who take wives not in view of pleasure but of offspring),[19] and indirectly by Tacitus' sarcastic allusion to the Jewish *generandi amor*.[20] As may be expected, adultery and sodomy are characterized as heinous crimes (199, 201).

Incidentally, the subject of marriage presents Josephus with a good opportunity for more of his customary misogynous remarks (cf. already 181). 'Woman, it is said in Scripture, is inferior to man in everything', consequently she must accept direction from him to whom God has given authority (201).[21] She is also harshly treated in connection with abortion. If she deliberately induces a miscarriage, or is found guilty of destruction of a foetus, she is to be counted as an infanticide, killer of a soul and responsible for diminishing the Jewish race (202).[22]

The final paragraph of this section discloses the philosophical principle uniting the three sources of uncleanness: sexual intercourse (leading to conception), childbearing and death all consist in a *psuchēs merismos*, a division of the soul, part of which passes from one place to another (203). This idea, which demands further elucidation, has Greek antecedents and appears also to be akin to Essene anthropology as depicted by Josephus.[23]

Some of the omissions in the domain of marriage laws are worth noting. For example, the only forbidden union mentioned by Josephus in *Contra Apionem* is that with near kin, whereas in *Antiquities* iv 244–45 he declares marriage to a slave-woman or a prostitute to be illicit. He fails also to refer either to divorce or to leviratic marriage, both of which are treated in *Antiquities* (iv 253–56)[24]

Interestingly, consideration of the uncleanness arising from childbirth prompts him to recommend sobriety when celebrating the arrival of a newly-born (drinking to excess is forbidden) and to stress the Jewish concern for the education of children. They must be taught to read and study the laws and history of their ancestors 'in order that they may imitate the latter, and, being grounded in the former, may neither transgress nor have any excuse of being ignorant of them' (204).[25]

Josephus' presentation of burial rites conforms to the rule laid down in the Hebrew Ecclesiasticus (7:34), which declares that all the passers-by are to join the funeral procession led by the relatives. Expensive ceremonies and monuments are, however, ostentatious and to be discouraged (205).[26]

III

The Mosaic doctrine of man's relation to his fellow-creatures forms the final section of Josephus' account. Reverting once more to the Decalogue, to the fifth commandment, he presents piety towards parents as the highest precept in the human sphere (206),[27] but points out that the Law further demands that the young should respect their elders in general, 'because God is the most ancient of all' (206).

The category of 'friends' follows immediately on that of parents and the old. Though he does not expressly say so, we may assume that in Josephus' eyes only fellow-Jews enjoyed this title.[28] He characterizes the correct treatment of a friend as one of unlimited trust: everything must be shared with, and nothing concealed from such a person.[29] He appends, in addition, sundry rules promoting community ties. Judges are not to accept bribes; if a Jew is able to help another, he must never refuse to do so; a man's property is not to be appropriated by another; no friend is to be charged interest on a loan (207–08).

The essential virtue to be exercised vis-à-vis strangers is generosity (*epieikeia*) (209). Moses insisted on safeguarding Jewish national customs but also on permitting Gentiles to participate in them. This is no doubt a reference by Josephus to proselytism with a view to suggesting that family bonds are not the only ties conducive to the formation of a community. It can be found also in a shared way of life. A close relationship of this sort is, however, not appropriate where casual visitors are concerned; they are to be excluded from the common customs (210). The latter clause can be interpreted in various ways,[30] but irrespective of its precise meaning it implicitly affirms the Jewish social exclusivism that was seen by Gentiles as a hatred of mankind, *misanthrōpia* (148, 291).[31]

Even though a share in the intimacies of Jewish life, so Josephus goes on, is extended to proselytes only, the Law imposes as a universal duty the provision of all persons in need with the basic necessities, such as fire, water and food. Travellers are to be directed on their way and all corpses are to be buried (211). Humane and civilized behaviour must also characterize any dealings with enemies. Jews at war must not wantonly destroy the orchards of their adversary, for trees are innocent, and if they could speak, they would decline all responsibility for the hostility. Indeed, if they had had knowledge of it, they would have migrated to another country (*Ant.* iv 299–300)! Furthermore, Jews are not to despoil the bodies of fallen enemies,[32] or ill-treat and abuse prisoners, especially captive women (212).[33]

The commandment to direct the lost traveller on his way[34] is often seen in modern literature as refuting the charge, echoed in a poem by Juvenal, that Jews assist only their co-religionists: *non monstrare vias eadem nisi sacra colenti*.[35] But an apologetical intent of this sort is far from certain. It should be recalled that the original biblical injunction (Deut. 27.18) seeks specifically to protect the blind and that the patently non-apologetical Palestinian Targums also understand the scriptural passage metaphorically: 'Cursed be he who deceives the foreigner (*'akhsanyā*) who is like a blind man'.[36]

Josephus claims, in brief, that the main message of the Law in the domain of human relations is philanthropy (*philanthrōpia*)[37] and a gentle disposition towards not only fellow-Jews but all mankind. Moreover – and in this respect he sounds singularly modern – he maintains that besides inculcating phil*anthropy* in the strict sense, Moses showed sympathy towards the animal world also.[38] In his highly eclectic summary of the Law, the historian finds place for the sabbatical rest to be enjoyed by domestic animals (Deut. 5.14) and for the duty of releasing parent birds caught together with their young (Deut. 22.6); and he even manages to insert two further cases without biblical antecedent. Thus a Jewish soldier in enemy territory must, in addition to sparing fruit trees, treat well all the working beasts. Most touching of all, he relates that Jews are forbidden to kill 'creatures which take refuge in our houses like suppliants' (213).[39] It may perhaps be useful to recall at this juncture that the biblical precept apropos of the fallen ox or donkey *belonging to a fellow-Jew* which must be helped to its feet, is transformed in *Antiquities* iv 275 to apply to *any* beast of burden in trouble.

This section of Josephus' summary of the Torah ends with an emphatic assertion of the kindness evinced by Judaism towards all – towards Gentiles, and enemies, and even plants and animals. '(Moses) had an eye to mercy . . . using the laws to enforce the lesson' (214).

This emphasis on mercy is nevertheless not incompatible with the concept of chastisement. Transgressors of the Torah, who cannot plead ignorance and are therefore without excuse, will receive their deserts. In his first appendix (215–17), Josephus outlines the penalties decreed by Moses, stating not without exaggeration that most offences carry the death sentence. He mentions in this paragraph adultery,[40] rape,[41] and male homosexual acts,[42] but elsewhere filial disobedience (206), the intention itself of wronging parents or of acting impiously towards God (217), abortion (202) and the acceptance of a bribe by a judge (207), are listed as capital crimes. But typically, Josephus omits any reference to idol-worship.[43] On the contrary, in a later passage (237), he reports that Moses enjoined tolerance towards alien deities: 'Our lawgiver has expressly forbidden us to deride or blaspheme the gods recognized by others, out of respect for the very word *god*'.[44]

The second appendix (217–19) deals with the reward awaiting the faithful who remain so firmly attached to the commandments that, like the many martyrs of past ages,[45] they are prepared to die for them.[46] These will enjoy a new and better life hereafter. Thus Josephus discloses his Pharisee belief,[47] though without distinguishing clearly between eternal life and the resurrection of the dead. Unlike the eschatology of the Essenes as he recounts it, which visits the wicked with unending suffering in dark, stormy places,[48] in *Contra Apionem* he envisages life after death as the privilege of the just. It is in consequence logical to infer that in his view the penalty of unrighteousness was annihilation.[49]

By way of conclusion it should be stressed that in this carefully conceived and simplified presentation of the Torah we are confronted with what is probably the earliest Jewish theological synthesis.[50] Its primary aim was manifestly to impress on educated Graeco-Roman readers the outstanding excellence of Judaism. This is apparent from the whole tone of *Contra Apionem*, from the introductory remarks relating to the calumnies of

Apollonius Molon, and as I have suggested, from the relatively detailed picture of the duties of the Jews towards aliens. But whilst striving to demonstrate the falseness of the fashionable anti-Jewish propaganda of misanthropy, it cleverly hints that full communion is practicable only among 'friends' (210), i.e., among Jews and proselytes.

At the opening of his summary, Josephus states: 'We possess a code excellently designed to promote piety, friendly relationship with each other, and humanity towards the world at large, besides justice, hardihood, and contempt of death' (146).[51] Is the special colouring of Josephus' version of the Torah, the bias adopted by him throughout the tractate, away from the strictly legal and ritual and towards the religious and ethical, due to his having a foreign readership in mind? For Kamlah, this goes without saying: the piety expressed in Josephus' composition is proclaimed entirely Hellenistic.[52] No doubt, Philo's allegorical treatment of the Law may be cited in support of such an argument. Nevertheless, it should be remembered that Jesus' teaching possesses a similar religious and ethical ring, yet it was addressed to a Jewish and not to a Gentile audience. Also, Josephus' remarks that virtue demands abstention from thoughts as well as from acts contrary to the Torah (183), and that the mere intention to do wrong incurs guilt (217), run parallel to the doctrine of Jesus concerning the primary causes of impiety when he represents anger and the lustful gaze as the sources of murder and adultery.[53]

It might be argued that contrary to providing Josephus' viewpoint with a Palestinian backing, the trend towards internalization characteristic of the Gospels reflects the same Hellenistic direction as that shown by *Contra Apionem* and Philo. That is to say, it did not originate with Jesus but with the Gentile church. Against such reasoning it has to be said that rabbinic literature is also partial to abridging the Torah, and in a similar sense. Nothing illustrates this better than the saying accredited to the third century Palestinian Amora, R. Simlai:

Six hundred and thirteen commandments were revealed to Moses . . . Then David came and comprehended them in eleven (Ps. 15) . . . Then Isaiah came and comprehended them in six (walking justly, speaking uprightly, despising ill-gotten gain, refusing bribes, not listening to encouragement to violence, turning one's eyes away from evil – Is. 33.15) . . . Then Micah came and comprehended them in three (doing justice, loving mercy and walking humbly before God – Mic. 6.8) . . . Then Isaiah came again, and comprehended them in two (observing justice and practising righteousness – Is. 56.1). Finally Amos came and comprehended them in one: *Seek me* and you shall live (Amos 5.4).[54]

10

New Light on the Sacrifice of Isaac from Qumran

While I was wading through the unexciting scraps of the Book of Jubilees from Qumran Cave 4, in view of the fifth edition of *The Dead Sea Scrolls in English*, I tumbled on 4Q225 and became truly excited. This Hebrew text, represented by medium-size fragments, contains an account similar to the Abraham section of the Book of Jubilees. The editors, J. C. VanderKam and J. T. Milik (*Discoveries in the Judaean Desert* XIII, Clarendon Press, Oxford, 1994[1], pp. 141–55), have given it the title, 'Pseudo-Jubilees[2]', but it may as well be an independent version of the pseudepigraphon previously known from Ethiopic, Greek and Latin translations.[2] Palaeographically the 'Herodian' script of 4Q225 is dated to the turn of the era (30 BCE – 20 CE). The two other 'Pseudo-Jubilees' manuscripts, 4Q226 and 4Q227, the former partly overlapping with 4Q225, are placed by the editors to the second half of the first century BCE. The actual composition, just like the traditional form of Jubilees, is likely to have originated in the middle of the second century BCE.[3]

Two features of the Ethiopic Jubilees are supplementary to the Genesis 22 story: the intervention of the angel Mastemah[4] and the date assigned to the intended sacrifice, 15 Nisan.[5] Of these, the first is paralleled in 4Q225: Mastemah not only initiates the trial of Abraham, but his angels comment on its outcome. By contrast, the date of the sacrifice is missing from the Qumran text. But 4Q225 includes broken references to further midrashic elements (printed in bold letters in the translation): mention of a fire (II, 1); a second address by Isaac (II, 4); reference to weeping holy angels (II, 5); mention of (Isaac's?) sons (II, 6); rejoicing among the angels of Mastemah (II, 7–8); God's comment on Abraham (II, 10); God's blessing of Isaac (II, 10–11); and chronological details (II, 12). The identity of several of these references is successfully determined by the editors with the help of targumic and midrashic parallels.[6] The impact of these on the ongoing debate on the interpretation of the Binding of Isaac and their possible influence on the New Testament theology of the cross has either escaped the editors or they did not consider them relevant to their editorial work.

The appropriate part of the manuscript is reproduced here. The editors have filled most of the gaps in the text from Genesis 22 and their reconstructions appear generally reasonable. However, I have deleted their purely hypothetical completion of the phrases which are without biblical parallels. Both the translation and the annotation are mine.

4Q225

I ... ⁸wywld bn 'ḥ[ry] kn
⁹[l'brh]m wyqr' 't šmw yshq wybw' sr hm[ś]ṭmh
¹⁰['l 'l]whym wyśtym 'brhm byshq wy'mr [']lwhym
¹¹['l 'br]hm qḥ 't bnkh 't yshq 't yhyd[kh 'šr]
¹²['th 'hb]th wh'lhw ly l'wlh 'l 'hd hhrym [. . .]ym
¹³['šr 'wmr] lkh wyq[wm wy]l[k] mn hb'rwt 'l h[r hmwryh]
¹⁴[   ]l[   ]wyś' 'b[rhm] 't

II
¹['y]ny[w whnh] 'š w[y]tn ['t h'ṣym 'l yshq bnw wylkw yḥdw]
² wywmr yshq 'l 'brhm ['byw hnh h'š wh'ṣym w'yh hśh]
³ l'wlh wywmr 'brhm 'l [yshq bnw 'lwhym yr'h 't hśh]
⁴ lw 'mr yshq 'l 'byw k...
⁵ ml'ky qʷdš 'mdym bwkym 'l . . .
⁶ 't bnyw mn h'rṣ wml'ky hm[śṭmh] . . .
⁷ śmḥym w'mrym 'kšyw y'bd w. . .
⁸ ymṣ' khš w'm l' ymṣ' n'mn '[brhm l'lwhym wyqr'] . . .
⁹ 'brhm 'brhm wy'mr hnny wy'mr '. . .
¹⁰ l' yhyh 'hb wybrk 'l yhwh 't ys[ḥq kwl ymy ḥyw wywlyd 't [cf. 4Q226 7.3]
¹¹ y'qwb wy'qwb hwlyd 't lwy dw[r šlyšy *vacat* [cf. 4Q226 7.4] whyw]
¹² ymy 'brhm wyshq wy'qwb wlw[y   šnh]

Annotated translation

I ... (8) And a son was born af[ter]wards (9) [to Abraha]m and he called his name Isaac. And the prince Ma[s]temah came (10) [to G]od and accused Abraham on account of Isaac.[7] And [G]od said (11) [to Abra]ham, 'Take your son, Isaac, [your] only (son) (12) [whom] you [love] and offer him to

me as a burnt offering on one of the . . . mountains (13) [which I will tell]
you.' And he ro[se and he we]n[t] from the wells[8] to Mo[unt Moriah]. (14)
. . . And Ab[raham] lifted up II (1) his [ey]es[9] [and behold there was] a
fire.[10] And he placed [the wood on Isaac, his son, and they went together].
(2) And Isaac said to Abraham, [his father, ' Behold there is the fire and the
wood, but where is the lamb] (3) for the burnt offering?' And Abraham said
to [Isaac, his son, 'God will provide a lamb] (4) for himself.[11] Isaac said to
his father, '*K*[. . . [12] . . . (5) the holy angels standing (and) weeping
over[13] . . . (6) his sons from the earth.[14] And the angels of M[astemah]
. . . (7) were rejoicing and saying,[15] 'Now he (Isaac) will be destroyed
. . . (8) whether he[16] will be found weak[17] and whether A[braham]
will be found unfaithful [to God. And he (God)[18] called,] (9) 'Abraham,
Abraham.' And he said, 'Here am I.' And he said, . . . (10) he (Abraham)
is not a lover (of God).'[19] And the Lord God blessed Is[aac[20] all the days
of his life (cf. 4Q226 7.3) and he begot] (11) Jacob, and Jacob begot Levi
(in the) [third (cf. 4Q226 7.4)] genera[tion. And all] (12) the days of
Abraham and Isaac and Jacob and Lev[i were . . . years].

4Q225 and the history of the early exegesis of Genesis 22

The interpretation of the biblical account of the sacrifice of Isaac in
rabbinic literature and its possible impact on the New Testament received
only scant attention in the course of the first half of the twentieth century.[21]
For about two decades the most comprehensive study, that of Spiegel, was
prevented from making the impact to which it was entitled by the fact that
it was written in Hebrew. It was only after its translation into English
by Judah Goldin that it began to be noticed in theological circles.[22] The
closing chapter of my *Scripture and Tradition in Judaism*, 'Redemption and
Genesis XXII: The Binding of Isaac and the Sacrifice of Jesus' (1961, pp.
193–227), reopened the debate and was followed by a number of fresh
attempts to investigate the issue.[23]

The chief findings I arrived at were as follows. 1. The simplest form of
the exegetical tradition concerning Genesis 22 is attested in the Palestinian
Targums in the narrative form of a 're-written Bible'. Its distinctive
features are that (a) Isaac was informed of his role as a victim; (b) he gave
his consent and asked to be bound; (c) he was favoured with a vision of
angels; and (d) God was to remember the binding of Isaac in favour of his
descendants.[24] Supplementary details are included in Ps. Jon. on Gen. 22.1
and 4, namely the adult Isaac's age (37 years) and the vision of a cloud of
glory designating the mountain of the sacrifice. 2. The expanded account
of the Aqedah-inspired theological reflections is recorded in Tannaitic and

Amoraic sources. These relate to the sacrificial character of the Aqedah (an allusion to the ashes and blood of Isaac),[25] and its saving effects.[26] Furthermore, the atoning power of the Temple sacrifices is attributed by the rabbis to God's remembering the sacrifice of Isaac on Mount Moriah = the Temple Mount.[27] The Aqedah is also associated with one of the principal Jewish feasts, first with Passover on account of the lamb symbolism during the existence of the Temple,[28] and subsequently with New Year and the blowing of the ram's horn recalling the binding of Isaac.[29]

I further argued that most of the narrative and even some of the speculative traditions are paralleled in the first-century CE writings of Josephus' *Jewish Antiquities*, i 222–36, Pseudo-Philo's *Liber Antiquitatum Biblicarum* (*LAB*) 18.5; 32.2–4; 40.2 and in IV Maccabees 13.12; 16.20,[30] as well as in the second century BCE Jubilees 17.15; 18.3 (dating the Aqedah to Passover), and that in consequence the essence of the post-biblical rewriting of the story is traceable back to at least the first century CE, which means that it was current at the time of the formation of the New Testament.[31] These views have found general favour among scholars during the last three decades, with the exception of Philip Davies and Bruce Chilton who set out in an article published in 1978 to substitute for them 'a revised tradition history'.[32] I believe that in the light of the evidence from 4Q225 their counter-argument can be finally refuted.

Here are the main items of their thesis. Instead of consisting in Isaac's conscious willing and meritorious participation in the sacrifice, the Aqedah was redefined as 'a haggadic presentation of the vicariously atoning sacrifice of Isaac in which he is said, e.g., to have shed his blood freely and/or to have been reduced to ashes'.[33] In other words, they arbitrarily selected the most advanced theological speculation of the rabbis and then claimed that this constituted the essence of the Aqedah. Next, the supporting external evidence (Josephus, Ps.-Philo and IV Macc.) adduced by me to argue for the first century CE currency of the Aqedah story was declared to be post-70 CE. Ps.-Philo and IV Maccabees, contrary to mainstream opinion, were dated to 70–135 CE,[34] and *Jewish Antiquities* was dated correctly to the end of the century, but without taking into account that Josephus regularly echoes traditional views. Such a revised chronology served as a precondition for the blunt assertion that 'the Aqedah was *invented* (my emphasis) by the Rabbis', mostly Amoraim, who 'went so far as to appropriate details of the Passion[35] to heighten the drama of Isaac's Offering and *to deny thereby the uniqueness of Jesus' offering*' (my emphasis).[36] Finally it was maintained that the Aqedah doctrine was introduced to replace the Tamid lamb offering, discontinued after the destruction of the Temple in 70 CE, by the symbolic sacrifice of Isaac;[37] and that the shift of emphasis from Abraham to Isaac, as well as most details of the targumic presentation of Genesis 22, had a rabbinic, and predominantly fourth century CE Amoraic, provenance.

I never felt that this 'revised tradition history' demanded an actual refutation, though others did issue firm and in my opinion convincing rebuttals.[38] But now, seventeen years after its publication, along came 4Q225, this apparently harmless scrap of a manuscript which, by revealing the pre-Christian skeleton of the targumic-midrashic representation of the sacrifice of Isaac, has rendered the hypothesis of an Amoraic origin of the Aqedah at least highly improbable. Hence, without further ado, I move to my peroration in the form of a chronologically arranged synoptic table of the exegetical evidence assembled in the foregoing pages.[39]

Synoptic table[40]

	BCE	1st CE	PT	Tan	Amor/later
1. Isaac adult		Jos	PsJ/FT/N		GenR
2. Fire/bright cloud	4Q225		PsJ		GenR, PRE
3. Isaac informed		Jos/*LAB*	FT/N		GenR
4. Isaac consents	4Q225?	Jos/*LAB*/ IVMacc.			GenR
5. Asks to be bound	4Q225?		PsJ/FT/N	SifDt	
6. Presence of angels	4Q225		FT, N		GenR
7. Crying angels	4Q225				GenR
8. Merit of Isaac	4Q225?	*LAB*		Mekh	GenR
9. Temple Mount	IIChr, Jub	Jos	FT/N		GenR
10. Passover	Jub		FT/N	Mekh	GenR
11. Lamb sacrifice			FT/N/PsJ		<LevR(bar.)>
12. Isaac's blood/ashes		*LAB*		Sifra	GenR/ y/bTaan

The Dead Sea Scrolls Fifty Years On

For nearly a hundred years, starting with the 1850 excavations by the French scholar F. de Saulcy, archaeologists laboriously searched every corner of the Land of Israel, but their spades failed to turn up anything written on perishable material, leather or papyrus. Then suddenly, in 1947 on the arid shore of the Dead Sea, a Bedouin shepherd accidentally stumbled on the greatest Hebrew manuscript discovery in history. In a cave south of Jericho and about two miles north of the ruins of Khirbet Qumran, he found seven leather scrolls. They were 1,000 years older than the most ancient Hebrew biblical codices previously known. Three manuscripts (an incomplete Isaiah Scroll, the War Scroll, and a Hymns Scroll) were purchased by E. L. Sukenik, professor of archaeology at the Hebrew University, and posthumously published by 1954. The other four (a complete Isaiah Scroll, the Community Rule, a commentary on the Book of Habakkuk and parts of an Aramaic paraphrase of Genesis) were acquired by the head of a Syrian Christian monastery in Jerusalem and entrusted to American scholars who edited the first three in 1950 and 1951. A few years later these scrolls were purchased by an anonymous buyer on behalf of the State of Israel and all the seven rolls from Cave 1 ended up in the Shrine of the Book, part of the Israel Museum in Jerusalem.

Between 1951 and 1956, the Qumran site and the neighbouring cemetery were excavated and ten more manuscript caves were identified. Cave 4 yielded tens of thousands of fragments and Cave 11 several further scrolls which were deposited in the Rockefeller Museum in East Jerusalem. To prepare the fragments for publication, the Jordanian archaeological authorities appointed Father Roland de Vaux, a French Dominican of the Ecole Biblique of Jerusalem, as chief editor. He in turn established a small international team of Christian, mostly Roman Catholic, Hebraists. They were faced with a monumental jigsaw puzzle of manuscript fragments. In the 1950s and early 60s the publication of the texts proceeded swiftly, but enthusiasm progressively abated. In 1967, the Six-Day War brought the fragments in the Rockefeller Museum under

Israeli control, but the former international editorial team was left in charge of the publishing process. By the thirtieth anniversary of Qumran in 1977, the procrastination, which was due to a lack of organization and sheer dilatoriness rather than incompetence or theological machinations, had turned into the academic scandal of the century. The situation was made worse by scholarly imperialism: for forty years the unpublished manuscripts were kept under lock and key, accessible only to the handful of official editors.

In 1991 the so-called 'Qumran revolution' erupted. Outraged public opinion, the unauthorized publication of some texts reconstructed by computer from a word list by a professor of Hebrew Union College, Cincinnati and one of his doctoral students, and the decision of a Californian research library to open its accidentally acquired Dead Sea photographic archive to all qualified scholars persuaded the Israel Archaeological Authority to lift their embargo on the unpublished Scrolls. A more detailed account of this sad story may be found in my book, *The Complete Dead Sea Scrolls in English* (1998). Since 1992, under the direction of Professor Emanuel Tov of the Hebrew University of Jerusalem, a team of some seventy scholars have been busy with the material still to be edited, and the work is expected to be completed by 2002–2003.

The Qumran finds consist of some eight hundred original compositions. Most of them were written in Hebrew, some in Aramaic, and a few in Greek.

The commonest writing material was skin, but papyrus was also used. One scroll is on copper and there are also a few inscribed potsherds. The size of the manuscripts varies from large scrolls to minute scraps. Books did not exist at Qumran; the scroll is the only form attested, consisting of several sheets of skin sewn together, written on one side only and rolled up with the text inside. Broken pots or ostraca, the cheapest writing material, were used for notes.

Complete or incomplete scrolls were found in Cave 1 (already listed), and Cave 11 (parts of a Leviticus manuscript written with old Hebrew letters, an incomplete Targum of Job, about a third of the Psalms with additions, and the Temple Scroll). The Copper Scroll from Cave 3 lists in cryptic language 64 hiding-places where gold, silver and precious stones are concealed. Whether the Copper Scroll deals with fact or with fiction is still debated.

The size and appearance of the manuscripts varies. Some of the scrolls are of considerable length. In its original form, the Temple Scroll stretched over 28½ ft (8.75 m) and the complete Isaiah Scroll from Cave 1 measures 24 ft or 7.34 m. But there are thousands of tiny fragments, too, containing only odd letters or parts of letters.

Of the 800 compositions, about 200 represent the Hebrew Bible. All its books, with the possible exception of Esther, are extant in Qumran. The text agrees in substance with the traditional Bible, but discloses a large number of stylistic differences, additions, omissions and changes in the order of the passages. Even before 1947 it was known that the text of the Bible existed in three shapes: the proto-Masoretic text which later became the traditional text of the Bible; the text reflected in the Samaritan Torah, and that which underlies the ancient Greek or Septuagint version. The biblical Dead Sea Scrolls prove that textual elasticity was even greater than we imagined.

The list of writings that constitute Holy Scripture was fixed in Palestine in the first half of the second century BCE, but remained open for another century in the Greek Diaspora. Hence the Greek Septuagint contains additional titles to the Hebrew Scripture known as the Apocrypha. Qumran Caves 4 and 11 have revealed the original Hebrew of the Book of Wisdom of Jesus son of Sira and extensive fragments of the Book of Tobit. Of the five Tobit manuscripts yielded by Cave 4, four are in Aramaic and one in Hebrew.

At the end of the Second Temple period, a large collection of further religious books circulated among Jews, known as the Pseudepigrapha. Before Qumran they were extant only in Greek, Latin, Syriac and Ethiopic translations. Now bits of Enoch and the Testament of Levi can be read in Aramaic, and Jubilees in Hebrew.

The Qumran caves also produced a large number of previously unknown compositions. A good many of these (such as the non-canonical Psalms and wisdom works) may have originated in mainstream Jewish circles, but there is also a group of sectarian writings: rules, religious poetry, biblical interpretation and a peculiar liturgical calendar.

The rules suggest that the movement had two branches. Both were governed by priests, but one male group pursued extreme asceticism, with common ownership of property and apparently celibacy; another, while insisting on especially rigorous faithfulness to the Law of Moses, permitted marriage and private possession of property.

The Hymns are mostly individual prayers. Qumran Bible exegesis often adopts the form of fulfilment interpretation. Scriptural prophecy is explained by pointing to persons and events in the community's recent history in whom the words of the prophets are said to have been realized. As for the calendars, they represent a time-reckoning based on a 364-day solar year, against mainstream Judaism's lunar calendar of 354 days, which is supplemented every three years by an extra month of 30 days. The distinctive outcome of this divergence was that the dates of the communities' feasts differed from those celebrated in the Jerusalem Temple.

Although none of the manuscripts is actually dated, their age is now universally accepted as ranging from the end of the third century BCE to the first Jewish uprising against Rome (66–70 CE). The palaeographical dating, arrived at in the 1950s, which also coincides with the archaeological data, has since been generally confirmed by radiocarbon tests.

From the early years of Qumran research a general consensus prevailed on three basic issues. 1. The manuscripts, the caves and the ruined establishment at Qumran are connected. 2. The Qumran establishment was occupied from the second half of the second century BCE to the time of its destruction (probably in 68 CE) by members of a Jewish group. 3. This ascetic community was that of the Essenes, located by Pliny the Elder on the western shore of the Dead Sea, somewhere between Jericho and Ein Gedi, and described in detail by the Jewish writers, Philo of Alexandria and Flavius Josephus.

The practical conclusion derived from these three statements and held during the early decades of scrolls studies was that probably all the manuscripts were copied, and most of the non-biblical documents composed, by the Essenes at Qumran. However, in more recent years, and especially since the lifting of the embargo on the unpublished texts in 1991, some of the former assumptions have been thrown open and a general reassessment of the Qumran problem as a whole is taking place.

From the early 1980s Norman Golb of the University of Chicago has persistently argued that the Dead Sea Scrolls did not originate at Qumran, but were sent there from Jerusalem to be hidden in caves when the Romans attacked the city. The texts therefore represent not the literature of the Essenes, but various ideologies of first-century Judaism.

Some writers have also rejected that the Qumran buildings corresponded to the Essene establishment described by Pliny. They argue that Pliny's words, *infra hos Engada* = below them (the Essenes) was Ein Gedi, indicate that the settlement in question was higher in altitude than Ein Gedi, and not that it was situated further to the north. Recently, an Israeli archaeologist discovered a small establishment in the Ein Gedi area which he claims belonged to the Essenes.

Once Pliny's testimony was thought (wrongly, in my view) to be out of the way, new hypotheses began to multiply. The Qumran complex was a small fortress. No, it was a villa built for a rich Jerusalem family seeking sunshine during the cold winter months. The room with a table and two ink wells, previously recognized as a *scriptorium* where the Essenes copied their scrolls, was identified with a Hellenistic or Roman dining-room furnished with beds on which hosts and guests reclined. Two Australian authors came up with the idea that Qumran was a customs post combined with a luxurious inn for travelling merchants who transported salt from the region, or imported incense from Arabia. In short, neither the ruins nor the scrolls have anything to do with the Essenes.

How does the common opinion of former years stand up to these onslaughts?

The denial of a link between the scrolls and the Qumran site leaves the presence of the manuscripts in the neighbourhood of the settlement unexplained. Why should they be brought to this distant place, when perfectly suitable hiding places could have been found closer to Jerusalem? By contrast, the connection between the site and the manuscripts is supported by the close proximity to the Qumran buildings of six of the eleven caves, including Cave 4 with its remains of 550 documents, and by the presence of the peculiar scroll jars both in Cave 1 and at the Qumran settlement, which had its own potter's workshop.

Neither have the recent theories shaken the common opinion that Qumran was a religious establishment. All the counter-proposals are unconvincing. It is conceivable that the Qumran buildings were erected on the site of an earlier rural fortification, but the large constructions subsequently built lack two essential characteristics of a fortress: the perimeter wall is flimsy and the crucial water conduits are unprotected. With regard to the suggestion that Qumran was a wealthy man's country house, the site is scarcely the right place for comfort and pleasure. Why not build a winter residence in the nearby fertile plain of Jericho? Also, the theory that the object identified by the archaeologists as a plaster table in a *scriptorium* was in fact a bed in a dining-hall does not stand up to serious examination. It is only 50 cm wide, hardly a place for comfortable reclining. As for the theory of a customs post next to a luxurious hostelry (jokingly referred to in the trade as the Dead Sea 'Hilton'), there is no evidence that the traffic in the Qumran area was ever busy enough to make such an institution viable.

Without a doubt, Qumran was constructed with communal occupation in mind. It contains a large meeting room/dining-hall with more than 1,000 simple pots, plates and bowls stacked in an adjacent room. The discovery of two inkpots, a rare commodity, indicates uncommon writing activity. By contrast, Father Roland de Vaux's conjecture that the Essenes used to write on the table found in the *scriptorium* is to be discarded. Ancient scribes normally wrote on their knees. The table, on the other hand, was necessary to prepare the leather which had to be lined horizontally and the width of the columns marked with vertical traces.

Finally, the unusual orientation and construction of 1,100 tombs in the Qumran cemetery point to a special group, a sect. So also do the numerous cisterns and the considerable water supply, which were meant for frequent ritual ablutions, one of the main characteristics of the Essenes.

The same conclusion may be drawn from the Qumran library itself. Sectarian rules and calendars are represented there in large numbers, suggesting a separatist religious community.

Can the ancient occupants of Khirbet Qumran still be identified with the Essenes? Hypothetically yes.

It may be argued that such an identification is superfluous because the community can be studied without an attached historical label. Analysis of the various rules invites us to distinguish two branches of a Jewish religious movement in the Qumran accounts. Both were directed by priests and inspired by an expectation of the imminent end, convinced that they formed God's elect in the last days. Both were directed by a *mebaqqer* or overseer, and both obeyed strict religious and moral regulations based on the teaching of their priestly leaders. In both groups, transgressors were subjected to a penal code, but the penalties differed. In both, new members went through a system of initiation, but again the systems varied. The main difference between the two consisted in the adoption of religious communism in the branch which followed the Community Rule, whereas the other branch admitted private property. Above all, one of the branches consisted of married members whose children were brought up according to the sect's laws and formally initiated at the age of twenty. The Community Rule, on the other hand, although supplying a detailed way of life, makes no allusion to women, marriage, divorce, children or education. Here the argument from silence speaks loud and clear.

The accounts of the Essenes display striking similarities, first and foremost in their attitudes to private property and marriage. Both also envisage a staged initiation process. Josephus, however, the best-informed ancient witness, notes that in addition to the male celibate communities some Essene groups adopted the married way of life, but permitted sex only for procreation. Josephus' allusion to the sexual abstinence demanded in this group during the months of pregnancy may be echoed by a Cave 4 copy of the Qumran Damascus Document. According to this text, a husband was expelled from the Community if he 'fornicated' with his wife (i.e. probably slept with her while she was expecting).

Opponents of the Essene identification have always emphasized that comparison between the Scrolls' accounts relating to the Qumran community and the classical notices about the Essenes shows noticeable differences. For example, the Qumran sectaries swore an oath at the first stage of their initiation, the Essenes of Josephus did so at the very end. However, it would be unreasonable to expect complete accord between two such sets of documents. The authors of the Scrolls possessed insider's knowledge of their Community, very different from that of the Gentile Pliny, the Egyptian Jew Philo, or even that of the Jerusalem priest Josephus. Also, the Scrolls were addressed to initiates, the classical accounts to Graeco-Roman intellectuals.

Regarding celibacy versus marriage, our present knowledge of the Qumran cemetery leads to uncertainty. Only about 40 tombs have been opened. The skeletons dug out from the main graveyard (consisting of some 1,100 tombs) are those of male subjects, but in the fringe cemeteries (with 100 tombs) the archaeologists found the remains of a handful of women and children. In the present political climate in Israel further excavations are unlikely.

To cut the argument short, I would continue to put my money on the Essenes.

Turning to the history of the community, the communal occupation of the site from the second half of the second century BCE to 70 CE provides us with a reliable chronological framework. Datable artefacts, especially hundreds of Seleucid, Hasmonaean, Herodian, Roman and revolutionary coins, testify to a more or less continuous sectarian presence from the late second century BCE to about 68 CE.

None of the Qumran manuscripts includes continuous historical narration. Most of the references to personalities are cryptic (e.g. Teacher of Righteousness, Wicked Priest, last priests of Jerusalem). The foreign conquering power is alluded to as the Kittim, almost certainly the Romans. The main sources for reconstructing the history of the community are the Damascus Document, which outlines in veiled language the sect's origins in the first half of the second century BCE and names a Hellenistic potentate as the foreign enemy, and the various biblical commentaries or *pesharim* which claim that contemporary events are the fulfilment of prophetic predictions. The Nahum Commentary gives actual names: the Greek kings Antiochus and Demetrius. A few further historical names appear in a very fragmentary calendric text: Aemilius (Scaurus), one of Pompey's generals in the 60s BCE; Shelamzion or Salome Alexandra, widow and successor of Jannaeus (76–67 BCE); Hyrcanus and John, probably John Hyrcanus II and the King Jonathan referred to in a poem (see below). According to the War Rule and the Book of War (4Q285), the final battle would oppose the community to the king of the Kittim-Romans.

The majority view concerning the history of the sect places the conflict between the founder-organizer of the community, the priestly Teacher of Righteousness and his chief opponent, the Wicked Priest, in the middle of the second century BCE. The Wicked Priest, described as good at the beginning of his career, turned ungodly on becoming the high priestly ruler of Israel. At the end he fell into the hands of his enemies (not the Kittim), who inflicted vengeance on him. In my doctoral thesis in 1952 I concluded that the only Jewish high priest of the relevant period in whom all these details can be verified was Jonathan Maccabeaus (152–143 BCE). Consequently, the last priests of Jerusalem who were finally defeated by the Kittim-Romans were Maccabaean–Hasmonaean priestly rulers.

The conflict between the Community and the Maccabees had a priestly inspiration. The sect originated among conservative Jews 'in the age of wrath' of the Hellenistic crisis in the early second century BCE. They were headed by traditionalist priests faithful to the Mosaic Law who accepted the leadership of the 'sons of Zadok', the members or associates of the ruling high priestly family. Over the years this Maccabaean historical reconstruction gained wide acceptance among Scrolls scholars.

Since 1991, when all the manuscripts became accessible to scholars, two new writings entered the historical debate. One of these, MMT or Some Observances of the Law, is interpreted by its editors as a document addressed by the Teacher of Righteousness to the Wicked Priest, Jonathan Maccabaeus. If correct, such an exposition would reinforce the mainstream historical thesis.

By contrast, another recently investigated fragment, the King Jonathan poem (4Q448), has been used as ammunition against the anti-Hasmonaean attitude of the Essenes on the grounds that the respected Jonathan is the Hasmonaean priest-king Alexander Jannaeus. I am, however, convinced that the details of the poem point, not to the less than admirable Jannaeus, whose career started with fratricide and finished with the crucifixion of 800 Pharisees, but to Jonathan Maccabaeus, who was first admired by the Community before being rejected as the Wicked Priest.

The Qumran community and Essenism as a whole left no recognizable traces in history after the late sixties of the first century CE. It is possible that after the destruction of their centre at Qumran they allowed themselves to be absorbed into mainstream rabbinic Judaism, but this explanation does not account for one important feature of the story. As there is no trace of a lasting Roman military presence at Qumran, why did not the original inhabitants return there to retrieve their eight hundred valuable manuscripts, if necessary in the middle of the night in the way that present-day Bedouin conduct their archaeological searches? Could it be that Flavius Josephus' gloomy portrayal of Essene martyrdom by the Romans relates the fate of the last inhabitants of Qumran?

To conclude this survey, let us glance at the doctrinal contents of the Scrolls in order to determine their contribution to our knowledge of contemporaneous Judaism and early Christianity.

First, let it be unequivocally stated that the Scrolls, the bulk of which originated in the second and first centuries BCE, are *Jewish* and not Christian. They are permeated by the fundamental characteristic of Jewish religion, the search for God through faithful obedience to the Torah of Moses. The Essenes observed this Law more strictly than most of their Jewish neighbours. MMT or Some Observances of the Law lists over two dozen cases where the sectarian halakhah was more demanding than that of their contemporaries. The Temple Scroll lays down the rules and the Damascus Document offers theological justification for the sect's particularly severe matrimonial laws.

Another important feature differentiating the members of the sect from mainstream Judaism was their withdrawal from the Temple. Not that they were opposed in principle to sacrificial worship; rather, they disagreed with the conduct of ceremonies by the Jerusalem priests. They expected to resume Temple service at the end, when Jerusalem would be under their control.

The calendar, which according to the sectaries reflected the eternal law of time issued from the mouth of God, was another particular cause of conflict. Those for whom the subject looks trivial need only recall the Easter dispute which nearly resulted in a schism between Rome and the churches of Syria and Asia Minor in the late second century, and that the eastern orthodox churches continue to this day to resist the reform of the calendar introduced by Pope Gregory XIII in 1582.

Religious ideas contained in the Scrolls have shed fresh light on primitive Christianity, too. Qumran and the early church represented 'sectarian' trends which considered themselves the true Israel. They were both organized on a biblical pattern, symbolically dividing their communities into twelve tribes led by twelve chiefs, or apostles. They both considered themselves the sole heirs of the divine promises recorded in the Bible. They both believed that the prophecies of Scripture were fulfilled in their respective communities.

Both the Essenes and the primitive church were animated by an intense expectation of the imminent coming of the Kingdom of God, and after the death of Jesus the early Christians anxiously waited for his impending glorious return. Since the hopes of both communities failed to materialize, both soon attempted to explain away this delay. At Qumran it was argued that the last age was longer than had been envisaged by the prophets, but that nevertheless one must patiently wait because 'all the ages of God will reach their appointed end' (*1QpHab* 7.13). In turn, the New Testament sees in the delay of the second coming a prolonging of the period granted for repentance (II Pet. 3.3–9).

Messianic hope flourished in both groups, but with notable differences. Thus in the Scrolls the idea of the Messiah is less pervasive than in the New Testament. Moreover, at Qumran two and even possibly three messianic figures were expected. In addition to the royal Messiah of traditional Judaism, the sectaries knew also of a priestly Messiah and possibly a Prophet, either a messianic Prophet or a prophetic Messiah. In mainstream Judaism and the New Testament these various figures coalesced into a single person. The 1991 media rumpus about a 'pierced' or crucified Messiah at Qumran was no more than a lot of hot air.

All these shared concepts may be attributable more to the religious ideology and language current during the first century CE in the Jewish world than any direct influence of Qumran on the New Testament. On the other hand, organizational similarities, e.g. monarchic leadership under a *mebaqqer* or overseer in the sect, or under a bishop in the church, are likely to be due to Christian borrowings from the Essenes, and so may also be the temporary adoption in the Jerusalem church of the practice of religious communism for which the Essenes were universally praised.

To sum up, in the course of fifty years of intense enquiry our understanding of a remarkable Jewish religious community has been improved and enriched. The writings of the Dead Sea sect can now be studied from its own manuscripts preserved in their original languages and supported by the undisturbed archaeological evidence from Qumran. The lifting of the veil of secrecy in 1991 has allowed many a gap in our knowledge to be filled and numerous obscurities to be clarified. However, contrary to the rash claims of a few misguided enthusiasts, the full evidence which is now at our disposal has disclosed nothing that might alter the basic understanding of the Qumran documents held by the large majority of manuscript experts.

12

Jesus the Jew and his Religion:
Autobiographical Reflections

Had I been told in the 1950s that one day I would be known as an expert on Jesus, I would have been greatly surprised. Before specializing in the Scrolls and in post-biblical Judaism, I considered myself a student of the Hebrew Bible. The New Testament lay outside my sphere of interest. As an undergraduate in Louvain, I showed no liking for it. This lack of enthusiasm may be attributed to the local circumstances. At the Jesuit College, the Gospels were taught in the first year of the four-year theology course, which in view of my previous studies I was allowed to skip. Even had I attended the relevant classes, the dry and technical discussion of the Synoptic problem – the literary relationship of Mark, Matthew and Luke – would no doubt have bored me to tears. Nor were the two years spent on St Paul in any way exciting. The lectures were aimed at expounding theological doctrine in the Letters to the Romans and the Corinthians rather than reconstructing the real world of Paul.

How then did I get involved with the New Testament? As a scholar, I first fleetingly encountered the Gospels when I began to focus on Bible interpretation at Qumran. As early as December 1951, I published a short essay in the *Cahiers Sioniens* (pp. 337–49), 'Le Commentaire d'Habacuc et le Nouveau Testament', investigating structural parallels between Qumran scriptural exegesis and the New Testament. A few similar efforts followed, but even in *Scripture and Tradition in Judaism* (1961), the New Testament section consisted only of the two final chapters.

My proper contact with the Gospels came in the mid-1960s when I switched to research in Jewish history in connection with the Schürer project. In an article published in the *Daily Telegraph* on 9 April 1966, on 'Neglected Facts in the Dead Sea Scrolls', I mentioned for the first time in the context of miraculous healing in the Gospels the example of the little known first-century AD Galilean charismatic, Hanina ben Dosa, who has since become, I suppose largely due to my studies, a household name among New Testament scholars. This was the first hint that was to lead to *Jesus the Jew*.

The idea of a book on the historical Jesus – and how revolutionary this idea was thirty years ago! – had a double beginning. In broad terms, it came as an offshoot of the Schürer project; that is to say, I intended to re-examine the Gospels as part of first-century AD Palestinian Jewish history and culture. I meant to portray Jesus against his genuine historical background, and not in the alien framework of Graeco-Roman culture *and* nineteen centuries of Christian elaboration. The second, more immediate, reason for launching into this search originated in an interview which I gave to the journalist and writer Colin Cross on the story of the birth of Jesus. It appeared in the *Observer Magazine* on 24 December 1967 under the title 'White Christmas, Black Christmas', anticipating the ideas which I later developed in *Jesus the Jew* on the Nativity story, the Gospel genealogies of Jesus, and the ancient Jewish understanding of the concept of virginity.

The article must have made some impact, for during my first return visit to Hungary in January 1968, a telephone call came from a London literary agent with the promise of a contract and a substantial advance (£500, a large sum in those days) for a book on Jesus along the lines of the *Observer* article. The agent kept his word, and I signed an agreement with a London publishing house, W. H. Allen, better known for its biographies and auto-biographies of stage personalities than for historical and religious scholar-ship. I was then too inexperienced and naive to realize the mismatch.

As the manuscript was to be delivered within three years, I set to work without delay. I was groping in the dark, but by the time I left for a visiting professorship at Brown University in Providence, Rhode Island, in January 1971, some chapters of the planned volume existed in written form. I gave several public lectures on the subject at various American uni-versities, and as the echoes were encouraging I felt I was on the right wave-length. But when, after my return to Britain, I despatched about half of the book in first draft to the publishers, without hesitation they terminated the agreement. Mine was not a book they could sell. In despair, I consulted Colin Cross who, helpful as always, introduced me to his agents, A. D. Peters, to whom on 5 February 1972 my complete typescript was handed over. The final settlement with W. H. Allen (including the return of the advance payment) took a little while, but by the late spring the book was accepted by William Collins, a leading publishing house. I remember my first visit to Lady Collins, who was in charge of their religious publications. The centre of her office, an unused fireplace, was occupied by a dog basket, the throne of a much-loved poodle, who attended all the business discus-sions. Lady Collins let me know that when her principal adviser, Canon (later Provost) David Edwards was asked to choose the manuscripts he wanted to read, she heard a 'Ho, ho. What's this?' and away went what was then called *Jesus and Christianity*. It was returned the next week with the reader's full endorsement. The only query was about the title, which they considered flat. 'Could it be retitled "Jesus and his Jewish background"?' I was asked. In that case, why not call it *Jesus the Jew*, I replied. That would be much stronger. Lady Collins enthusiastically agreed.

The book appeared on 20 August 1973, almost simultaneously with Volume I of the new English Schürer. The two together made something of a splash. The following year, a separate American edition followed under the imprint of Macmillan, New York.

Like most significant episodes of my life, *Jesus the Jew* was the product of a providential accident. Since it is generally believed that books on Jesus owe their existence more to the religious experiences of their authors than to problems surrounding the subject, it was automatically assumed by many that the same rule applied to me, too, especially in the light of my (presumed) spiritual wanderings. However, in my conscious knowledge, the purpose of writing the book had nothing to do with theological pre-occupations or with self-justification, a kind of *Apologia pro vita sua*, but was the unplanned outcome of the preliminary research which produced the first part of the revised *History of the Jewish People in the Age of Jesus Christ* (the new Schürer), coupled with a historian's desire at last to put the record straight. The present investigation, as I wrote in *Jesus the Jew* (p. 17), 'is prompted by a single-minded search for fact and reality and undertaken out of feeling for the tragedy of Jesus of Nazareth. If, after working his way through the book, the reader recognizes that this man, so distorted by Christian and Jewish myth alike, was *in fact* neither the Christ of the Church, nor the apostate and bogey-man of Jewish popular tradition, some small beginning may have been made in the repayment to him of a debt long overdue.'

The main problem facing a sympathetic, yet religiously detached, historian who confronts the New Testament results from the fact that the pocket book which contains the specifically Christian Scriptures offers two substantially different pictures of Jesus. All their subsequent theological colouring about Messianism and redemption notwithstanding, the Gospels of Mark, Matthew and Luke, the Synoptic Gospels, still allow a genuine glimpse of a first-century AD Jewish holy man, portrayed as a preacher, healer and exorcist, delivering special moral exhortations concerning the impending arrival of the 'kingdom of God'. By contrast the Fourth Gospel, that of John, and the letters of Paul sketch an increasingly other-worldly saviour figure, the paramount centre of all the religious speculations of the primitive church. When one sketch is superimposed on the other, it becomes clear that they have hardly anything in common.

The purpose of *Jesus the Jew* was to rebuild the picture of the historical Jesus, a task considered to be beyond the scholar's means during the preceding half century because, according to the then current views, hardly anything could be known 'concerning the life and personality of Jesus, since the early Christian sources show no interest in either'.[1] To achieve this aim, I endeavoured to explore the figure of Jesus as preserved in the Synoptic Gospels, in the framework of the political and social history of first-century BC–first-century AD Galilee, and especially in that of contemporaneous popular, charismatic Judaism of prophetic derivation. The hero of this type of Palestinian religion was not the king, the rabbi or the priest, but the man of God, believed to be capable of working miracles and mastering the forces of evil and darkness, namely the devil and sickness. In the first century BC, Honi the rain-maker was such a holy man, and so also was Jesus' younger Galilean contemporary, Hanina ben Dosa, renowned for curing the sick, even from a distance, and helping the needy. His many wondrous interventions earned him the title of protector, saviour and benefactor of humankind. The Galilean Jesus of the Synoptic Gospels is perfectly at home in such a company.

Having thus sketched the background and setting of Jesus' existence, I needed a checking mechanism, which I found in a historical and linguistic analysis of the titles borne by Jesus in the Gospels. Of these, three – 'prophet', 'lord' and 'son of God' – when examined in their Semitic (Aramaic/Hebrew) context are found in biblical and post-biblical Jewish literature applied to charismatic holy men.[2] Hence I concluded that the historical Jesus could be best situated 'in the venerable company of the Devout, the ancient Hasidim' (*Jesus the Jew*, p. 223). I hastened to add, however, that compared to the portrait of minor charismatic figures preserved in post-biblical Jewish sources, Jesus stood out as incomparably superior.

> Second to none in profundity of insight and grandeur of character, he is in particular an unsurpassed master of the art of laying bare the inmost core of spiritual truth and bringing every issue back to the essence of religion, the existential relationship of man and man and man and God. (p. 224)

Having produced a book on Jesus which I thought would be judged 'unorthodox' by Christians, Jews and New Testament scholars alike, I was greatly surprised by an overall lack of hostility. Of course, some unkind words were printed. A Jewish critic, violently resenting my refusal to classify Jesus as a Pharisee, put me among the anti-Semites. A well-known

English Jesuit now deceased described the book's learning as 'at times . . . oppressive'. He blamed the 'overcrowded' character of the volume on my 'apparent desire' to show off my familiarity with Christian biblical criticism! An American Bible expert, taking exception to my light-hearted remark that New Testament scholars often wear the blinkers of their trade, haughtily dismissed the book with 'Jesus the Jew deserves better than this'. A French woman writer, contributing to a right-wing magazine, settled for the double denunciation of 'scandal and blasphemy'. But on the whole the findings oscillated between warm approval and an open verdict. The former reached its pinnacle in a dithyrambic assessment published in the *Jewish Chronicle* (24 August 1973): 'In a field as well trodden as New Testament exegesis it is extremely rare to encounter a new book which can only be characterised as epoch-making.' As for the open verdict, I have always cherished the splendidly equivocal last phrase in the review appearing in Oxford's *Journal of Theological Studies* (1974, p. 489): 'The result is a valuable contribution to scholarship, but it is hard to assess exactly how successful it is.' But more explicitly, various reviewers, among them Henry Chadwick, then Dean of Christ Church in Oxford,[3] indicated that the absence of any treatment of the teaching of Jesus prevented them from arriving at any firm conclusion concerning my actual findings. Needless to say, I was fully aware of the need to tackle the problem of the sayings of Jesus and indicated in the Preface of the first edition that I hoped to deal with this important issue in another volume, entitled *The Gospel of Jesus the Jew*.

It took some time for the continuation of the Jesus project to reach the top of my writing agenda. It was preceded by the compilation of a volume of essays, entitled *Post-Biblical Jewish Studies* (1975) and consisting of three sections (Qumran – Bible Exegesis – Rabbinic History), a volume that was meant to mark, but missed, my fiftieth birthday in 1974. The second half of the 1970s was occupied by work on the second volume of the new Schürer, published in 1979, and from 1978 to 1980 I was chairman of the Board of Oriental Studies, which demanded much time for administrative and committee work. Some slight distraction was provided by lecture trips to Providence, Rhode Island (1976) and to Vancouver (1980), and especially to Israel in 1979, where I lectured at the University of Tel Aviv, paid my first visit to Qumran under Israeli control, and spent a couple of hours with Yigael Yadin, the deputy prime minister, who was convalescing after a first heart attack. We discussed his forthcoming English edition of the Temple Scroll, the Yadin *Festschrift* which the *Journal of Jewish Studies* was preparing for him, to appear in 1982, and my work on revising Schürer. Like most academics kicked upstairs to high administration, he seemed to be hankering after scholarly debate.[4] This was the last time I saw him alive. He died five years later, aged sixty-seven.

However, an unforeseen powerful impetus directing my attention to the dormant promise came from the Vice-Chancellor of the University of Newcastle who, on the recommendation of the relevant committee, invited me to deliver the 1981 Riddell Memorial Lectures. I had an instant title at hand, *The Gospel of Jesus the Jew*, and delivered the three addresses on 17–19 March 1981 (see Chapters 2–4 above). The constraints of time and space imposed by the form of three one-hour talks meant that the Newcastle lectures could only be a succinct preliminary presentation of the piety preached and practised by Jesus. The opening lecture wrestled with the problem of how to distinguish the authentic message of Jesus from the many later accretions superimposed on it by the primitive church. Lectures two and three sketched the portrait of a person who, while remaining identifiable as a first-century Jewish holy man, nevertheless stands out as a teacher entirely inspired by faith-trust (*emunah*) and dedicated to a call for repentance (*teshuvah*) preparatory to the coming of the Kingdom of God. He also appears uniquely aware of his filial relation to the Father in heaven (*Abba*), and to believe passionately that his mission was to communicate the same sense of relationship with God among his fellow men and women.

It was a curious experience to be back in Newcastle. Both the city and the university had changed enormously since I left in 1965. In the staff club strange faces stared at me from every side. Nevertheless, at the lectures I met a few old friends. The former Vice-Chancellor, Charles Bosanquet, and his wife kindly came along to listen, and my old friends Colin and Barbara Strang offered me hospitality in their refurbished disused railway-station house in the back of beyond of the Northumbrian countryside. Those were delightful days.

In 1982 I tried out the Gospel lectures in Britain, in Ireland (North and South),[5] and during a three-week trip in the United States which included, in addition to Tulane University in New Orleans (where I was distinguished visiting professor in Judaeo-Christian studies), Emory University in Atlanta; Duke University in Durham, North Carolina; Rochester University, New York; and North Western University in Evanston, Illinois. The Riddell Lectures, reshaped in the light of the experience gained in the course of the exchanges at home and abroad, and enlarged by further studies previously published in *JJS*, resulted in 1983 in the second part of the trilogy, *Jesus and the World of Judaism*.[6] In a new preface, I attempted to respond to a frequently encountered objection: 'If Jesus was so steeped in Jewish piety and so fundamentally non-political in his outlook as you depict him, why did he clash with the representatives (or at least some representatives) of Judaism and with those of Rome?' My answer was that Jesus was seen, as (according to Flavius Josephus) was John the Baptist before him, as a *potential* threat to law and order and consequently to the well-being of the Jewish people, and in the authorities' judgement as such had to be eliminated for the common good. 'The trial ... of Jesus of Nazareth, a ... serious affair because of the affray which he caused in the Temple [in the merchants' quarter], and because of the suspicion that some of his followers were Zealots, led to a miscarriage of justice and one of the supreme tragedies in history' (pp. viii–ix). Ten years later, in the Preface of *The Religion of Jesus the Jew*, I reformulated this answer:

> The arrest and execution of Jesus were due, not directly to his words and deeds, but to their possible insurrectional consequences feared by the nervous authorities ... in that powder-keg of first-century Jerusalem ... Had Jesus not caused an affray in the Temple by overturning the tables of the merchants and money-changers, or had he even chosen to do so at a time other than Passover – the moment when the hoped-for Messiah ... was expected to reveal himself – he would most probably have escaped with his life. He died on the cross for having done the wrong thing (causing a commotion) in the wrong place (the Temple) at the wrong time (just before Passover). Here lies the real tragedy of Jesus the Jew. (p. x)

The Gospel of Jesus the Jew slightly advanced my argument, but I was still far from resting my case. Once more the Jesus subject had to be laid aside because of the urgency of the Schürer work. With the publication of Volume III, Part 2, this reached completion in June 1987, during the London symposium on the Dead Sea Scrolls. The whole assembled company of Qumran experts was invited by the publishers of the English Schürer to a celebratory party after more than twenty years of hard labour, with speeches from Ramsay Clark, Fergus Millar, Martin Goodman and myself. The idea of a gaudy came from the Clarks (the publishers), but this did not prevent one of the senior Scrolls editors present from later reproaching me for using the Qumran symposium for self-aggrandizement. From 1987 onwards I got increasingly deeply involved in the Qumran war and the Yarnton Scrolls affair, so that the final instalment of the Jesus trilogy, contractually scheduled for 1989, was further and further postponed. Moreover, from 1991 my first wife's deteriorating health added to the worry and delayed progress. I put in a big effort in 1992, perhaps urged on by my participation in the television documentary, *Jesus before Christ*, prompted by A. N. Wilson's successful book, *Jesus*, and filmed on location in Bethlehem, Galilee and Jerusalem. By the autumn, the typescript of *The Religion* was finished and the publication of the final volume of the trilogy was fêted at Wolfson College on 1 March 1993.

While *Jesus the Jew*, which was novel, even revolutionary, in its self-assurance that the historical Jesus is within the reach of scholarly research and combative in style and inspiration, is probably the part of the trilogy which made the deepest impact, *The Religion of Jesus the Jew*, more mature, mellow, constructive and 'spiritual', is my favourite of the three. It portrays Jesus as a faithful observer of Judaism and of the Jewish Law, 'perceived, primarily and essentially and positively, not as a juridical, but as a religious–ethical reality, revealing what he thought to be the right and divinely ordained behaviour towards men and towards God' (p. 45).

The exposition of the authentic Judaism practised by Jesus is followed by a sketch of the teaching of Jesus which took the form, not so much of Bible interpretation – most of the passages of polemical scriptural exegesis originated in the early church – as of authoritative statements by a master possessing spiritual power. 'It was the people's belief in the heavenly origin of Jesus' . . . teaching, reinforced . . . by his apparent mastery over corporal and mental sickness, that dispensed [him] from the need to demonstrate the truth of [his] teaching' (p. 74). In short, the words of Jesus were endowed with authority not because they were backed by Scripture, but because he was revered as a prophet, inspired by the spirit of God.

If the form of the message of Jesus was charismatic, its literary style was that of popular proverbs and parables. The latter, particularly typical of the teaching of Jesus, had focused on three radical topics: repentance, confidence in God, and total self-dedication to the kingdom of heaven.

The two main topics of Jesus' preaching concerned his particular perception of the kingdom of God and of God as Father. As regards the kingdom, his approach was oblique and his outline hazy; he never distinctly spelled out his concept of 'kingdom'. Two features stand out: 1. The God of Jesus is not a regal figure but rather 'a well-to-do landowner and paterfamilias of rural Galilee'; and 2. The expectation of, and work for, the kingdom took place in an atmosphere of eschatological enthusiasm. Jesus and his disciples

entered whole-heartedly into the eschatological age and recognized a fundamental difference between their own time with no future, and the centuries that preceded it. From the moment when Jesus obeyed the

Baptist's call to repentance, time for him became the end-time demanding a decisive and irrevocable *teshuvah* [return to God]. (p. 148)

The Father image is at the heart of Jesus' representation of the Deity. It is a characteristic Jewish concept which, as usual, has gained personal and individual colouring in the mind of Jesus.

Needless to say, the picture of a loving and solicitous Father does not tally with the human experience of a harsh, unjust and cruel world. Then as now, fledglings fell from the nest, little ones perished and, as Jesus himself was soon to experience, the innocent suffered. It would be a mistake to imagine that he offered to his followers a kind of sentimentally anthropomorphic image. But what lies at the heart of his intuition and gives individuality and freshness to his vision is the conviction that the eternal, distant, dominating and tremendous Creator is also and primarily a near and approachable God. (p. 180)

All this naturally leads us to 'Jesus, the religious man'.[7] This religious personality was characterized by an all-pervasive eschatological spirit, one imparting enthusiasm, inspiring urgency and absoluteness in action. It also stimulates the individual to a constant imitation of God.

Through his three ancient witnesses, Mark, Matthew and Luke, the real Jesus, Jesus the Jew, challenges traditional Christianity as well as traditional Judaism. Jesus cannot be represented as the founder of Christianity.

For . . . if he meant and believed what he preached . . . namely that the eternal Kingdom of God was truly at hand, he simply could not have entertained the idea of . . . setting in motion an organized society intended to endure for ages to come. (pp. 214–5)

Only the future will show if and how Christians and Jews will respond. Standardized bodies usually shy off such confrontations. But there is one constituency which is earmarked for Jesus in the present as it was in the past. The 'magnetic appeal of [his] teaching and example . . . holds out hope and guidance to those outside the fold of organized religion, the stray sheep of mankind, who yearn for a world of mercy, justice and peace lived in as children of God' (p. 215).

Always foreseeing the worst, I was amazed by the warm reception granted to *The Religion of Jesus the Jew* in all shades of public opinion. On 2 March 1993, the day after its publication, in a full-page piece in the *Evening Standard* headed 'The scholar who found the real Jesus', A. N. Wilson wrote:

Of Jesus the man, perhaps we still know very little – but of the kind of teacher and healer he was, the kind of religion he preached, the kind of audience he addressed, we now know infinitely more, thanks to Vermes; and once one has absorbed the message of Vermes's books, it is impossible ever to view Christianity in the same light.

In a different vein, but no less encouragingly, the renowned Cambridge theologian, Don Cupitt, summed up the book's challenge to Christian scholars. They have 'to accept that Jesus' own religion was simply Jewish, and he had no thought of stepping outside it. So a Jewish account of Jesus is bound to be the best – which leaves Christians permanently one down.' Also, though here and there he himself finds fault with the book, he declares that 'Vermes in effect wins the main argument' (the *Guardian*, 27 March 1993). Again, to follow A. E. Harvey, a friend and former Oxford colleague, now Canon and Sub-Dean Emeritus of Westminster, who strongly disagrees with my thoroughly eschatological approach, 'many readers may find that Jesus comes freshly alive' and in *The Religion of Jesus the Jew* his essential portrait appears 'credible – even, at times, arresting' (*TLS*, 9 April 1993).

As could be expected, there were some dissenting voices in the confraternity of transatlantic New Testament scholars, particularly quibbling with my lack of 'methodology' in the use of rabbinic literature in the interpretation of the Gospels. Missing the humoristic tone in the characterization of my approach to the issue as 'true *British* pragmatism', with a distinct preference for 'muddling through', because 'innovative [research] should not be bound by fixed, predetermined rules' (*Religion*, 7), a recent critic of the Jesus trilogy, John P. Meier, felt entitled to deliver a little sermon in my direction and for my benefit: 'Any scholarly investigation that is not totally erratic operates by certain rules.'[8] If Meier had taken the trouble to glance at 'Jewish Studies and New Testament Interpretation', referred to on the same page as an account of my method in Gospel exegesis, his readers could have been spared such a pompous remark.[9]

Jewish reactions have also been essentially positive. In the *Jewish Chronicle* (6 August 1993), Tessa Rajak, a friend and former pupil, provocatively presents Jesus as 'probably the most famous Jew of all time. Yet [he] is a Jew who rarely gets discussed in (Jewish magazines).'

Geza Vermes gives us a Jesus who is ready to claim his place in the line of the great Jewish people of God, irrespective of what later became of his teaching. The low-key, meticulous, fair-minded – positively British

– investigations of the now emeritus professor of Jewish studies at Oxford have a way of shaking things up, so that they never look the same again.

A powerful revolutionary echo came from Israel, too. Reviewing *The Religion of Jesus the Jew* in the country's leading newspaper, *Ha'aretz*, Magen Broshi, director of the Shrine of the Book, called the age-old ban by virtue of which the name of the Nazarene was never to pass through Jewish lips 'patently absurd'.

The tangible proof that the trilogy made some mark was provided by the fact that between 1977 and 1995, *Jesus the Jew* was translated into Spanish, French, Italian, Japanese, Portuguese, German and Hungarian.[10] *Jesus and the World of Judaism*, already extant in Portuguese, reached the Hungarian market during the Budapest book week in June 1997, and *The Gospel of Jesus the Jew* has been included in *Jesus der Jude*, the German translation of *Jesus the Jew*. As for *The Religion of Jesus the Jew*, it has already appeared in Spanish, Portuguese and Hungarian, and a translation into Korean is in the making.

Thirty years ago, anyone foolhardy enough to confront the problem of the Jesus of history appeared an innovator. Since then an increasing number of scholars have ventured in that direction, first in Oxford, and more recently in the United States, too.[11] When Lady Collins and I decided to call my original contribution to the Jesus story 'Jesus *the Jew*', the title enunciating what should be patent to all still sounded striking and pioneering. According to Paula Fredriksen, it caused a 'small revolution' (*JJS* 44, 1993, p. 319). During the intervening years the phrase 'Jesus the Jew' became more and more familiar. Ten years after the publication of the book, a long leader in *The Times* published on Easter Saturday (2 April 1983) was entitled 'Jesus was a Jew'. This progressive headline was far ahead of the more conventional theological views expressed in its correspondence column by a world-famous Cambridge New Testament scholar: 'Jesus was indeed a Jew, but one whom his own fellow-Jews could not tolerate. This is a fact' (*The Times*, 7 April 1983). This was a yesterday's theologian's fact. *The Times* signalled the way of the future. Today 'Jesus the Jew' almost ranks as a cliché.

The same *Times* leader foresaw another new line of development by announcing that 'Jesus the Jew may become a symbol of some ultimate unity in the quest for truth between Christian and Jew, just as he is between Christian and Christian.' The admirable progress shown during the last thirty years in the Christian–Jewish dialogue constitutes the fulfilment of the dream of Jules Isaac concerning *friendship (amitié)* between individual Christians and Jews and, who knows?, one day between church and synagogue.

In Britain, the Council of Christians and Jews, established during the war against Hitler, has been remarkably revived in recent years. The Oxford branch may be a good illustration. The late Anglican archdeacon Carlyle Witton-Davies, closely associated with the running of the national Council over the years, unsuccessfully tried a number of times to set up a local branch. He made a fresh effort in 1980 and encountered an enthusiastic response. He proposed me as chairman, an office which I held until 1985, and the Oxford branch, a kind of Fabian Society, organized *avant-garde* debates in Wolfson College on all aspects of Judaeo-Christian relations. The Council, both the national and the international, is flourishing and slowly paving the way towards the recognition of the 'real' Jesus by Christians and Jews.

Have *Jesus the Jew* and its sequels played a small part in the developments that have taken place over the last couple of decades in both Christian and Jewish circles? A change in the attitude of the churches to Judaism and the Jews is noticeable. It is particularly welcome that the new spirit of the dialogue is concerned not only with fighting Christian anti-semitism but also with the study of the Jewish understanding of the Bible and of the figure of Jesus of Nazareth. It is particularly significant that the Christian stand is now expressed not only in the work of enlightened theologians, but also in official documents.

Thus, in its statement on inter-faith dialogue issued in 1988, the Lambeth Conference of the Anglican Communion formulated the new outlook with characteristic clarity:

> Modern biblical scholarship is increasingly becoming a joint enterprise between Jews and Christians . . . Some Jews have become very aware of Jesus as part of their own history, and their writings have brought home to Christians his Jewishness. Renewed study of Jewish sources by Christian scholars has led them to see first-century Judaism in a new and more positive light.

The 'conversion' of the Roman Catholic Church is if anything even more noteworthy. Its new stance is put forward by none other than the Pontifical Biblical Commission, which in the first half of the twentieth century was the mouthpiece of the most fundamentalist and retrograde opinions on all matters pertaining to the Bible.[12] In a document agreed by its learned members in 1983, and written up by one of them, Professor Henri Cazelles, whom I knew well in my Paris days, the Biblical Commission set out to outline the church's teaching about the Christ–Messiah under the title *Scripture and Christology*. Published in Latin and French in 1984, it has also been available in English since 1986, thanks to the work of my former classmate from Louvain, the Jesuit Joseph A. Fitzmyer, now himself a member of the Commission.[13]

In its survey of methodologies used today in christology, the Commission dwells on historical research (quite necessary, we are told, but never neutral or objective), and more specifically on 'the approach to Jesus from Judaism'. It is there that a point of view, inconceivable just a few decades ago and no doubt still shocking for backwoods Christians, expresses itself with clarity and vigour.

> After the First World War some Jewish historians, abandoning centuries-old animosity – of which Christian preachers were themselves not innocent – devoted studies directly to the person of Jesus and to Christian origins (J. Klausner, M. Buber, C. G. Montefiore, etc.) . . . Some Jewish historians . . . have set in relief certain lines of his personality; they have found in him a teacher like the Pharisees of old (D. Flusser) or a wonder-worker similar to those whose memory Jewish tradition has preserved (G. Vermes). Some have not hesitated to compare the passion of Jesus with the Suffering Servant, mentioned in the Book of Isaiah (M. Buber). All these attempts (at interpretation) *are to be accorded serious attention by Christian theologians engaged in the study of Christology.* (p. 9, my emphasis)

A little later, the same point is repeated with equal stress: 'The diligent study of Judaism is of the utmost importance for the correct understanding of the person of Jesus' (p. 23). Not even the *caveat* that follows[14] – the Commission seems to have come to the realization that it had been carried away too far by scholarly enthusiasm – can undo the massively positive effect of this epoch-making church document. Incidentally, I find it quite comforting that, although at least half a dozen members of the Commission, among them Pierre Benoit and Dominique Barthélémy from the world of the Scrolls, knew me and my Catholic and priestly past, they did not shrink from including my name among those *Jewish* experts whose views 'are to be accorded serious attention by Christian theologians engaged in the study of Christology'.

Since Judaism has no institutions similar to the Lambeth Conference or the Pontifical Biblical Commission, it would be useless to look for a Jewish authority to issue official statements on Jesus. Nevertheless, here too signs of a thaw may be detected. Naturally, sympathetic utterances are more often heard from progressive Jews than from Orthodox quarters, but in academic circles one witnesses a notable metamorphosis. For instance,

when in 1965 Professor Shmuel Safrai of the Hebrew University, a strictly observant Jew, devoted a fascinating study to the *Hasidim* (or Devout) in
early rabbinic literature, it never occurred to him to include Jesus under
this heading. Yet when he returned to the same subject three decades later.
Jesus figures prominently among the ancient pietists from Galilee.[15] Moreover, when – as I have noted earlier – one can read in the leading Israeli
daily, *Ha'aretz*, in a review of *The Religion of Jesus the Jew*, that the age-old,
traditional ban on Jesus is 'patently absurd', it is difficult not to sense there
the beginning of a wind of change.

So we can look forward with burning expectation to the new millen-
nium. If, as Pope John Paul II has promised, the Catholic Church will
belatedly express her sorrow over Christian injustice inflicted on the
Jewish people, the people of Jesus the Jew,[16] and if, by a miracle, *any*
modern book on Jesus is offered in modern Hebrew to Israeli readers, I will
begin to believe that the hope formulated in the Introduction of *Jesus the
Jew* will have come true and 'a small beginning [will] have been made in the
repayment to [Jesus] of a debt long overdue' (p. 17).

Shortly before I had to relinquish my Oxford University chair in 1991 due
to age, I received an invitation from the late Dr John Sykes, one of the general editors of *The New Shorter Oxford English Dictionary*, to act as an
adviser on all matters relating to Judaism. I gladly accepted this retirement
job: the pay was a pittance, but the task intrigued me. So for about a year,
batches of entries – hundreds of them – taken from the previous edition
kept on reaching me. My task was either to approve them or to suggest
alterations. I quite enjoyed the challenge, but foolishly failed to record for
myself the changes I put forward to the editors, who made the final decision. So at the end I could not check the number of my proposals which
ended up being accepted.

The work progressed fast, the two gigantic volumes (3,801 tightly set
pages) were completed, and a monumental press launch was scheduled at
Claridge's on 7 September 1993 with a luncheon party arranged for editors, guests, leading media personalities, and us humble advisers. I found
myself sitting at a round table in the company of a dozen people, all
unknown to me. To make conversation, I asked the white-haired lady on
my right about her connection with the *Dictionary*. 'Oh, I'm Burma,' she
declared without hesitation, having dealt with all the words of Burmese
origin. I could not think anything better to reply than 'How d'you do? I'm
Judaism.' Emboldened, I enquired from the septuagenarian on my left
what his line was. 'I'm snooker,' he said. 'A famous player?' 'No, no, I'm
the author of the rule book. Mind you, I can play, but my highest break was

fifty-eight, which I managed on my fifty-eighth birthday.' Further to the left a familiar-looking woman with large glasses turned out to be 'wine'. She was Jancis Robinson of TV fame, and in the process of completing *The Oxford Companion to Wine*. I even discovered an academic, a Cambridge professor of linguistics, in charge of all the grammatical terms in the *Dictionary*. The meal was sumptuous, but when we left Claridge's, I assumed that this was the end of my involvement with *The Shorter Oxford English Dictionary*. I was mistaken.

What I did not realize was that my suggestion regarding the name Jesus had been adopted by the editors, and this in turn provoked quite an outcry on the part of old-fashioned Christians and much hilarity in the editorial circles of *The Times*. Instead of the old definition 'The name of the Founder of Christianity', the new one runs '(The name of) the central figure of the Christian faith, a Jewish preacher (*c*.5 BC–*c*.AD 30) regarded by his followers as the Son of God and God incarnate.' 'Jesu, joy of man's defining', was the front page headline in *The Times* (9 October 1993), which reported, among other things, that the Reverend Tony Higton, a senior evangelical and a member of the General Synod [of the Church of England] found 'the idea of Jesus as a "Jewish preacher" to be a rather derogatory term'. Since someone no doubt made him aware of the possible antisemitic connotations of his statement, the unfortunate clergyman then tried to extricate himself from the mess of his own making by welcoming the fact that the *Dictionary* 'helpfully records for the first time that Jesus is Jewish', but objecting to the designation 'preacher' (letter to *The Times*, 13 October 1993)! But the third leader of *The Times* (9 October), under another humorous headline, 'The game of the name', came out firmly in my support: '*The New Shorter Oxford English Dictionary* . . . has defined the name of Jesus accurately and more economically than before.'

I have the strange feeling that my best known and most lasting contribution to a better perception of the historical Jesus may be this dictionary definition which does not carry my name.

Abbreviations

ab.	*Aboth*
Ant.	Flavius Josephus, *Antiquitates*
APOT	R. H. Charles, *The Apocrypha and Pseudepigrapha of the Old Testament* I–II, 1912–13
b	Babylonian Talmud followed by the name of the tractate
BA	*Biblical Archaeologist*, New Haven, Conn.
BB	*Baba Bathra*
Ber.	*Berakhoth*
BJ	Flavius Josephus, *Bellum Judaicum*
BM	*Baba Mezi'a*
CBQ	*Catholic Biblical Quarterly*, Washington
CDSSE	G. Vermes, *The Complete Dead Sea Scrolls in English*, 1998
Decal.	Philo, *De Decalogo*
DJD	*Discoveries in the Judaean Desert* I, 1955
DSS	G. Vermes, *The Dead Sea Scrolls: Qumran in Perspective*, 1977, 1981, 1982
EH	Eusebius, *Ecclesiastical History*
Enc. Jud.	*Encyclopaedia Judaica* 1–16, Jerusalem 1971
ET	English translation
Flor.	*Florilegium*
GenAp	*Genesis Apocryphon*
History	Emil Schürer, *The History of the Jewish People in the Age of Jesus Christ* I, rev. and ed. G. Vermes and F. Millar, 1973; II, rev. and ed. G. Vermes, F. Millar and M. Black 1979; III, rev. and ed. G. Vermes, F. Millar and M. Goodman, 1986–87
HTR	*Harvard Theological Review*, Cambridge, Mass.
IDB	*The Interpreter's Dictionary of the Bible* I–IV, New York, Nashville 1962
IDBS	*The Interpreter's Dictionary of the Bible, Supplementary Volume*, Nashville 1976
JAOS	*Journal of the American Oriental Society*, New Haven, Conn.
JBL	*Journal of Biblical Literature*, Philadelphia
JE	*The Jewish Encyclopaedia* I–XII, New York 1901f.
JJS	*Journal of Jewish Studies*, Oxford
JQR	*Jewish Quarterly Review*, London

JSJ	*Journal for the Study of Judaism*, Leiden
JSNT	*Journal for the Study of the New Testament*, Sheffield
JTS	*Journal of Theological Studies*, Oxford
Jub.	*Book of Jubilees*
m	Mishnah followed by the name of the tractate
M	*Milḥamah* (War Rule)
Makk.	*Makkoth*
Meg.	*Megillah*
Mekh.	*Mekhilta*
Ned.	*Nedarim*
NT	*Novum Testamentum*, Leiden
NTS	*New Testament Studies*, Cambridge
p	*Pesher*
PAAJR	*Proceedings of the American Academy for Jewish Research*, New York
PEQ	*Palestine Exploration Quarterly*, London
PG	Patrologia Graeca, ed. J. P. Migne
PL	Patrologia Latina, ed. J. P. Migne
Ps. Jon.	Pseudo-Jonathan
Q	Qumran Cave preceded by its number
R.	Rabbah preceded by the name of the biblical book
RB	*Revue Biblique*, Paris
S	*Serekh* (Community Rule)
Sᵃ	*Serekh*, first annex (Messianic Rule or Rule of the Congregation)
Sᵇ	*Serekh*, second annex (Benedictions)
Sanh.	*Sanhedrin*
Shabb.	*Shabbath*
Sheb.	*Shebi'ith*
Sheq.	*Sheqalim*
Sot.	*Soṭah*
Spec. Leg.	Philo, *De Specialibus Legibus*
Strack–Billerbeck	H. Strack and P. Billerbeck, *Kommentar zum Neuen Testament aus Talmud und Midrasch* I–IV, 1922–28
t	Tosefta followed by the name of the tractate
TDNT	*Theological Dictionary of the New Testament* I–X, ed. G. Kittel and G. Friedrich, 1964–76
TLS	*The Times Literary Supplement*
TWNT	*Theologisches Wörterbuch zum Neuen Testament* I–X, 1933–76
y	Palestinian Talmud followed by the name of the tractate
Yad.	*Yaduyim*
Yom.	*Yoma*
ZDPV	*Zeitschrift des deutschen Palästina-Vereins*, Wiesbaden
ZNW	*Zeitschrift für die neutestamentliche Wissenschaft*, Berlin

Notes

Preface

1. Doubleday, New York., vol. II, p. 14. So far three volumes of the series have appeared. Volume I: *The roots of the problem and the person* (1991, x, 484 pp.); Volume II: *Mentor, message and miracles* (1994, xvi, 1118 pp.); Volume III: *Companions and competitors* (2001, xiv, 703 pp.). The work, which contains an encyclopaedic survey of the secondary literature on this inexhaustible subject, has been greeted with fulsome praise by theologians, but was given a less than enthusiastic welcome by ancient historians.

2. *A Marginal Jew*, vol. II, p. 14, n. 7. The same lengthy note is repeated word for word in his vol. III, p. 16, and n. 21.

3. It first appeared in the Festschrift for Yigael Yadin, edited jointly by Jacob Neusner and myself, see *JJS* 33 (1982), pp. 361–76. It was included in *Jesus and the World of Judaism* in the following year. The theory is built on my earlier research published in *Scripture and Tradition in Judaism* (1961, reprinted in 1973 and 1983).

4. For the full text, see below pp. 68–80.

5. Volumes I–III, T. & T. Clark, Edinburgh, 1973–1987.

6. Vol. II, pp. 1044–47.

7. *The Religion of Jesus the Jew*, 1993, p. 7. The oddity of John Meier's argumentation is matched by another American author, Bruce Chilton, in 'Jesus within Judaism' (see *Judaism in Late Antiquity*, edited by Jacob Neusner, 1995, p. 265). Taking exception to my characterization of Jesus as a 'charismatic Hasid', Chilton launches into a kind of psychoanalytical dissection of my latent motives. 'Vermes', he claims, 'does not explain the sources of his thought . . ., but they are plain enough. The neo-orthodox mode of Protestant thought (and, in its wake, Catholic thought) after the Second World War made Martin Buber a companion saint with Karl Barth, and the image of the prayerful Hasid appealed both to theologians such as Reinhold Niebuhr and to historians such as Roland de Vaux and André Dupont-Sommer in their work on the Dead Sea Scrolls. . . . Vermes, at first active within the French-speaking Catholic circles which propagated the Hasidic–Essene hypothesis, worked on the scrolls during the period in which the hypothesis was most in vogue.' I have never encountered in an academic work such a hilarious hotchpotch of irrelevancies. Martin Buber's eighteenth and nineteenth century neo-Hasidim have nothing to do with the pre-Christian ancient Hasidim of de Vaux and Dupont-Sommer, neither was the openly agnostic and anticlerical

Dupont-Sommer under the influence of French Catholic thought. Those who are better informed than Chilton about the early stages of Scrolls research know that the first proponent of the Essene identification of the Qumran community was the famous Israeli archaeologist Eleazar Lipa Sukenik, who was certainly not inspired by 'French Catholicism'. Another prominent Israeli researcher of ancient Hasidism, Shmuel Safrai, is also clearly innocent of French Catholic or even Buberian influence ('The Teaching of Pietists in Mishnaic Literature', *JJS* 16, 1965, pp. 15–33; 'Jesus and the Hasidim', *Jerusalem Perspective* 42–44, 1994, pp. 3–22).

8. 'Who He Was' in *The New Republic*, 15 October, 2001, p. 51. Bruce Chilton also calls *Jesus the Jew* a 'popular book', but the context shows that 'popular' for him means the opposite of 'scholarly' (see op. cit. p. 264).

9. 'In Quest of the Historical Jesus', *The New York Review of Books*, vol. 48, no.18, 15 November, 2001, p. 35.

1. Jesus the Jew

Delivered as the twenty-first Claude Goldsmid Montefiore Lecture at the Liberal Jewish Synagogue in London on 14 November 1974.

1. Geza Vermes, *Jesus the Jew: A Historian's Reading of the Gospels*, 1973, ²1976, 1981, 1983, 1994, 2001.

2. The *Guardian*, 10 October 1969.

3. Rudolf Bultmann, *Jesus and the Word*, 1962, p. 14. (He died in 1976.)

4. Syme, 'The Titulus Tiburtinus', *Vestigia*, vol. 17, p. 600.

5. *Jewish Antiquities*, viii, 45.

6. *Jewish Antiquities*, viii, 46–47.

7. *Financial Times*, 1 February 1974.

8. It may come as a surprise to many that at the time of the birth of Jesus, the Pharisaic confraternity numbered according to Josephus (*Jewish Antiquities*, xvii, 42), only a little over six thousand members, as against four thousand Essenes (ibid., xviii, 20), whereas the total Jewish population of Palestine is estimated to have amounted to two to two and a half million.

9. *Jewish Antiquities*, xviii, 117–118.

10. *The Times Literary Supplement*, 7 December 1973.

11. *JJS* 25, 1974, p. 336.

12. *Theology* 77, 1974, p. 277. The same journal carried a rejoinder to Horbury by A. E. Harvey (pp. 376–77).

13. *The Tablet*, 8 December 1974, p. 1179.

14. *The Month*, January 1974.

15. L. E. Keck, *JBL* 95, 1975, p. 509.

16. D(enise) J(udant), *La Pensée catholique*, no. 176, 1978, p. 88.

17. Michel Bouttier, *Etudes théologiques et religieuses* 54, 1979, p. 299.

18. *JTS* 25, 1974, p. 489.

2. *The Gospel of Jesus the Jew I: A Historian's Reading of the Gospels*

Originally delivered together with chapters 3 and 4 as the Riddell Memorial Lectures in March 1981 and published by the University of Newcastle upon Tyne under the title *The Gospel of Jesus the Jew*, 1981.

1. One of the major problems facing any scholar concerned with Jesus is that the accumulated mass of literature devoted to him not only leaves little room for new insights but positively tends to block the way to a fresh understanding of the Gospels. I have therefore decided to re-read the Synoptics with my mind on their teaching content and to determine the main lines of my thesis in these chapters on that foundation before looking into the views of contemporary New Testament scholarship. I have however made use of the latter afterwards, checking and correcting initial conclusions in the light of current theories and debate.

It is important to note that this study of 'The Gospel of Jesus the Jew' cannot include a complete bibliographical survey or discuss all relevant opinions. A detailed account of recent academic work on Jesus is available in the series of review articles published by W. G. Kümmel in *Theologische Rundschau* between 1975 and 1980: 'Ein Jahrzehnt Jesusforschung (1965–1975)', vol. 40, 1975, pp. 289–336; vol. 41, 1976–77, pp. 198–258, 295–363; 'Jesusforschung seit 1965', vol. 43, 1978, pp. 105–161, 232–265; vol. 45, 1980, pp. 48–84, 293–337.

2. Typical of this kind of presentation is one of the introductory objections in Thomas Aquinas's *Summa Theologiae*. The section, 'Utrum Deus sit' (Is there a God), begins as follows: 'Videtur quod Deus non sit' (It would seem that there is no God). See St Thomas Aquinas, *Summa Theologiae. Latin Text and English Translation*, Pars prima, quaestio secunda, articulus tertius, Blackfriars (1964), pp. 12–13.

3. On the history of New Testament exegesis, see *The Cambridge History of the Bible* I–III, 1963–1970; S. C. Neill, *The Interpretation of the New Testament 1861–1961*, 1963; Robert Davidson and A. R. C. Leaney, *Biblical Criticism* 1970; W. G. Kümmel, *The New Testament: The History of the Investigation of its Problems*, ²1970.

4. The attitude of the so-called quality press to works of sound scholarship on religion, including the study of the New Testament, is distinguished by a shyness oddly at variance with a laudable interest in academic books on archaeology, classics and ancient history. Only such topics as *The Sacred Mushroom and the Cross* and the Turin Shroud seem to attract the large headlines in the national dailies and weeklies nowadays.

5. I hope I shall be forgiven if I reproduce here the opening lines of the original 1973 Preface to *Jesus the Jew*, no longer contained in the current paperback edition: 'During the last few years I have often been asked whether I was writing my book on Jesus from a Jewish point of view. The answer is yes – and no. It is not inspired by traditional Jewish attitudes towards the "Founder of Christianity", and is decidely not intended to depict a "Jewish" Jesus as a denominational counterpart of the Jesus of the various churches, sects and parties that claim allegiance to him. On the other hand, insofar as it insists that a convincing study of Jesus of Nazareth must take into account that the Gospels containing the story and teaching of this

first-century Galilean demand a specialized knowledge of the history, institutions, languages, culture and literature of Israel, both in Palestine and the Diaspora, of the age in which he lived, then it is a very Jewish book indeed.' An example of the extreme opposite of the historian's approach to the Gospels is that of fundamentalist Christians who insist as an absolute condition for the understanding of the gospel message that one shares the evangelist's outlook. See ch. 1, p. 2 above.

6. Up to until the end of the last century, expertise in the Bible, both in the Old and the New Testaments, was regarded as part of the Christian theologians' indispensable appurtenance. It was for such men, familiar as a matter of course not only with Latin and Greek but also with Hebrew and Aramaic, that the highly technical presentation of Jewish history, institutions, doctrine and literature from 175 BC to AD 135 by Emil Schürer was intended. Cf. *Geschichte des jüdischen Volkes im Zeitalter Jesu Christi* I ($^{3-4}$1901), p. 1. As the scope of the scriptural field broadened and the need grew for more and wider linguistic, archaeological and historical skills, an autonomous (or quasi autonomous) biblical discipline came into being. To begin with, it embraced the whole of scripture; the giants of those days, say Wellhausen or Lagrange, excelled in both Testaments, not to mention other branches of orientalism and the classics. Later, a growing trend towards specialization resulted in a divorce between Old Testament and New Testament research and the appearance on the scene of two distinct species, 'Alttestamentler' and 'Neutestamentler'. Today the separation seems complete. The run-of-the-mill New Testament specialist rarely possesses more than a rudimentary knowledge of Hebrew: biblical Hebrew, that is, for post-biblical and rabbinic Hebrew is seldom taught in (English and North American) Christian theology courses. As for Aramaic, the spoken language of Jesus, I myself heard a distinguished New Testament professor declare at a professional gathering that the special study of Aramaic is quite unnecessary since it is 'the same as Hebrew'. In 1975, the Oxford Theology Board seriously attempted to make even the Greek text of the Gospels optional – biblical Hebrew, as far as I know, has never been compulsory there for theology students – but after lengthy public debate the Board's plan was frustrated through a formal vote by Congregation, the University's parliament. A verbatim report of the speeches may be found in the *Oxford University Gazette*, Supplement (3) to No. 3625, of 11 June 1975, pp. 973–84.

7. P. S. Alexander describes my approach to the Gospels as a 'method of moving inwards to the New Testament from a firm control of the surrounding literature'. He considers this method preferable to 'the sorties in search of parallels' adopted by 'many New Testament scholars'. (Review of G. Vermes, *Post-biblical Jewish Studies*, in *JTS* 27, 1976, p. 172.)

8. The interpreter's primary task is to assess the evidence contained in the gospels, detect the basic material, and then form it into a coherent whole. Historical reconstructions based on the (hypothetical) identification of a single trait – a method not uncommon in Dead Sea Scrolls research – are unlikely to provide anything substantial by way of conclusions.

9. This same idea is to be found in various guises in the traditional or conservative branches of Judaism (cf. Louis Jacobs, *A Jewish Theology* (1973), pp. 215–18) and in Christianity, Roman Catholic or Protestant. As recently as 18 November

1893, Pope Leo XIII was able to write in his encyclical, *Providentissimus Deus*, that all the canonical books of the Bible derived directly from the Holy Spirit: 'Spiritu Sancto dictante conscripti sunt'. On the Protestant attitude to the question, see James Barr, *Fundamentalism*, 1977, pp. 286–303. This author notes that in much Calvinist and Lutheran orthodoxy, the Masoretic vowel signs (invented by Jewish scholars between AD 600 and 900) are also held to be part of the inspired content of the Hebrew Bible and that such a doctrine implies a concept of inspiration entailing 'dictation' (ibid., pp. 297–98).

10. For a brief general survey, see G. B. Caird, 'Chronology of the NT', *IDB* I, pp. 601–2.

11. See G. Vermes, 'Bible and Midrash', *The Cambridge History of the Bible* I, 1970, pp. 209–14; *Post-biblical Jewish Studies*, 1975, pp. 69–74.

12. On the *Diatessaron* (literally, 'through four') of Tatian, a second-century Syrian Christian apologist, see Bruce M. Metzger, *The Early Versions of the New Testament*, 1977, pp. 10–36.

13. For a brief sketch of the emergence and development of New Testament criticism in the eighteenth and nineteenth centuries, see A. R. C. Leaney, *Biblical Criticism*, pp. 233–36; W. G. Kümmel, *The New Testament*, ²1970.

14. See ibid., pp. 236–43; W. G. Kümmel, op. cit., pp. 147–55; *Introduction to the New Testament*, ²1975, p. 48.

15. Wrede, *Das Messiasgeheimnis in den Evangelien*, 1910. ET *The Messianic Secret*, 1971. Another highly influential study was Albert Schweitzer's *Von Reimarus zu Wrede*, 1906, better known as *The Quest for the Historical Jesus*, 1910, ³1954, 2000.

16. Cf. *Jesus and the Word*, 1958, pp. 17, 48–51; *New Testament Theology* I, 1952. p. 1. 'Bultmann gives the impression that Jesus neither preached nor believed anything specifically Christian. Wellhausen's remark that Jesus was the last of the Jews and Paul the first Christian could be Bultmann's: Jesus belonged to late Judaism, while Christ was first recognized by the primitive church.' (Otto Betz, *What do we know about Jesus?*, 1968, p. 17).

17. Wellhausen, 'Jesus war kein Christ sondern Jude' (Jesus was not a Christian but a Jew), *Einleitung in die drei ersten Evangelien*, 1905, p. 113.

18. Bultmann, *Jesus and the Word*, p. 14.

19. I Cor. 12.28; 14.29, 32; Eph. 2.20; 3.5; 4.11. See G. Friedrich, *Prophētēs* TDNT VI, pp. 848–55; E. E. Ellis, 'Prophecy in the Early Church', *IDBS*, p. 701.

20. Bultmann, *The History of the Synoptic Tradition*, 1963, p. 105. On form criticism, see Leaney, op. cit., pp. 246–65; E. V. McKnight, *What is Form Criticism?*, 1975; C. E. Carlston, 'Form Criticism, NT', *IDBS*, pp. 345–48.

21. Bornkamm, op. cit., p. 13.

22. Manson, *The Teaching of Jesus, Studies of its Form and Content*, 1931, ²1935.

23. The first edition appeared between 1948 and 1955. See also E. Stauffer, *New Testament Theology*, 1955; K. Stendahl, 'Biblical Theology', *IDB* I, pp. 420–22; Rudolf Schnackenburg, *New Testament Theology Today*, 1963; Hans Conzelmann, *An Outline of the Theology of the New Testament*, 1969; W. G. Kümmel, *The Theology of the New Testament*, 1969; Joachim Jeremias, *New Testament Theology* I, 1971.

24. Bultmann, *Theology of the New Testament* I, p. 1.

25. See Birger Gerhardsson, *Memory and Manuscript: Oral Tradition and Written Transmission in Rabbinic Judaism and Early Christianity*, 1961, ²1964; *Tradition and Transmission in Early Christianity*, 1964; *The Origins of the Gospel Traditions*, 1977.

26. Cf. Norman Perrin, *What is Redaction Criticism?* 1969; R. T. Fortna, 'Redaction Criticism, NT', *IDBS*, pp. 733–35.

27. It is worth pointing out that even a work as exaggerated as Morton Smith's *Jesus the Magician*, 1978 implicitly testifies to the possibility that gospel data confronted with external evidence can lead to historically admissible conclusions.

28. Talmud and Midrash have preserved biographical fragments in the framework of haggadic stories concerning the rabbis of the Tannaitic and Amoraic age, but no connected narration is associated with their sayings. Cf. W. S. Green, 'What's in a Name? – The Problematic of Rabbinic "Biography"', *Approaches to Ancient Judaism: Theory and Practice*, 1978, pp. 77–96; Jacob Neusner, 'The Present State of Rabbinic Biography', *Hommage à Georges Vajda*, ed. G. Nahon and Ch. Touati, 1980, pp. 85–91. The teachings of the sages were memorized, handed down, and no doubt at an early stage recorded in script. But biography as such or autobiography, like Philo's *Life of Moses* or Josephus's *Vita*, is attested only in the Greek language in Jewish literature. It is therefore not unreasonable to conclude that the gospel is essentially a Hellenistic literary form. The question of the non-appearance of historical compositions among the Qumran manuscripts is raised in my *Jesus and the World of Judaism*, 1983, pp. 137–39. See also *DSS*, pp. 136–37.

29. See below, p. 49.

30. Cf. *Jesus the Jew*, pp. 145–49.

31. Cf. above n. 18.

32. The book appeared in 1967. Perrin, a British scholar, studied under T. W. Manson and Joachim Jeremias and taught New Testament until his death at the University of Chicago.

33. Cf. Perrin, *Rediscovering the Teaching of Jesus*, pp. 39–47.

34. Perrin, *The New Testament: An Introduction*, 1974, p. 281.

35. I discuss this topic in 'Jewish Studies and New Testament Interpretation', below, pp. 53–67. The two principal sources of danger are Hermann Strack and Paul Billerbeck, *Kommentar zum Neuen Testament aus Talmud und Midrasch* I–IV (1922–28), and G. Kittel–G. Friedrich, *Theological Dictionary of the New Testament* I–X (1964–76). The original German edition, *Theologisches Wörterbuch zum Neuen Testament*, was published between 1933 and 1976.

36. Cf. below, pp. 48–49.

37. *Jesus the Jew*, pp. 83–222.

38. A good case has been made out, I believe, for asserting that the titles 'prophet', 'lord' and 'son of God' possess a definite association with the charismatic of a Hasidic healer and teacher. See *Jesus the Jew*, ibid.

39. Ibid., pp. 160–91. See further 'The Present State of the "son of man" Debate', below, pp. 81, 89. Cf. also J. A. Fitzmyer's rejoinder, 'Another View of the "Son of Man" debate', *JSNT* 4, 1979, pp. 58–68.

40. If, that is, either of them is genuine! It is natural for any New Testament interpretation produced within ecclesiastical circles always to select alternatives serving the long-term interests of the church.

41. This statement does not overlook Gospel passages recording real or fictional encounters between Jesus and Gentiles such as the Gerasene demoniac (Mark 5.1ff. par.), the Syro-Phoenician woman (Mark 7.24–30 par.) and the centurion from Capernaum (Matt. 8.5–13 par.). But none of these episodes reveal a deliberate missionary purpose; they are all accidental meetings. In fact, Mark 7.24 explicitly asserts that Jesus wished to remain incognito during his short stay in Tyrian territory. The Synoptics never ascribe to Jesus himself proselytizing intentions in Gentile lands. Only in John 7.35 is there such an allusion in the form of a question asked by an unsympathetic audience: 'Where does this man intend to go that we shall not find him? Does he intend to go to the Dispersion among the Greeks and teach the Greeks?' My assessment of the evidence coincides with that of F. C. Grant: 'Jesus never began a ministry among the Gentiles . . . Did Jesus intend (at least eventually) a mission to Gentiles? Luke 4.25–27 may be understood to point that way, and also 13.29; but the evidence as a whole is against the theory' ('Jesus Christ', *IDB* III, pp. 885–86). As for Matt. 28.18–20, it is so patently a church formulation that it requires no direct consideration in the context of Jesus' own thought. Cf. Bultmann, *The History of the Synoptic Tradition*, p. 157.

42. Mark 15.34 par. This Aramaic exclamation, corresponding to the opening verse of Ps. 22, was found disturbing enough by Luke and John for them to substitute for it, 'Father, into thy hands I commit my spirit' (Luke 23.46; cf. Ps. 31.5), and, 'It is finished' (John 19.30). The Marcan/Matthean form of Jesus' last words seems to suggest that although he foresaw resistance and hostility Jesus was convinced that God would at the last moment snatch him out of the hands of his enemies. As will be indicated later (p. 155, n. 71), this is the sole prayer of Jesus in the synoptics in which he does not address God as 'Father'.

43. Paul's 'gospel' preaching salvation through the crucified Christ was 'scandal' to Jews and 'stupidity' to Gentiles (I Cor. 1.23). Among contemporary writers, Michael Grant lays particular emphasis on the failure of Jesus. Cf. *Jesus: An Historian's Review of the Gospels*, 1977, especially chapters 7 and 9.

44. I know of no real evidence prior to the New Testament of belief among Jews in a suffering/dying Messiah. See *Jesus the Jew*, pp. 139–40; *History* II, pp. 547–49.

45. 'This is not a belief that grew up within the church . . . It is the central belief about which the church itself grew . . . If the resurrection is the dénouement of the whole story and not a "happy ending" tacked on to a tragedy . . .' *The Founder of Christianity*, 1971, pp. 28–29.

46. *Jesus the Jew*, pp. 37–41, 234–35.

47. Luke 24.11. A canon enacted by an eighth-century Irish synod denies validity to any testimony brought by a woman on the grounds that the apostles themselves refused to accept female witnesses. 'Testimonium feminae non accipitur, sicut apostoli testimonium feminarum non acceperint de resurrectione Christi.' (*Capitula selecta ex antiqua canonum collectione facta in Hibernia c. saeculo VIII*, Liber XVI, cap. III in Migne, PL 96, col. 1286). I owe this piece of information to my friend, Bernard S. Jackson.

48. On this see A. Oepke, 'Parousia', *TDNT* V, pp. 858–71; A. L. Moore, *The Parousia in the New Testament*, 1966; cf. also E. Fiorenza Schlüsser, 'Eschatology of the NT', *IDBS*, pp. 271–77.

49. 'But their eyes were kept from recognizing him' (Luke 24.6). 'Jesus himself

stood among them. But they supposed that they saw a spirit' (Luke 24.36–37). In the Fourth Gospel, Mary Magdalene 'saw Jesus standing, but she did not know that it was Jesus' (John 20.14). C. H. Dodd stresses that the 'appearances' are 'centred in a moment of *recognition*' (*The Founder of Christianity*, p. 40). But the important feature, unacknowledged by him, is that this is not a *visual* recognition.

50. 'Now concerning the coming of our Lord Jesus Christ and our assembling to meet him (cf. I Thess. 4.15–17), we beg you, brethren, not to be quickly shaken in mind or excited, either by spirit or by word, or by letter purporting to be from us, to the effect that the day of the Lord has come' (II Thess. 2.1–2).

51. Regarding delay in eschatological fulfilment, see E. Grässer, *Das Problem der Parousieverzögerung in den synoptischen Evangelien und in der Apostelgeschichte,*[2] 1960; A. Strobel, *Untersuchungen zum eschatologischen Verzögerungsproblem*, 1961.

52. See below pp. 34–35, 46–47.

53. *Habakkuk Commentary* (1QpHab) vii. 1–14.

54. Compared with the radical scepticism of much contemporary New Testament scholarship, the stand taken here may be defined as middle-of-the-road. For even such a moderate writer as Norman Perrin proclaims his overall principle to be, 'When in doubt, discard', and states categorically that 'the burden of proof always lies on the claim of authenticity'; that is to say, whatever is not proved to be genuine is to be presumed inauthentic (*Rediscovering the Teaching of Jesus*, pp. 11–12). Bearing in mind the basic Jewish respect for tradition in general, and attachment to the words of a venerated master in particular, I myself would advocate *a priori* an open mind, and would not tip the balance in favour of inauthenticity.

55. Cf. *Jesus the Jew*, p. 84.

56. Hengel, *Judaism and Hellenism*, 1974, pp. 104–05.

57. 'The Background of the Maccabean Revolution: Reflections on Martin Hengel's "Judaism and Hellenism"', *JJS* 29, 1978, p. 9.

58. In *theory*, this opinion is shared by most New Testament scholars. For example, Rudolf Bultmann writes: 'Critical investigation shows that the whole tradition about Jesus which appears in the three synoptic gospels is composed of a series of layers which can on the whole be clearly distinguished . . . The separating of these layers . . . depends on the knowledge that the gospels were composed in Greek within the Hellenistic Christian community, while Jesus and the oldest Christian group lived in Palestine and spoke Aramaic. Hence everything in the synoptics which for reasons of language or content can have originated only in Hellenistic Christianity must be excluded as a source for the teaching of Jesus.' (*Jesus and the Word*, p. 17).

59. Against those New Testament scholars who, for chronological reasons, consider the Dead Sea manuscripts wholly superior to Mishnah, Tosefta, Talmud, Midrash and Targum, I continue to maintain that 'if the Qumran Scrolls are invaluable in shedding new light on early Christianity, rabbinic literature skilfully handled, is still the richest source for the interpretation of the original message, and the most precious aid to the quest for the historical Jesus' (*Jesus and the World of Judaism*, p. 125).

60. On Judaeo-Christianity and the Ebionites, see Hans Joachim Schoeps, *Theologie und Geschichte des Judenchristentums*, 1949; *Urgemeinde, Judenchristentum,*

Gnosis, 1956; Marcel Simon *et al., Aspects du Judéo-Christianisme*, 1965; Marcel Simon and André Benoit, *Le judaïsme et le christianisme antique*, 1968, pp. 258–74; (Jean Daniélou), *Judéo-Christianisme – Recherches historiques et théologiques offertes en hommage au Cardinal Jean Daniélou*, 1972. Marcel Simon, 'Réflexions sur le Judéo-Christianisme', *Christianity, Judaism and other Greco-Roman Cults. Studies for Morton Smith at Sixty* II, ed. J. Neusner, 1975, pp. 53–76.

61. Cf. *Jesus the Jew*, pp. 22–25, 58–82. On the charismatic type, see Rudolf Otto, *Gottesreich und Menschensohn*, ³1954, pp. 267–309; ET *The Kingdom of God and the Son of Man*, 1943, pp. 333–76.

62. J. B. Segal, 'Popular Religion in Ancient Israel', *JJS* 27, 1976, pp. 1–22; esp. pp. 8–9. Cf. also W. S. Green, 'Palestinian Holy Men: Charismatic Leadership and Rabbinic Tradition', *Aufstieg und Niedergang der römischen Welt*, ed. W. Haase. II *Principat.* 19. 2. *Religion – Judentum: Palästinisches Judentum*, 1979, pp. 619–47.

63. Cf. *Jesus the Jew*, pp. 80–82.

64. On the rabbinic 'man of deed', see my study, 'Hanina ben Dosa', *JJS* 23, 1972, pp. 28–50; 24, 1973, pp. 51–64; *Post-biblical Jewish Studies*, 1975, pp. 178–214.

65. Cf. *Jesus the Jew*, pp. 58–69.

66. Cf. below, pp. 29, 35.

67. *Jewish Antiquities* xviii. 63–64. Cf. pp. 91–98 below.

68. Cf. *Jesus the Jew*, pp. 42–57.

69. Segal, art. cit., p. 20.

70. S. Freyne, *Galilee from Alexander the Great to Hadrian*, 1980, pp. 373, 388, n. 92. 'It is only hypercritical scholarship that ignores or rejects Jesus' teaching as unimportant in locating him within the spectrum of Galilean life of his own day.' The appended note reads: 'This is one of the main criticisms that can be levelled against Vermes's study . . . A subsequent volume is promised that will study the teaching of Jesus . . . but already by focussing on the deeds alone and the suggested parallels with the *hasid* tradition the lines would appear to have been irrevocably drawn.' I remain somewhat perplexed by Seán Freyne's comment for I have never thought or said or written that the teaching of Jesus was 'unimportant' or that the label 'Hasid' could explain all about him. The 'Postscript' to *Jesus the Jew* is scarcely equivocal in this regard: 'The discovery of resemblances between the work and words of Jesus and those of the Hasidim . . . is however by no means intended to imply that he was simply one of them and nothing more. Although no systematic attempt is made here to distinguish Jesus' authentic teaching – this is an enormous task that will, it is hoped, be undertaken on another occasion – it is nevertheless still possible to say, even in the absence of such an investigation, that no objective and enlightened student of the Gospels can help but be struck by the incomparable superiority of Jesus' (pp. 223–24).

3. The Gospel of Jesus the Jew II: The Father and His Kingdom

1. Cf. *Jesus the Jew*, pp. 26–28.

2. Cf. ibid., p. 115. For a detailed survey, see Gustaf Dalman, *Die Worte Jesu*, ²1930, pp. 272–80; ET *The Words of Jesus*, 1902, pp. 331–36; E. Lohse, 'Rabbi,

Rabbouni, *TDNT* VI, pp. 961–65; Ferdinand Hahn, *The Titles of Jesus in Christology*, 1969, pp. 73–81.

3. On the scribes, see *History* II, pp. 322–29; Joachim Jeremias, '*Grammateus*', *TDNT* I, pp. 740–42; Stephen Westerholm, *Jesus and Scribal Authority* (1978) pp. 26–31. For the Pharisees, see *History* II, pp. 388–403 (cf. the bibliography on pp. 381–82 to which add, Ellis Rivkin, 'Pharisees', *IDBS*, pp. 657–63 and *A Hidden Revolution*, 1978). Cf. in particular Jacob Neusner, *The Rabbinic Traditions about the Pharisees before 70*, I–III, 1971.

4. Bultmann, *Jesus and the Word*, p. 49.

5. *History* II, pp. 325–26.

6. The bulk of the controversies appears in the Marcan tradition. Explicit scriptural argument will be indicated by italics.

Mark 2.5ff. par./2.17 par./2.19ff. par./2.25ff par./3.4 par./3.24 par./3.33ff. par./7.6f. par./10.2ff. par./10.18ff. par./11.27 par./11.29 par./12.1ff. par./ 12.15ff. par./12.24ff. par./12.29ff. par./12.35ff. par./12.38ff. par./14.20f. par./ 14.48f. par.

Matt. 4.4ff.–Luke 4.ff./Matt. 5.39ff.–Luke 6.27ff./Matt. 12.27f.–Luke 11.18ff./ Matt. 23.4ff. – Luke 11.39ff.

Matt. 5.21ff./5.27f./5.33ff./11.28f.

Luke 13.12ff.

In Matt. 5.21–48, Jesus' teaching on murder, adultery, divorce, oaths, revenge and love of one's enemies is presented in the form of controversy, but this is likely to be the responsibility of Matthew. The Lucan parallels lack the formula: 'You have heard that it was said to the men of old . . . But I say to you' and the appropriate biblical quotations.

7. See *Jesus the Jew*, pp. 42–57.

8. In two passages, the Pharisees/scribes met by Jesus in Galilee are expressly said to have been visitors from Jerusalem: Mark 3.22 – Matt. 12.24 and Mark 7.1 – Matt. 15.1. Similarly, Josephus refers to a delegation of four persons, three of whom were Pharisees, despatched from Jerusalem to Galilee to effect his dismissal from the post of regional commander-in-chief. See *Vita* 196–97. As far as I know, this is the only mention of a Pharisee presence in the northern province in the whole of Josephus' work.

It used to be commonly held that during the era of the Second Temple there was no Pharisee influence in Galilee. In 1977, Aharon Oppenheimer advanced a theory denying any basic distinction between Judaean and Galilean Judaism. Expounded in *The 'Am Ha-Aretz*, 1977, and in particular in its chapter VI (pp. 200–17), his thesis appears to have impressed some scholars. Thus John Riches, *Jesus and the Transformation of Judaism*, 1980, believes himself entitled, on the basis of an uncritical acceptance of Oppenheimer's work, to 'treat with considerable caution' views reflecting an alleged Judaean sentiment of superiority towards Galileans (p. 85). Likewise Eric M. Meyers and James F. Strange declare in *Archaeology, the Rabbis and Early Christianity*, 1981, that Oppenheimer's arguments are convincing (p. 36). But these authors do not seem to realize that none of Oppenheimer's proofs actually relate to the pre-Yavneh age. This flaw has been noticed by Seán Freyne (*Galilee from Alexander the Great to Hadrian*, p. 339, n. 48) and fully exposed by Martin D. Goodman in his review of *The 'Am Ha-Aretz*: 'Nothing that

O(ppenheimer) presents would preclude the more extreme interests of the Judaean rabbinical academies in purity and tithing being confined in Galilee to those few rabbinic figures . . . of whom the texts tell . . . O. has very few passages to cite of Galilean communities expressing interest before 132 in purity, tithing or sabbatical year and even of those that are given not all are safe . . . What is left? Some Galileans joined Judaean rabbinic schools before 132 . . . and a few issued halakha on return to Galilee to a more or less indifferent populace. Some Judaean rabbis visited Galilee . . . for reasons unspecified . . . Certainly Galileans were Jews, and the Gospels and Josephus confirm their use of synagogues and conformity with the control of the Temple before 70. But O's need to claim any more than that comes from his own apologetic: the assertion that before 132 Palestinian Jews considered the rabbinic Judaism of the sages whose words are recorded in the Mishnah as some sort of "orthodoxy" accepted by all as an essential part of being Jewish' (*JJ* 31, 1980, p. 248–49).

9. The title, 'village scribe' (*kōmogrammateus*) is used sarcastically in Josephus, *Ant.* xvi. 203; *BJ* i. 479.

10. Cf. *Jesus the Jew*, pp. 52, 54.

11. The exegetical arguments appearing in the Gospel of Matthew are most probably the work of this rabbinically trained evangelist. Cf. K. Stendahl, *The School of St Matthew*, 1954, [2]1968.

12. On the activity of the scribes and rabbis in the domain of legal development, see *History* II, pp. 330–32. Cf. also my *Post-biblical Jewish Studies*, pp. 80–81.

13. Mark 1.22 par. Cf. *Jesus the Jew*, pp. 28–29. The link between exorcism/ healing and the concept of *exousia* is manifest in Mark 3.15; 6.7; Matt. 10.1; Luke 10.19. For a detailed exposition (which is not altogether satisfactory), see W. Foerster, '*Exousia*', *TDNT* II, pp. 562–75, esp. 568–69.

14. Matt. 12.25–28; Luke 11.17–20; Mark 7.14–23; Matt. 15.10–20.

15. Cf. R. Bultmann, *The History of the Synoptic Tradition*, 1963, pp. 39–54 (Controversial Dialogues): 'This means, in my view, that we can firmly conclude that the formation of the material in the tradition took place in the *Palestinian Church*' (p. 48). Apropos of 'scholastic dialogues', Bultmann writes: 'But we must raise the question whether the *Palestinian or the Hellenistic Church* was responsible for formulating the scholastic dialogues. Their form and their relation with both the controversy dialogues, and the Rabbinic scholastic dialogues, show that the former was the case' (p. 55).

16. For an outline of the educational system in Palestine, see *History* II, pp. 417–22. Cf. also S. Safrai, 'Education and Study of the Torah', *The Jewish People in the First Century*, II, 1977, pp. 945–69; M. Hengel, *Judaism and Hellenism* I, pp. 65–83. On Babylonian Jewish religious education, see D. M. Goodblatt, *Rabbinic Instruction in Sasanian Babylonia*, 1975.

17. Whether a special class of wandering teachers existed is uncertain, but it may be worth noting that the Talmud mentions itinerant Galilean exegetes (*bSanh.* 70a; *bHull.* 27b).

18. It seems to be correct to assert, in fact, that systematization in Judaism reflects foreign cultural influences: Hellenism in the case of Philo, and Islamic and Christian philosophy and theology in medieval or modern Judaism. Even a contemporary author is compelled to write: 'Many Jewish thinkers have written on

theological topics since Kohler (*Jewish Theology*, 1918) but there is a real lack of systematic treatment which this book seeks, however inadequately, to fill' (Louis Jacobs, *A Jewish Theology*, 1973, p. vii).

19. This is a kind of litany recited between New Year and the Day of Atonement. Cf. *JE* I, p. 65; *Enc. Jud.* 3, cols. 973–74.

20. Cf. Joseph Heinemann, *Prayer in the Talmud: Forms and Patterns*, 1977, pp. 173–74.

21. A. E. Harvey, 'Christology and the Evidence of the New Testament', in *God Incarnate: Story and Belief*, ed. A. E. Harvey, 1981, p. 50.

22. N. Perrin, *Rediscovering the Teaching of Jesus*, p. 54.

23. Cf. O. E. Evans, 'Kingdom of God, of Heaven', *IDB* II, pp. 17–26; R. H. Hiers, 'Kingdom of God', *IDBS*, p. 516; J. Hering, *Le royaume de Dieu et sa venue*, 1959; Martin Buber, *Kingship of God*, 1967; John Gray, *The Biblical Doctrine of the Reign of God*, 1979. For a full survey of the views expressed by New Testament scholars, see N. Perrin, *The Kingdom of God in the Teaching of Jesus*, 1963; ibid., *Jesus and the Language of the Kingdom*, 1976; J. Schlosser, *Le règne de Dieu dans les dits de Jésus* I–II, 1980.

24. For a comprehensive discussion of the subject, see Sigmund Mowinckel, *He That Cometh*, 1956. The latest study is Joachim Becker's *Messianic Expectation in the Old Testament*, 1980.

25. On the Psalms of Solomon, see Otto Eissfeldt, *The Old Testamen. An Introduction*, 1965, pp. 610–13, 773–74. Cf. also Paul Winter, 'Psalms of Solomon', *IDB* III, pp. 958–60; James H. Charlesworth, *The Pseudepigrapha and Modern Research*, 1976, ²1981, pp. 195–97. For the Greek text, see A. Rahlfs, *Septuaginta* II, pp. 471–89. For an English translation, cf. G. Buchanan Gray in *APOT* II, pp. 631–52.

26. *Ps. of Solomon* 17.23–32. Cf. R. H. Charles, *APOT* II, pp. 645–50.

27. *1QS* v, 20–25 in D. Barthélemy and J. T. Milik, *Discoveries in the Judaean Desert* I, 1955, pp. 127–28; *CDSSE*, p. 376. On the Blessings, see *DSS*, p. 261.

28. On the *Tefillah* or *'Amidah* or *Shemone 'Esre*, see *History* II, pp. 455–63; J. Heinemann, 'Amidah', *Enc. Jud.* 2, cols. 838–46; *Prayer in the Talmud*, 1977, pp. 218–27. The text has been preserved in a Palestinian and a Babylonian recension. Both are translated in *History* II, *loc. cit.*

29. 15th benediction in the Babylonian recension; cf. *History* II, p. 458.

30. On Jewish apocalyptics see Paul Volz, *Eschatologie der jüdischen Gemeinde im neutestamentlichen Zeitalter*, ²1934; D. S. Russell, *The Method and Message of Jewish Apocalyptic*, 1964; P. D. Hanson, *The Dawn of Apolcalyptic*, 1975; 'Apocalypticism', *IDBS*, pp. 28–34.

31. *1QS* iii, 13 – iv, 26; *CDSSE*, pp. 101–03.

32. *1QS* iv, 25; *CDSSE*, p. 103.

33. *1QM* xviii, 1; *CDSSE*, p. 181.

34. *1QM* xvii, 7–8; *CDSSE*, p. 181.

35. Dalman, *Die Worte Jesu*, ²1930, pp. 75–83. ET *The Words of Jesus*, 1902, pp. 96–101.

36. *Sifra* (ed. Weiss) 93d. Cf. Dalman, op. cit., p. 80. (ET p. 97). In interpreting, 'I have separated you from the peoples that you should be mine', in this sense, the midrashist presumes that the Gentiles as a rule are sinners.

37. *Sifre on Num.* (ed. Horovitz), 115 (p. 126).

38. *mBer.* 2.2. Cf. E. E. Urbach, *The Sages. Their Concepts and Beliefs* I, 1975, p. 400.

39. *Tanhuma* (ed. Buber), I, p. 63.

40. I have reached a negative conclusion in my examination of the messianic character of Jesus in the sense that he does not appear to have given much weight to the question of Messianism or to have seen himself as fulfilling such a function. Cf. *Jesus the Jew*, pp. 129–159. Here I am in agreement with Bultmann, who wrote: 'I am personally of the opinion that Jesus did not believe himself to be the Messiah' (*Jesus and the Word*, p. 15). My own judgement is based on the strict definition of 'Messiah' as a valorous, holy, just and mighty Davidic king of the end of time. Lack of precision in this domain is bound to blur the issue. Yet it is not uncommon among New Testament scholars of today to add to the essential notion of the King Messiah various others arising from diverse circles at different times, some held by many, others by only a few, or even by a single individual. A medley of this sort, proclaimed Jewish Messianism, provides ample scope for detecting features which match up to the 'Christ Jesus' of the New Testament. Some go so far as to recognize all the data relating to Jesus in the Gospels as pertaining to christology/messianism without asking whether they are in any way associated with the historical expectation of the Jewish people, let alone with Jesus' self-awareness.

41. 'It is impossible to avoid thinking that Matt. 25. 31–46 derives from Jewish tradition. Perhaps when it was taken up by the Christian Church the name of God was replaced by the title of the Son of Man'. R. Bultmann, *The History of the Synoptic Tradition*, p. 124.

42. *yBer.* ii 5c. Comparison of the two parables yields significant results. In both cases, all the workmen receive the same wage irrespective of the number of hours of actual work, but whereas in the rabbinic story an industrious and skilful person is discharged after two hours' work because, in the king's words, he has achieved more in that short time than the others during the whole day, Jesus' teaching, emphasizes generosity towards the unworthy. According to Joachim Jeremias (*The Parables of Jesus*, ²1972, p. 138), the Talmudic parable, given in the name of R. Ze'era (*c.* AD 300), is secondary to that of Jesus. But this estimate, described as a 'probability bordering on certainty', depends on the presumption that Ze'era was the actual author of the story. In fact, this type of material is more likely to have circulated as part of popular wisdom for centuries and to have been used and interpreted by preachers according to their lights and varying didactic needs. In connection with the change from king to landowner in the Gospels, see also an identical shift in *bSanh.* 91ab from a 'king of flesh and blood' to an 'orchard owner' (*ba'al pardes*).

43. Cf. above, pp. 25–26.

44. Mark 4.3ff. par; Mark 4.26ff; Matt. 13.24ff.

45. Matt. 20.1–16. Apropos of this parable Bultmann writes: 'Matt. 20. 1–16 obviously teaches God's impartial goodness to all his servants; but against whom was the parable directed originally?' (*The History of the Synoptic Tradition*, p. 199). No doubt against conceited and ambitious early disciples?

46. Mark 4.30ff. par. The mustard plant, *brassica nigra* (cf. J. Feliks, 'Mustard', *Enc. Jud.* 12, col. 720), was apparently very successful in Galilee. R. Simeon ben Halafta (*c.* AD 200), praising the fertility of the province, reports that he has one

growing in his field which is as tall as a fig tree and which he can actually climb (cf. *yPea* vii 20b).

47. Matt. 5.3; Luke 6.20. – Mark 10.23ff. par. Jesus' saying is only very slightly less exaggerated than the Talmudic metaphor of passing an elephant through the eye of a needle (*bBer.* 55b; *bBM* 38b).

48. N. Perrin, *The Kingdom of God in the Teaching of Jesus*, 1963, provides a general survey Cf. also H. Schürmann, 'Eschatologie und Liebesdienst in der Verkündigung Jesu' in *Vom Messias zu Christus*, ed. K. Schubert, 1964, pp. 203–32; A. Strobel, *Kerygma und Apokalyptik*, 1967; G. E. Ladd, *The Presence and the Future*, 1974.

49. See in particular *The Quest for the Historical Jesus*, 2000.

50. See especially *The Parables of the Kingdom*, 1935, 1978.

51. Cf. *The Parables of Jesus*, ²1972. See also W. G. Kümmel, *Promise and Fulfilment*, 1957.

52. Otto, *The Kingdom of God and the Son of Man*, 1943, pp. 59–63.

53. Albert Schweitzer's thesis that Jesus expected the coming of the kingdom during the first mission of the disciples is based on his interpretation of Matt. 10. When Jesus' hope failed to materialize, he changed his teaching. Cf. *The Quest of the Historical Jesus*, 2000, p. 326–27. This exegesis is purely artificial and unsubstantiated: cf. W. G. Kümmel, *Promise and Fulfilment*, pp. 62–63.

54. In the *Testament of Levi* 17, seven periods in the history of the priesthood are to be followed by the new area of the Priest-Messiah (ch. 18). Cf. R. H. Charles, *APOT* II, pp. 313–15. 1 Enoch 93.1–10; 91.12–17 divides world history into ten weeks. Cf. M. A. Knibb, *The Ethiopic Book of Enoch* II, 1978, pp. 219–25. According to J. T. Milik's reconstruction of the 11Q Melchizedek document, the final epoch of history will consist of ten jubilees. Cf. 'Milkisedeq et Milkî-reša' dans les anciens écrits juifs et chrétiens', *JJS* 23, 1972, pp. 98–99, 124.

55. These are (1) Abraham to David; (2) David to the Babylonian exile; (3) Babylonian exile to the birth of the Messiah. See Matt. 1.17.

56. Cf. B. Rigaux, *Les Epîtres aux Thessaloniciens*, 1956, pp. 653–61, 671–73.

57. Various interpretations of these difficult passages are listed by N. Perrin in *The Kingdom of God in the Teaching of Jesus*, pp. 171–74 and *Rediscovering the Teaching of Jesus*, pp. 74–77. Some exegetes see in the 'violent' the hostile rulers of the world of the spirits or the Jewish opponents of Jesus. Cf. W. G. Kümmel, *Promise and Fulfilment*, p. 123. Others seek to identify them with the Zealots or Sicarii. Cf. S. G. F. Brandon, *Jesus and the Zealots*, 1967, pp. 78, 300. Note however M. Hengel's disagreement in *DieZeloten*, ²1976, p. 345. Perrin adheres to E. Käsemann's conclusion expressed in *Essays on New Testament Themes*, 1964, p. 42: 'The Kingdom of God . . . is hindered by men of violence.' Perrin comments: 'What we have here is the reverse of the situation envisaged in the interpretation of the exorcisms: there the Kingdom of Satan is being plundered, here that of God' (*Rediscovering*, p. 77). I prefer to see in these sayings, and especially in the more original logion of Matthew, one of Jesus' typical exaggerations. The apparent success of John's mission and his own in Galilee, with crowds elbowing their way forward to reach the teacher, suggests to Jesus the simile of troops storming the kingdom to seize it.

58. Incidentally I agree with Jeremias, *The Prayers of Jesus*, 1977, p. 91, that

Jesus may have spoken the 'Our Father' 'on different occasions in slightly differing form', which would imply that the Matthean addition may also have originated with Jesus. For a recent detailed bibliography of the Lord's Prayer, see Jean Carmignac, *Recherches sur le 'Notre Père'*, 1969.

59. Cf. Joseph Heinemann, *Prayer in the Talmud*, 1977, pp. 32–33, 78–80, 93–95, etc.

60. Bultmann (*History of the Synoptic Tradition*, p. 160) attributes the saying to a lost Jewish writing. It does not figure among the logia recognized as authentic by N. Perrin.

61. *Jesus the Jew*, pp. 194–99. For a thorough analysis of the 'Father' concept in the Old Testament and Judaism, see G. Quell and G. Schrenk, *'Patēr'*, *TDNT*, V, pp. 959–82; R. Hamerton-Kelly, *God the Father, Theology and Patriarchy in the Teaching of Jesus*, 1979.

62. Cf. Charles, *APOT* II, pp. 12–13.

63. *Mekh. on Ex.* 20:6 (ed. Lauterbach II, p. 247).

64. Cf. J. M. Allegro, *Discoveries in the Judaean Desert* V, 1968, p. 53; *CDSSE*, p. 494.

65. Heinemann, op. cit., pp. 189–90.

66. *History* II, p. 460.

67. On the Hasidim, see A. Büchler, *Types of Palestinian Jewish Piety from 70 B.C.E. to 70 C.E.*, 1922; S. Safrai, 'The Teaching of Pietists in Mishnaic Literature' *JJS* 16, 1965, pp. 15–33; G. Vermes, 'Hanina ben Dosa', *JJS* 23, 1972, pp. 28–50; 24, 1973, pp. 51–64; *Post-biblical Jewish Studies*, 1975, p. 178–214.

68. Cf. G. Schrenk, *'Patēr'*, *TDNT*, V, pp.982–1014; J. Jeremias, *Prayers*, pp. 11–65. For the rabbinic usage, see G. Dalman, *Die Worte Jesu*, pp. 150–59 (ET pp. 184–89).

69. Cf. Jeremias, *Prayers*, p. 32.

70. Cf. G. Dalman, *Worte*, p. 155. (ET p. 189).

71. One departure from the norm is, 'My God, my God, why hast thou forsaken me?' (Mark 15.34 par.), an expression not spontaneous but borrowed from the Aramaic translation of Ps. 22. The other is the Matthean beginning of the Lord's Prayer, *'Our Father who art in heaven'* (Matt. 6.9).

72. Cf. Jeremias, *Prayers*; N. Perrin, *Rediscovering*, pp. 40–41.

73. N. Perrin, *Rediscovering*, p. 41.

74. Jeremias, *Prayers*, pp. 57–62.

75. Dan. 5:13; *1QGenAp* ii, 19, 24; iii, 3 (J. A. Fitzmyer, *The Genesis Apocryphon of Qumran Cave 1*, ²1971, pp. 44, 46); 6Q8 1.4 (M. Baillet, *Discoveries in the Judaean Desert* III, 1962, p. 117).

76. Jeremias, *Prayers*, p. 59.

77. *Targum Neofiti* to Gen. 44.18.

78. D. Flusser, *Jesus*, 1969, p. 145, n. 159.

79. Among the rabbis of the Tannaitic age, we find Abba Hanin (or Hanan), Abba Shaul, Abba Yose ben Dostai in addition to the grandsons of Honi. Cf. G. Dalman, *Worte*, pp. 278–79 (ET, p. 339). Jesus disapproves of such a metaphorical use of the title – *patēr* is preceded by 'rabbi' and followed by 'master' – when he instructs his followers not to call any man 'father' (Matt. 23.9). Jeremias (*Prayers*, pp. 41–43) sees this prohibition as an attempt to protect 'the address "Abba" from

profanation', but I think Jesus is more likely to have been intending to deflect from religious teachers the veneration due to God alone. Cf. *Jesus the Jew*, p. 211.
80. Cf. *Jesus the Jew*, p. 211.
81. On the *Kaddish*, see *Enc. Jud.* 10, cols 660–62; A. Z. Idelsohn, *Jewish Liturgy and its Development*, 1932, pp. 84–88; J. Heinemann with J. J. Petuchowski, *Literature of the Synagogue*, 1975, pp. 81–84.
82. According to R. Simeon ben Yohai (mid-second century AD), no bird is caught in a fowler's net without a decree from heaven (*ySheb.* ix 38d; *Gen. R.* 79:6, etc. Cf. Vermes, *Post-biblical Jewish Studies*, pp. 162–63)

4. The Gospel of Jesus the Jew III: Jesus and Christianity

1. T. W. Manson, *The Teaching of Jesus*, ²1935, p. 101.
2. The most remarkable feature of this kind of reaction is that the unhistorical nature of belief causes no concern to upholders of a so-called historical religion. Manson did not think it necessary to explain why he could 'rightly' ignore the evidence of the 'earliest records'. The classic justification of such 'apparent' departures from the testimony of the Synoptics is sought in a combination of unwritten (supplementary) tradition and in the work of the Holy Spirit in the church (cf. Acts 1.3–5; John 14.26; 16.13). The modern justification consists in denying the reliability of the 'earliest evidence' in connection with the authentic teaching of Jesus, and in asserting that it also mirrors the thought of the church. Cf. p. 19 above, and *Jesus the Jew*, pp. 224–25.
3. On Jewish religion in the inter-testamental era, see *History* II, pp. 464–554; Wilhelm Bousset, *Die Religion des Judentums im späthellenistischen Zeitalter*, ²1926; G. F. Moore, *Judaism in the First Centuries of the Christian Era. The Age of the Tannaim* I–III, 1927–30; J. Maier, *Geschichte der jüdischen Religion*, 1972; E. E. Urbach, *The Sages. Their Concepts and Beliefs* I–II, 1975; E. P. Sanders, *Paul and Palestinian Judaism*, 1977; Wolfgang Haase (ed.), *Aufstieg und Niedergang der römischen Welt – Principat – Religion (Judentum: Allgemeines; Palästinisches Judentum)* II 19.1–2, 1979; Jacob Neusner, 'Judaism after Moore: A Programmatic Statement', *JJS* 31, 1980, pp. 141–56; *Judaism: The Evidence of the Mishnah*, 1981.
4. Cf. above, pp. 31–32.
5. Cf. 'Law of God' (Josh. 24.26); 'Law of the Lord' (II Kings 10.31); 'Law of Moses' (Josh. 8.31), etc.
6. *Pace* A. Oppenheimer and his followers (see ch. 3 n.8 above), I still maintain that because of its distance from the Temple and the centres of study in Jerusalem the Galilean practice of Judaism was less sophisticated and punctilious than that prevailing in general in Judaea in the pre-70 era. Cf. *Jesus the Jew*, pp. 54–55.
7 See Mark 6.56 par. and Num. 15.38–39; Deut. 22.12. Cf. also *History* II, p. 479; J. Schneider, '*Kraspedon*', *TDNT* III, p. 904; Strack–Billerbeck IV, pp. 277–92; Rudolf Schnackenburg, *The Moral Teaching of the New Testament*, 1965, p. 56.
8. It may be asked whether the phrase, 'they make their fringes large' (*megalunousin*), has some midrashic connection with Deut. 22.12, 'You shall make yourselves fringes (*gᵉdilim*)'. The Hebrew word meaning 'twisted threads', used instead

of the familiar *ẓiẓiyoth* of Num. 15.38–39, recalls the root *GDL*. 'to be great, large, to grow'.

9. *bMakk*. 24a.

10. 'The Ten Words, as they are called, the main heads under which are summarized the Special Laws, have been explained in the preceding treatise (*The Decalogue*). We have now . . . to examine the particular ordinances' (*The Special Laws* I, 1, trans. F. H. Colson, *Philo* VII, Loeb Classical Library, 1958, p. 101).

11. It is curious to note that when Philo intends to illustrate a point in the Decalogue, viz. that the 'oracles' are addressed to individuals in the second person singular, he quotes the same three commandments as Jesus. 'Thou shalt not commit adultery, thou shalt not kill, thou shalt not steal' (*Decal*. 36; *Philo* VII (Loeb), p. 25). The main difference is that Philo does not adopt the order of the commandments given in the Hebrew Bible and followed by Jesus, or that of the Septuagint, but quotes freely, no doubt from memory.

12. On the subject of love, see C. Spicq, *Agapè dans le Nouveau Testament* I–III, 1958–59. For the somewhat idiosyncratic view that the dual commandment is a Jewish-Hellenistic creation and has nothing to do with Jesus, see Chr. Burchard, 'Das doppelte Liebesgebot in der frühen christlichen Überlieferung' in *Der Ruf Jesu und Antwort der Gemeinde – Joachim Jeremias Festschrift*, 1970, pp. 39–62.

13. 'What is hateful to you, do not do it to your neighbour. This is the whole Torah; all the rest is only interpretation' (*bShabb*. 31a). Cf. also Philo, *Hypothetica* 7, 6. For a single principle summarizing perfect moral behaviour even more simply, see the test set by Yohanan ben Zakkai for his five disciples: 'Go forth and see which is the good way to which a man should cleave. R. Eliezer said, A good eye. R. Joshua said, A good companion. R. Jose said, A good neighbour. R. Simeon said, One that sees what will be. R. Eleazar said, A good heart' (*mAb*. 2.9). Yohanan ben Zakkai is said to have approved of the latter (ibid.).

14. According to Bultmann (*The History of Synoptic Tradition*, p. 103), 'The saying, as an individual utterance, gives moral expression to a naif egoism'. But this view appears totally to misrepresent the thrust of the logion and the underlying concept of religiousness. If one of the chief purposes of the Torah is the creation of a society of brothers, children of the heavenly Father, is it not reasonable to assume that in such a family each individual member may use his own sensitivity as an instinctive norm for correct fraternal behaviour?

15. 'Christ redeemed us from the curse of the law, having become a curse for us' (Gal. 3.13). On the connection between Paul's thought and Deut. 21.22–23, cf. Max Wilcox, ' "Upon the Tree" – Deut. 21.22–23 in the New Testament', *JBL 96*, 1977, pp. 85–99.

16. This is one of the thorniest of Gospel passages for Christian exegetes. For recent monographs see H. Hübner, *Das Gesetz in der synoptischen Tradition*, 1973; Robert Banks, *Jesus and the Law in the Synoptic Tradition*, 1975. In both the Lucan and the Matthean versions, Jesus appears to stress the permanency of the whole Torah with its iotas and tittles, i.e. decorative penstrokes. On the latter, see G. F. Moore, *Judaism* III, p. 83. For Bultmann (*The History of the Synoptic Tradition*, p. 138), the saying reflects, not the thought of Jesus, but 'discussions between the more conservative (Palestinian) communities and those that were free from the law (Hellenistic)'. But since Luke, addressing Gentile Christians, depicts Jesus as

taking a wholly unconditional stand in favour of the Law, the total unsuitability and embarrassing nature of his version commends itself as genuine. By contrast, Matthew's wording (5.17–18) entails obscure allusions to some kind of fulfilment or accomplishment after which, presumably, changes are expected to occur: 'I have not come to abolish (the Law and the Prophets) but to fulfil them (*plērōsai*). Till heaven and earth pass away, not an iota, not a tittle, will pass from the Law until all is accomplished' (*genētai*). This formulation probably reflects an adaptation of Jesus' saying to the post-70 situation when the destruction of the Temple put an end to the practicability of the sacrificial legislation. As for the concept of fulfilment, it is taken by some scholars in the sense of a realization of prophecy: cf. for example R. Banks, *Jesus and the Law*, pp. 204–13; B. S. Jackson, 'Legalism', *JJS* 30, 1979, pp. 3–4. However, the phraseology, 'to abolish – to fulfil' (Matt. 5.17), clearly mirrors the rabbinic *ľbattel-ľqayyem*, i.e. to abolish – that is, to consider cancelled – the Torah in wealth, but fulfil it in poverty (*mAb.* 4.9), and is therefore best interpreted in that sense. For a detailed discussion of this question, see G. Dalman, *Jesus – Jeschua* (1922), pp. 51–62; ET *Jesus-Jeshua: Studies in the Gospels*, 1929, repr. 1971, 56–66. The Matthean addition to the basic logion (Matt. 5.19) may well represent, as Bultmann proposes, 'the attitude of the conservative Palestinian community in contrast to that of the Hellenists' (*The History of the Synoptic Tradition*, p. 138). If Matt. 5.20, proclaiming that the righteousness of Jesus' disciples should exceed that of the scribes and Pharisees, belongs to the present pericopa – as I think it does against Bultmann (ibid.) and others (cf. B. Przybilski, *Righteousness in Matthew and his World of Thought*, 1980, p. 80), then it may be argued that the original saying of Jesus (5.18) is conveyed by Matthew both in an anti-Hellenistic Christian (5.19) and in an anti-Pharisaic (5.20) polemical setting. For Jesus' stress on inwardness in fulfilling the Torah, see p. 43 above. The idea of the perpetuity of the Law is expounded by G. F. Moore, *Judaism* I, p. 269–80.

17. For the Jewish custom, see *m Yad.*, Strack–Billerbeck I, pp. 695–704.

18. Mark 2.25ff. par.; 3.1ff. par.; Luke 13.15f.; 14.3ff. Cf. E. Lohse, '*Sabbaton*', *TDNT* VII, pp. 21–26.

19. Cf. among others, G. Bornkamm, *Jesus of Nazareth*, 1960, pp. 97–98; N. Perrin, *Rediscovering the Teaching of Jesus*, p. 150; H. Hübner, *Das Gesetz in der synoptischen Tradition*, 1973, p. 154. See further *Jesus the Jew*, pp. 28–29.

20. See *Jesus the Jew*, p. 29. Cf. M. Black, *An Aramaic Approach to the Gospels and Acts*, ³1967, pp. 217–18. According to W. D. Davies, the Matthean version makes 'the whole discussion turn around the question of the oral tradition rather than the written Law' (*The Setting of the Sermon on the Mount*, 1964, p. 104).

21. Cf. n. 18 above.

22. A highly significant discussion of this issue is preserved in the *Mekhilta* on Ex. 31.13 (ed. Lauterbach III, pp. 197–99): 'Whence do we know that the duty of saving life supersedes the Sabbath laws? ... R. Eleazar ben Azariah ... said: If in performing the ceremony of circumcision, which affects only one member of the body, one is to disregard the Sabbath laws, how much more should one do so for the whole body when it is in danger! ... R. Akiba says: If punishment for murder sets aside even the Temple service, which in turn supersedes the Sabbath (cf. Matt. 12.5: the priests in the Temple profane the Sabbath), how much more should the

duty of saving life supersede the Sabbath laws! . . . R. Simeon ben Menasiah says: Behold it is said, "And you shall keep the Sabbath for it is holy for you" (Ex. 31.14). This means: The Sabbath is given you but you are not surrendered to the Sabbath. R. Nathan says: Behold it is said, "Wherefore the people of Israel shall keep the Sabbath, observing the Sabbath throughout their generations" (Ex. 31.16). This implies that we should disregard one Sabbath for the sake of saving the life of a person so that he may be able to observe many Sabbaths' (trans. Lauterbach).

23. *bSanh.* 74a. The general principle is laid down in *b Yom.* 85b: 'Regard for life supersedes the Sabbath'.

24. Cf. J. Klausner, *Jesus of Nazareth*, 1925, p. 279. For a lenient rabbinic ruling, see *m Yom.* 8.6, 'If a man has a pain in his throat, they may drop medicine into his mouth on the Sabbath, since there is doubt whether life is in danger, and whenever there is doubt whether life is in danger, this overrides the Sabbath' (trans. H. Danby, *The Mishnah*, 1933, p. 172). On '*Pikkuah nefesh*' (regard for life), see *Enc. Jud.* 13, cols. 509–10.

25. See further Mark 8.36 par.; Matt. 6.25; Luke 12.33, indicating that Jesus bases his teaching on the principle that life is the supreme good (cf. Bultmann, *The History of the Synoptic Tradition*, p. 83). The plucking of grain on the Sabbath is presented as admissible relief from starvation (Mark 2.23–26 par.). It follows naturally from this that to surrender one's life to God is the greatest sacrifice (Mark 8.34–35 par.). This applies also to the poor widow who, by depositing two small coins into the Temple treasury, offers to God 'her whole living' (Mark 12.44 par.).

26. The scribes and the Pharisees sit on Moses' seat; so practise and observe what they tell you'. The 'chair of Moses' was the seat of the president of the synagogue; cf. *History* II, p. 442.

27. As E. R. Goodenough points out, for Philo 'each law is justified on the basis of its symbolical value' (*An Introduction to Philo Judaeus*, ²1962, p. 42). As an illustration of this principle it may be recalled that for the Alexandrian sage circumcision is 'a symbol of two things most necessary to our well-being. One is the excision of pleasures which bewitch the mind . . . The other reason is that a man should know himself and banish from the soul the grievous malady of conceit' (*Spec. Leg.* I, 8–9). Nevertheless, this emphasis on the allegorical meaning of laws goes hand in hand with an insistence on a simultaneous literal observance of the biblical commandments. Here again Philo and Jesus appear to represent the same religious stand. 'There are some who, regarding the laws in their literal sense in the light of symbols of matters belonging to the intellect, are over punctilious about the latter, while treating the former with easy-going neglect. Such men I for my part should blame for handling the matter in too easy and offhand a manner: they ought to have given careful attention to both aims, to a more full and exact investigation of what is not seen and in what is seen, to be stewards without reproach . . . It is quite true that the Seventh Day is meant to teach the power of the Unoriginate and the non-action of created beings. But let us not for this reason abrogate the laws laid down for its observance, and light fires or till the ground or carry loads or institute proceedings in court or act as jurors or demand the restoration of deposits or recover loans, or do all else that we are permitted to do as well on days that are not festival seasons. It is true that the Feast is a symbol of gladness of soul and thankfulness to God, but we should not for this reason turn our backs on the general gatherings of

the year's seasons . . . Why, we shall be ignoring the sanctity of the Temple and a
thousand other things, if we are going to pay heed to nothing except what is shewn
us by the inner meaning of things. Nay, we should look on all these outward observances as resembling the body, and the inner meanings as resembling the soul. It
follows that, exactly as we have to take thought for the body, because it is the abode
of the soul, so we must pay heed to the letter of the laws.' (*The Migration of
Abraham* 89, 91–93; trans. F. H. Colson and G. H. Whitaker, *Philo* IV (Loeb),
pp. 183, 185). On Josephus see below, pp. 99–108.

28. Cf. G. F. Moore, *Judaism* II, pp. 6–7. E. E. Urbach, *The Sages* I, pp. 365–99
(passim). The paramount reason for observing the commandments is that they
have been decreed by God; hence the performance of every statute, ceremonial or
moral, is ultimately an act of obedience. Cf. *Pesiqta de-R. Kahana* (ed. Buber) 40ab;
Tanhuma (ed. Buber) IV, pp. 118–19, quoted in *Jesus the Jew*, pp. 64–65.

29. *1QS* ii, 25 – iii, 5 (*CDSSE*, p. 100): 'No man shall be in the Community of
His truth who refuses to enter the Covenant of God so that he may walk in the
stubbornness of his heart . . . He shall not be reckoned among the perfect; he shall
neither be purified by atonement, nor cleansed by purifying waters, nor sanctified
by seas and rivers, nor washed clean by any ablution . . .' *1QS* v, 13–14 (*CDSSE*,
p. 104): '(The men of falsehood) shall not enter the water to participate in the
Purity of the saints, for they shall not be cleansed unless they turn from their
wickedness.'

30. Such an emphasis on the individual rather than the community is not
difficult to understand in the eschatological context outlined above, pp. 34, 35.
Communal legislation can have no meaning where a society is not destined to
endure.

31. Homicide and anger are represented as liable to the same punishment.
Likewise, seriously to insult a brother is to commit an offence belonging to the
same category of crime as murder. At Qumran, words spoken to a priest in wrath
(*1QS* vi, 26), short-temper shown towards a superior (vii, 2) and insulting a fellow-
sectary (vii, 4) are also singled out as serious infringements of the rule entailing a
full year's penance but not permanent expulsion. Cf. *CDSSE*, p. 107. For a highly
speculative view of a possible anti-Qumran polemic in Matthew, see W. D. Davies,
The Setting of the Sermon on the Mount, 1964, pp. 235–239.

A saying similar to Matt. 5.21ff., attributed to a pupil of the fourth-century
Amora, R. Nahman b. Isaac, appears in the Babylonian Talmud: 'Whoever causes
his companion's face to lose colour (i.e. humiliates him) in public, he is as though
he had shed his blood' (*bBM* 58b).

32. *The Mekhilta of R. Simeon ben Yohai* on Ex. 20.14 (ed. Hoffmann, p. 111),
advances a point of view similar to that of Jesus: 'Do not commit adultery': he is not
to commit adultery . . . either by the eye or by the heart. Whence do we know that
the eye and the heart fornicate? As it is written, 'Not to follow after your heart and
eyes' (Num. 15.39). Cf. also *Pesiqta Rabbati* 24.2: 'Thou shalt not commit adultery'
(Ex. 20.14). R. Simeon ben Laqish said, You are not to say that only he is called
adulterer who uses his body in the act. We find scripture saying that even he who
visualizes himself in the act of adultery is called an adulterer. And the proof? The
verse, 'The eye of the adulterer waits for the twilight' (Job 24.15) (trans. W. G.
Braude, *Pesikta Rabbati* I, 1968, pp. 505–6).

33. Whilst the generosity of the rich towards the poor is praiseworthy – 'the assembly will relate his acts of charity' (Ecclus 31.11; 'his renown' according to the Hebrew text) – Jesus warns against the danger of self-aggrandizement. On alms-giving in secret, see the mention in *mSheq.* 5.6 of the 'chamber of secrets' in the Temple where the diffident could help themselves to gifts deposited there by tact-ful benefactors. Again, the concentration of the ancient Hasidim, whose prayers recited in public places could not be disturbed by greetings addressed to them even by the king himself, was greatly admired (*mBer.* 5.1; *tBer.* 3.20). On the other hand, the *tameion*, or hidden room, is where the patriarch Joseph prays (*Testament of Joseph* 3.3). Similarly, Philo's Therapeutai, or contemplative Essenes, are said to have closeted themselves in consecrated rooms where only scripture was allowed (*The Contemplative Life* 25; F. H. Colson, *Philo IX* (Loeb), p. 127). The Hasidim, Abba Hilkiah and Hanina ben Dosa, are also depicted as retiring when they intended to pray, either to the flat roof of the house, or to the upper chamber (*bTaan.* 23b; *yBer.* v9d; *bBer.* 34b). As for fasting, in certain circumstances (e.g. drought or famine) it was a public act, a social duty regulated by Jewish law: 'They are forbidden to wash themselves, to anoint themselves, to wear sandals or to have marital intercourse; and the bath-houses are closed' (*mTaan.* 1.6). Jesus represents fasting as essentially an expression of personal piety.

34. Here again, a code of ethical behaviour composed for a community is replaced by an individual approach to morality. But as soon as Christianity became aware of its social dimensions, church rules came into existence and rapidly grew into a body of complex canon law.

35. On Qumran parallels, see Herbert Braun, *Qumran und das Neue Testament* I, 1966, pp. 23–24.

36. Bultmann, *The History of the Synoptic Tradition*, p. 166. Cf. H. Conzel-mann, *An Outline of the Theology of the New Testament*, 1969, pp. 102–04.

37. G. Dalman, *Die Worte Jesu*, pp. 231–33 (ET pp.282–85). On p. 233 (ET pp. 284–85) the saying is rendered into Aramaic.

38. W. D. Davies, *The Setting of the Sermon on the Mount*, pp. 206–7.

39. The embarrassing nature of the saying is revealed by its disappearance from Luke's discourse. Bultmann's hypothesis that the verse is extracted from a Jewish apocalypse and supplemented by a Christian editor (*The History of the Synoptic Tradition*, p. 123) is difficult to reconcile with ecclesiastical aims. 'An assertion of Jesus' ignorance is unlikely to have been created by the Church' (C. E. B. Cran-field, *The Gospel according to St Mark*, 1959, p. 410). Later church fathers (Jerome, Ambrose) declared the verse to be an Arian interpolation. Cf. E. Klostermann, *Das Markusevangelium*, ⁴1950, p. 138.

40. Again Bultmann characterizes the logion as 'a community product' (op. cit., p. 24), but the denial of Jesus' right to allocate seats in 'his' kingdom does not seem to be an invention of the church.

41. The image appears also in rabbinic literature. Mordecai's genealogy is traced to Qish and from this fact it is deduced by means of a pun that he 'knocked (*heqish*) on the gate of mercy' and it was opened to him (*bMeg.* 12b).

Total trust is the key element in the child-father context of the Gospel. In the parallel adult setting represented by the parable of the Prodigal son (Luke 15.18–24), the same attitude is linked to repentance-*teshuvah*. It is worth noticing that in an oft-quoted rabbinic parable attributed to the mid-second-century R. Meir, the initiative comes, not from the son, as in Jesus' version, but from the father. The son, though ashamed of his life of wickedness, lacks the confidence to return and confront his father. See *Dt. R.* 2.3 to Deut. 4.30; cf. Strack–Billerbeck II, p. 216; I Abrahams, *Studies in Pharisaism and the Gospels* I, 1917, p. 142; N. Perrin, *Rediscovering*, pp. 91, 95–96.

42. On the meaning of the Greek adjective *epiousios* and its Semitic substratum, see G. Dalman, *Die Worte Jesu*, pp. 321–34; W. Foerster, '*Epiousios*', *TDNT* II, pp. 590–99; M. Black, *An Aramaic Approach to the Gospels and Acts*, [3]1967, pp. 203–7. The fundamental teaching is that one prays for a single day's needs.

43. With all respect to J. Jeremias (*The Parables of Jesus*, pp. 157–59) and N. Perrin (*Rediscovering*, pp. 128–29), this is a better exegesis of the parable. According to them, it 'is not concerned with the importunity of the petitioner, but with the certainty that the petition will be granted' (Jeremias, p. 159).

44. Buber, *Two Types of Faith*, 1951, pp. 28–29.

45. 'A righteous man and dear to God' (*Ant.* xiv. 22).

46. On Honi, see *Jesus the Jew*, pp. 69–72.

47. The saying is based on the Balaam story (Num. 22.12 and 20) where God first refuses the prophet permission to accompany the envoys of Balak, but when he persists, allows him to go.

48. A warning against concern for material possessions is voiced in *Mekh.* on Ex. 13.17 (ed. Lauterbach I, p. 171). The Israelites were not led directly to Canaan so that they would not be immediately absorbed in their fields and vineyards. They were kept by God for forty years in the desert, miraculously provided there with food and drink, and were thus enabled to assimilate the Torah.

49. J. Jeremias's identification of the death mentioned in the parable as 'the approaching eschatological catastrophe' (*The Parables of Jesus*, p. 165) is quite unnecessary. The message has a timeless significance.

50. A similar counsel is given in the Talmud: 'Do not be anxious about the worry of the morrow for you do not know what the day will bring. For one may no longer exist tomorrow and he worries himself over a world (or "a day") that is no more' (*bSanh.* 100b).

51. Buber, *Two Types of Faith*, p. 76.

52. Cf. S. G. F. Brandon, *Jesus and the Zealots*, 1967; J. H. Yoder, *The Politics of Jesus*, 1972; Paul Lehmann, *The Transfiguration of Politics: Jesus Christ and the Question of Revolution*, 1975; Milan Machoveč, *A Marxist looks at Jesus*, 1976; Richard J. Cassidy, *Jesus, Politics and Society*, 1978.

53. I believe it worth mentioning that when I delivered the Riddell Memorial Lectures at the University of Newcastle in March 1981 this was the only remark to provoke audible disagreement in certain quarters of my audience. My questioning of the divinity of Jesus and the reality of his resurrection was received, by contrast, in stoical silence.

54. Wisdom/cunning (*phronēma*, *phronēsis* *phronimos*), the quality of the serpent in the Garden of Eden (Gen. 3.1), scarcely tallies with Jesus' spiritual ideal even when combined with the 'innocence' of a dove (Matt. 10.16). The saying may reflect an old Jewish proverb ascribed to Jesus by the Palestinian church. It has also been inserted into *Cant. R.* 2.14, 'The Holy One blessed be He said to Israel:

Towards me they are innocent like doves, but towards the nations of the world they are as crafty as serpents.'

55. It is curious that although J. Jeremias carefully examines details of the parable such as ancient Palestinian wedding customs, he has nothing to say about its moral aspect, maybe because it has no rôle to play in what he believes to be an 'eschatological crisis' story (*The Parables of Jesus*, pp. 171–75).

56. Search for the kingdom overrides family bonds; cf. below.

57. This is a rhetorical exaggeration: the coming of the kingdom of God being imminent, all attention must be centred on it. The dead will be looked after by the dead! To see in this logion a head-on clash between Jesus and the law and pious custom is, I believe, a complete misunderstanding of the gospel message, *pace* A. Schlatter, *Der Evangelist Matthäus*, 1929, p. 288; N. Perrin, *Rediscovering*, p. 144 and M. Hengel, *Nachfolge und Charisma. Eine exegetische-religionsgeschichtliche Studie zu Mt. 8:21f. und Jesu Ruf in die Nachfolge*, 1968, p. 16. Equally mistaken, in my opinion, is the exegesis interpreting 'the dead' metaphorically as 'the wicked' (cf. I Tim. 5.6 and *Gen. R.* 39.7). See Strack–Billerbeck I, p. 489; P. Joüon, *L'Evangile de Jésus-Christ*, 1930, p. 49. For a possible, though not very likely, mistranslation of Aramaic words, see M. Black, *An Aramaic Approach to the Gospels and Acts*, pp. 207–8.

58. The Copper Scroll from Qumran (3Q15) lists sixty-four locations of hidden treasure. Cf. J. T. Milik, *Discoveries in the Judaean Desert* III, 1962, pp. 284–99; *CDSSE*, pp. 583–89. Mishnaic civil law does not envisage the case alluded to in the Gospel, but it would be included in the category of a field purchased with 'all that is in it' (*mBB* 4.9).

59. According to J. Jeremias (*The Parables of Jesus*, pp. 200–201) and N. Perrin (*Rediscovering*, p. 89), the main emphasis is on joy, or surprise and joy, rather than on the man's determination to acquire the much-desired object at any price. But not only is such an interpretation contrary to the natural movement of the simile; it overlooks the fact that joy figures only in the story of the hidden treasure and not in that of the pearl. The sole element common to both parables is the sale of everything possessed in order to buy the field or the precious object. The same unreserved devotion inspires the widow to offer to God 'all that she had' (Mark 12.41–44 par.). Similarly, willingness to accept trials and difficulties – the taking up of one's cross (Mark 8.34 par.; Matt. 10.38; Luke 14.27) – is essential to the pursuit of the kingdom. For Jesus, this carrying of the cross symbolizes submission to the Father's will and not self-imposed mortification. He declares fasting at a wedding inappropriate. Indeed, no doubt because of his habit of attending banquets, he was spoken of as 'a glutton and a drunkard' by his opponents (Matt. 11.19; Luke 7.34).

60. Cf. S. Schechter, *Some Aspects of Rabbinic Theology*, 1909, pp. 199–205; A. Marmorstein, 'The Imitation of God (Imitatio Dei) in the Haggadah', *Studies in Jewish Theology*, 1950, pp. 106–21; M. Buber, 'Imitatio Dei', *Israel and the World*, 1963, pp. 66–77; Pamela Vermes, *Buber on God and the Perfect Man*, 1980, pp. 141–44.

61. *Mekh.* on Ex. 15.2 (ed. Lauterbach II, p. 25).

62. The fullest version of the rabbinic doctrine appears in the Talmud and the Palestinian Targum. 'R. Hama son of R. Hanina (third-century Palestinian sage) said: It is written "Follow the Lord, your God" (Deut. 13.5). How can a man

follow the Shekhinah? Is it not written, "The Lord, your God, is a devouring fire" (Deut. 4.24)? But follow the attributes of the Holy One blessed be He. As he clothes the naked . . . (Gen. 3.21) so you too must clothe the naked. The Holy One . . . visited the sick . . . (Gen. 18.1), so you too must visit the sick. The Holy One . . . comforted the mourners . . . (Gen. 25.11), so you too must comfort the mourners. The Holy One . . . buried the dead . . . (Deut. 34.6), so you too must bury the dead' (*bSot.* 14a). Cf. also *Ps. Jon.* on Deut. 34.6 on pp. 76–78 below. For a Christianized version of this doctrine, see Matt. 25.31–46. Cf. R. Bultmann, *The History of the Synoptic Tradition*, pp. 123–34.

63. I find Bultmann's assessment of this passage quite incomprehensible: 'This saying is much more akin to the grudging spirit of the last chapter of Eth. Enoch than to the preaching of Jesus' (*The History of the Synoptic Tradition*, p. 103).

64. For a select bibliography, see W. Klassen, 'Love in the NT', *IDBS*, p. 558. See also the monograph on the subject by John Piper, *'Love Your Enemies': Jesus' Love Commandment in the Synoptic Gospels and the Early Christian Paraenesis* (1979) with extensive bibliography, pp. 235–48.

65. Luke 14.26. The Matthean parallel reads: 'He who loves father and mother more than me is not worthy of me' (Matt. 10.37).

66. The real meaning seems simply to be: Do not hit back.

67. The contrast between the conduct of John the Baptist and that of Jesus is stressed by the evangelists. Whereas the ascetic John, while ready to exhort tax-collectors to act justly (Luke 3.12), remained socially aloof from them, Jesus took part in their rejoicings. Conventional Jews who criticized both John and Jesus are alluded to in the parable of children who blame their companions for refusing to join in any of their games (Matt. 11.16–19; Luke 7.31–34). The interpretation of the parable proposed by Jeremias (*The Parables of Jesus*, pp. 161–62) and Perrin (*Rediscovering*, pp. 85–86) following F. F. Bishop (*Jesus of Palestine*, 1955, p. 104), appears to be a complete distortion of the obvious meaning of Matt. 11.17; Luke 7.32.

68. Enlightened Jews such as Martin Buber are fully aware of this distinction: 'Christianity – by which I do not mean the teaching of Jesus . . .' (M. Buber, *Israel and the World – Essays in a Time of Crisis*, ²1963, p. 178).

69. C. H. Dodd, *The Founder of Christianity*, 1970.

70. See for example Martin Buber, *Two Types of Faith*, 1951.

71. For rabbinic association of dogs and Gentiles, see *tYom Tov* 2.6; *bMeg.* 7b. Cf. Strack–Billerbeck I, pp. 724–25.

72. Regarding the hypothesis that 'holy thing' (*to hagion*) is a mistranslation of the Aramaic *q'dasha* (ring), confused with *qudsha* (holiness), see M. Black, *An Aramaic Approach³*, pp. 200–02; J. A. Fitzmyer, *A Wandering Aramean*, 1979, pp. 14–15 and p. 73 below.

73. For the metaphor, 'swine' = Gentiles, see *Gen. R.* 44.22; *bShab.* 155b. In I Enoch 89.12 the black boar refers to the detested Esau/Edom.

74. For an attempt at conciliation, see W. D. Davies, *The Setting of the Sermon on the Mount*, 1964, pp. 326, 331.

75. This is one of the universalistic features of Matthew. Cf. W. D. Davies, *The Setting of the Sermon on the Mount*, pp. 327–30. Since, as has been suggested earlier (p. 20), the particular and the universal stand can hardly reflect the mind of

the same person, it is more likely that the latter derives from editorial activity in a Church open to Jews as well as to Gentiles.

76. On the Church's representation of itself as the true Israel, see in particular Marcel Simon, *Verus Israel*, ²1964.

77. See also Rom. 7.5–6: 'While we were living in the flesh our sinful passions, aroused by the Law, were at work in our members to bear fruit of death. But now we are discharged from the Law, dead to that which held us captive, so that we serve not under the old written code but in the new life of the spirit.'

78. Cf. above, pp. 34–35, 46.

79. Cf. e.g. Rom. 7.21–25.

80. Thanks to the redemption achieved by the real Son, the believer is granted the title of adopted son.

81. On the few, equivocal, New Testament passages applying the word 'God' to Jesus, see O. Cullmann, *The Christology of the New Testament*, 1959, pp. 306–14. How such an evolution could have occurred in connection with a teacher who not only protested against being called 'good' since 'No one is good but God alone' (Mark 10.18), but for whom the twice-daily recitation of the *Shema*' ('Hear O Israel, the Lord our God is *One* Lord') was the cornerstone of religion (Mark 12.29–30), remains for the historian the most disconcerting feature of all in the formation of Christianity.

5. Jewish Studies and New Testament Interpretation

Originally published in *JJS*, vol. XXI, no. 1, 1980, pp. 1–17.

1. Wellhausen, 'Jesus war kein Christ, sondern Jude', *Einleitung in die drei ersten Evangelien*, 1905, p. 113.

2. The most penetrating study of the Judaeo-Christian conflict is that by Marcel Simon, *Verus Israel*, Paris ²1964 (ET, 1986). See also James Parkes, *The Conflict of the Church and the Synagogue*, 1934, 1961.

3. Among recent publications see N. R. M. de Lange, *Origen and the Jews*, Cambridge 1976, and J. N. D. Kelly, *Jerome: His Life, Writings and Controversies*, 1975.

4. 'Memini me . . . Lyddaeum quemdam praeceptorem . . . non parvis redemisse nummis'; *Praef. in Iob*, PL XXVIII, 1140.

5. Jerome, *Comm. in Ezech.* 24.15, PL XXV, 230; *Comm. in Matth.* 23.5, PL XXVI, 174.

6. Cf. O. S. Rankin, *Jewish Religious Polemic*, 1956; B. Blumenkranz, *Juifs et chrétiens dans le monde occidental*, 1960; *Les auteurs chrétiens latins du moyen âge sur les juifs et le judaïsme*, 1963; K. H. Rengstorf – S. von Kortzfleisch, *Kirche und Synagoge* I–II, 1968; F. E. Talmage, *Disputation and Dialogue: Readings in Jewish–Christian Encounter*, 1975.

7. Raymundus Martini, *Pugio fidei adversus Mauros et Iudaeos*, 1687, reprinted 1967.

8. Cf. H. H. Ben-Sasson, 'Disputations and Polemics', *Enc. Jud.* 6, pp. 79–103.

9. Ioh. Christophorus Wagenseilius, *Tela ignea Satanae*, 1681, reprinted 1970.

10. Out of respect towards a highly praised senior scholar, I will keep his identity undisclosed. The quotation appears in a book published in 1965.

11. J. J. Wettstein, *Novum Testamentum graece* I–II, 1751–2.

12. A. Souter, *Text and Canon of the New Testament*, 1913, p. 99.

13. G. F. Moore, 'Christian Writers on Judaism', *HTR* 14, 1921, p. 221.

14. R. Laurence, *Libri Enoch prophetae versio aethiopica*, 1838; A. Dillmann, *Liber Jubilaeorum aethiopice*, 1859.

15. This work first appeared in 1874 under the title, *Lehrbuch der neutestamentlichen Zeitgeschichte*; a second edition, renamed *Geschichte des jüdischen Volkes im Zeitalter Jesu Christi*, was published between 1886 and 1890, and a third/fourth edition followed (1901–1909). Three volumes of a fully revised and modernized English edition have been issued by Geza Vermes, Fergus Millar and Martin Goodman, with Pamela Vermes as literary editor, under the title *The History of the Jewish People in the Age of Jesus Christ*, 1973, 1979, 1986–87 (*History*). A third volume with an index is in preparation.

16. Ferdinand Weber, *System der altsynagogalen palästinischen Theologie aus Targum, Midrasch und Talmud dargestellt*, 1880. A second edition appeared under the title, *Jüdische Theologie auf Grund des Talmud und verwandter Schriften gemeinfasslich dargestellt*, 1897.

17. E. Kautzsch, *Die Apokryphen und Pseudepigraphen des Alten Testaments* I–II, Tübingen 1900.

18. R. H. Charles, *The Apocrypha and Pseudepigrapha of the Old Testament* I–II, Oxford 1912–13. For a more recent anthology, see J. H. Charlesworth (ed.), *Old Testament Pseudepigrapha* I–II, 1983, 1985.

19. The latter requirement no longer applies to one of the works as it has since been translated into bad English.

20. H. L. Strack – P. Billerbeck, *Kommentar zum Neuen Testament aus Talmud und Midrasch* I–IV, 1922–28. Two further volumes of indices were compiled and published in 1956 and 1960 by Joachim Jeremias and Kurt Adolph.

21. Gerhard Kittel, *Theologisches Wörterbuch zum Neuen Testament* I–X, Stuttgart 1933–76; ET by G. W. Bromiley, *Theological Dictionary of the New Testament* I–X, 1964–76.

22. Stephen Neill, *The Interpretation of the New Testament 1861–1961*, 1964, p. 292.

23. Julius Wellhausen, *Israelitische und jüdische Geschichte*, [8]1958, p. 193.

24. Cf. note 16 above. The quotation is taken from the 1897 edition p. xiii.

25. In the English revised version vol. II, § 27 is restyled as 'Life and the Law', and the contents are thoroughly cleansed.

26. E. P. Sanders, *Paul and Palestinian Judaism*, 1976, pp. 234–5.

27. For a severe criticism of the linguistic misconceptions in this Dictionary, see J. Barr, *The Semantics of Biblical Language*, 1961, pp. 206–62.

28. Martin Buber, *Der Jude und sein Judentum*, 1963, pp. 621–4. For an English version see Talmage, *Disputation and Dialogue*, pp. 49–54.

29. Martin Buber, *Briefwechsel aus sieben Jahrzehnten. II (1918–1938)*, 1972, p. 499.

30. G. Kittel, 'Die Entstehung des Judentums und die Entstehung der

Judenfrage', *Forschungen sur Judenfrage* 1, 1937; 'Das Konnubium mit den Nicht-Juden im antiken Judentum', ibid., 2, 1937; 'Die ältesten Judenkarikaturen', ibid., 4, 1940; 'Die Ausbreitung des Judentums bis zum Beginn des Mittelalters', ibid., 5, 1941; 8, 1944; 'Das antike Weltjudentum', ibid., 7, 1943. See also 'Die historische Voraussetzung der jüdischen Rassenmischung', *Schriften des Reichsinstituts für Geschichte des neuen Deutschland*, 1939.

31. On anti-Jewish utterances in modern theological literature see Charlotte Klein, *Theologie und Anti-Judaismus*, 1975. ET *Anti-Judaism in Christian Theology*, 1978.

32. Jules Isaac, *Jésus et Israël*, Paris 1946.

33. Paul Winter, *On the Trial of Jesus*, Berlin 1961. A second (posthumous) edition was issued by T. A. Burkill and G. Vermes, 1974.

34. For the latest general introduction to the Scrolls see G. Vermes, *An Introduction to the Complete Dead Sea Scrolls*, 1999, 2000. A handy translation of the non-biblical texts may be found in G. Vermes, *The Complete Dead Sea Scrolls in English*, 1998.

35. A. Dupont-Sommer, *Aperçus préliminaires sur les manuscrits de la Mer Morte*, 1950. ET *The Dead Sea Scrolls. A Preliminary Survey*, Oxford 1952; *Nouveaux aperçus sur les manuscrits de la Mer Morte*, 1953. ET *The Jewish Sect of Qumran and the Essenes*, 1954.

36. J. L. Teicher in a series of articles published in *JJS*, vol. 2, 1951 onwards.

37. For detailed bibliographical information see the relevant sections in B. Jongeling, *A Classified Bibliography of the Finds in the Desert of Judah: 1958–1969*, 1971; J. A. Fitzmyer, *The Dead Sea Scrolls. Major Publications and Tools for Study*, ²1977, 1990; F. Garcia Martinez and D. W. Parry, *A Bibliography of the Finds in the Desert of Judah 1970–1995*, 1996.

38. On Qumran messianic doctrine see *History* II, pp. 489–92, 550–54.

39. See in particular J. A. Fitzmyer. 'The Contribution of Qumran Aramaic to the Study of the New Testament', *NTS* 20, 1974, pp. 382–407; 'Methodology in the Study of Jesus' Sayings in the New Testament', *Jésus aux origines de la christologie*, ed. J. Dupont, 1975, pp. 73–102.

40. For a reasonably up-to-date introduction to the rabbinic literature including the Targums see *History* I, pp. 68–118. B. Grossfeld, *A Bibliography of Targum Literature* I–II, 1972–77.

41. The Aramaic text with Spanish, French and English translations has now been edited in full by A. Díez Macho, *Neophyti I. Targum Palestinense MS de la Biblioteca Vaticana* I–VI, 1968–79. For a French translation with introduction and notes of Targum Neofiti and Targum Ps.-Jonathan see R. Le Déaut and J. Robert, *Targum du Pentateuque* I–V, 1978–81.

42. For a full exposition see Z. W. Falk, *Introduction to Jewish Law in the Second Commonwealth* II, 1978, pp. 307–16. A brief discussion may be found in G. Vermes, *Post-Biblical Jewish Studies*, 1975, pp. 65–67. Cf. also J. A. Fitzmyer, 'The Matthean Divorce Texts and some new Palestinian Evidence', *Theological Studies* 37, 1976, pp. 197–226.

43. See D. Daube, *The New Testament and Rabbinic Judaism*, 1956, pp. 365–68; for an argument in the opposite direction cf. J. D. M. Derrett, *Law in the New Testament*, 1979, pp. 362–88. According to Josephus, when Herod's sister, Salome, despatched a document (*grammateion*) to her husband to dissolve their marriage,

she acted against the law of the Jews. 'For only a man is allowed among us to do this' (*Ant.* XV, 259).

44. Cf. *History* II, p. 321.

45. See Vermes, *Jesus the Jew*, pp. 192–222.

46. J. Barr puts forcefully the same ideas in his criticism of Kittel's Dictionary: 'It could be argued that this emphasis upon the Hebraic background of ideas may indeed have been present in the minds of instructed Jews like St Paul, but that the words which had this series of associations for him could for the most part be *understood* by Gentile Christian hearers especially by the less instructed among them, in the normal Hellenistic sense of the words.' *Semantics of Biblical Language*, p. 250.

47. This is a two-year course entailing a written examination which consists of a general paper (Jewish literature, history, and institutions from 200 BC to AD 425) and three further papers chosen from the following topics: Jewish historiography, Jewish law, Jewish Bible interpretation, Jewish eschatology, Jewish liturgy, Jewish wisdom literature. The topics are studied from prescribed texts in Hebrew, Aramaic and Greek. Candidates must also submit a short thesis (30,000 words) on an approved subject. (Since 1983, a simplified one-year course, qualifying for a Master of Studies (MSt) degree, is also available.)

6. *Jewish Literature and New Testament Exegesis*

Delivered as the presidential address at the first Congress of the European Association for Jewish Studies at Hertford College, Oxford on 19 July 1982. Published in *JJS*, vol. XXXIII, no. 2, 1982, pp. 361–76.

1. See above pp. 53, 67.

2. Cf. Martin Hengel, *Judaism and Hellenism*, 1974, pp. 104–5; see above p. 24–25.

3. Cf. above p. 65.

4. The subsequent outline partly relies on evidence adduced in the previous chapter.

5. Cf. above p. 54.

6. Atque hinc aeque indubitanter a me conclusum est etiam secundo, quod in locis istius Testamenti obscurioribus (quae sunt quamplurima) optimus & summe genuinus sensum eruendi modus est inquirendo, quomodo & quonam sensu intellectae sunt istae phraseologiae & locutiones, secundum vulgarem & communem gentis istius dialectum et sententiam, et ab iis quae eas protulerunt, & ab auditoribus. Non enim valet, quid nos de istiusmodi locutionibus a conceptus nostri incude fingere possimus; sed quid illae apud eos sonuerint vulgari sermone. Quod cum nullo alio modo perquiri possit, quam auctores Talmudicos consulendo; qui et vulgari loquuntur Judaeorum dialecto; atque omnia Judaica tractant & patefaciunt. Johannis Lightfooti, *Horae Hebraicae et Talmudicae in Quatuor Evangelistas*, Lipsiae MDCLXXV (*In Evangelium Matthaei*) 173–74.

7. Strack–Billerbeck, vols I–IV, 1922–28.

8. Kittel, vols I–X, 1933–76; ET vols I–X, 1964–76.

9. First published in 1883 and revised in 1915.

10. *TDNT*, vol. X, p. 649.

11. On the Targums see *History* I, pp. 99–114.

12. P. Kahle, *Masoreten des Westens* II, 1930.

13. *Neophyti 1. Targum Palestinense MS de la Biblioteca Vaticana* I–VI, 1968–79.

14. First issued in Oxford in 1946 and subsequently revised and re-edited in 1954 and 1967.

15. For an introduction see G. Vermes, *An Introduction to the Complete Dead Sea Scrolls*, 1999, 2000.

16. His most important papers have been assembled in *A Wandering Aramean: Collected Aramaic Essays*, Missoula 1979. See also 'The Aramaic Language and the Study of the New Testament', *JBL* 99, 1980, pp. 5–21.

17. Fitzmyer, *A Wandering Aramean*, p. 8.

18. Ibid., p. 86.

19. Ibid., p. 96.

20. See my comments in *JTS* 31, 1980, pp. 581–82.

21. Joseph A. Fitzmyer and Daniel J. Harrington, *A Manual of Palestinian Aramaic Texts*, 1978. For my review see *JTS* 31, 1980, pp. 580–82.

22. *Manual*, p. xii.

23. M. Black, *An Aramaic Approach to the Gospels and Acts*, [3]1967, p. 139.

24. Fitzmyer, *A Wandering Aramean*, p. 11.

25. Josephus, *Contra Apionem* i, 167.

26. Of course this remark does not apply to the Greek transliteration *korbanas* or *korbōnas* used in the sense of Temple treasury in Matt. 27.6 and expressly interpreted as *hieros thēsauros* by Josephus (*Ant.* ii, 175).

27. Cf. B. Mazar, *Eretz-Israel* 9, Albright Volume, 1969, pp. 168–70.

28. Black, *Aramaic Approach*, pp. 139–40.

29. *IQS* 6.2; *IQ*27 ii, 5 (*DJD* I.105); *CD* 14.20.

30. Fitzmyer, *A Wandering Aramean*, p. 12, reproducing 'Methodology in the Study of the Aramaic Substratum of Jesus' Sayings in the New Testament' from *Jésus aux origines de la christologie*, ed. J. Dupont, 1975.

31. J. P. M. van der Ploeg et al., *Le Targum de Job de la grotte XI de Qumrân*, Leiden 1971, col. XI, 8, p. 32. Reproduced in *Manual*, p. 20.

32. See *Manual*, p. 327.

33. *A Wandering Aramean*, p. 13.

34. See below pp. 81, 90.

35. Fitzmyer, 'Another View of the Son of Man Debate', *JSNT*, 1979, pp. 58–68. Cf. also 'The Aramaic Language and the Study of the New Testament', *JBL* 99, 1980, pp. 5–21.

36. 'Another View', p. 65.

37. Ibid., p. 59.

38. *A Wandering Aramean*, p. 15.

39. A similar criticism applies to Professor Fitzmyer's comments on *ma'ʾmara – memra*, ibid., pp. 94–95.

40. See *Manual*, p. xii. For Fitzmyer's comments on my criticisms, see his 'Problems of the Semitic Background of the NT', in *The Yahweh–Baal Confrontation*, 1995, pp. 86–93.

41. See Vermes, *Post-Biblical Jewish Studies*, pp. 121–24.

42. Cf. above p. 57, n. 16.
43. See also above p. 161, n. 41.
44. Bultmann, *The History of the Synoptic Tradition*, 1963, pp. 69–108.
45. Jeremias, *The Parables of Jesus*, ³1972.
46. Cf. above Chapter 4, n. 41, pp. 161–62.
47. See for instance, P. R. Davies and B. D. Chilton, 'The Aqedah: A Revised Tradition History', *CBQ* 40, 1978, pp. 515, 517. Cf. below, pp. 109–13.
48. Cf. Matt. 19.28; Luke 22.30; James 1.1.
49. See e.g., *1QS* 8; *1QM* 2 etc.
50. Cf. *1QpHab* 7; II Peter 3 etc.
51. See Mark 2.5–7 par.; *4QPrNab* fr. 1–4. Cf. above p. 9.
52. For further discussions, see Robert Hayward, 'The Present State of Research into the Targumic Account of the Sacrifice of Isaac', *JJS* 32, 1981, pp. 127–50; James Swetnam, *Jesus and Isaac: A Study of the Epistle to the Hebrews in the Light of the Aqedah*, 1981.
53. Cf. above pp. 47–48 and 163, notes 60–62.
54. *Mekh.* in loc. (ed. Lauterbach II, 25). Abba Shaul sees in 'I (man) and He (God)' a mystical correspondence demanding that man should model his actions on the conduct of his Creator.
55. This is an illustrated reworking of the problem first raised in *JTS* 31, 1980, p. 582.
56. S. Safrai et al. (eds), *Compendia Rerum Iudaicarum ad Novum Testamentum. Section One. The Jewish People in the First Century* I–II, 1974, 1976.
57. Cf. above pp. 64, 65.
58. Strack–Billerbeck, I, pp. 513–14.
59. *DJD* II, 1961, no. 19, pp. 104–9.
60. As is well known, the original Schürer – and the revised English version does not differ from it in this respect devotes only two chapters to religious ideas: 'Life and the Law' and 'Messianism'; cf, *History* II, pp. 464–554.

7. The Present State of the 'Son of Man' Debate

An expanded version of a paper read at the Sixth International Congress of Biblical Studies in the Examination Schools at Oxford on 6 April 1978. Published in *JJS* vol. XXIX, no. 2, 1978, pp. 123–34.

1. See 'Appendix E' in Matthew Black, *An Aramaic Approach to the Gospels and Acts*, pp. 310–28, reprinted with an additional footnote in my *Post-biblical Jewish Studies*, pp. 147–65. For an abridged presentation of the evidence, see *Jesus the Jew* pp. 163–68, 188–91.
2. F. Hahn, *The Titles of Jesus in Christology*, 1969, p. 15.
3. F. H. Borsch, *The Son of Man in Myth and History*, 1967, p. 22.
4. Carsten Colpe, article on *huios tou anthrōpou*, *TWNT* VIII, p. 406, *TDNT* VIII, p. 404.
5. This view is reiterated by C. F. D. Moule, *The Origin of Christology*, 1977, p. 13, with special reference to Dan. 7.13, a matter to be considered presently. Cf. note 17 below.

6. Cf. *Jesus the Jew*, pp. 162, 256 n. 8.

7. Meyer, *Jesu Muttersprache*, 1896.

8. Lietzmann, *Der Menschensohn*, 1896.

9. Dalman, *Die Worte Jesu*, Leipzig 1898, ²1930. ET *The Words of Jesus*, 1909.

10. Fiebig, *Der Menschensohn*, 1901.

11. Campbell, 'The Origin and Meaning of the Term Son of Man', *JTS* 48, 1947, pp. 145–55.

12. Bowman, 'The Background of the Term "Son of Man"', *Expository Times* 59, 1947/48, pp. 283–88.

13. Black, '"The Son of Man" in the Teaching of Jesus', *Expository Times* 60, 1948/49, pp. 32–36.

14. Sjöberg, '*Ben 'adam und bar 'enash* im Hebräischen und Aramäischen', *Acta Orientalia* 21, 1950/51, pp. 57–65, 91–107.

15. Rejected by Lietzmann and Sjöberg, the circumlocutional use has been advocated by Meyer, Campbell and Black among the authors cited, and also by P. Joüon, *L'évangile de Notre-Seigneur Jésus-Christ*, 1930, p. 604, and later on by R. E. C. Formesyn, 'Was there a Pronominal Connection for the Bar Nasha Self-designation?', *NT* 8, 1966, pp. 1–35. However, apart from M. Black, none of these writers has felt it necessary to look for Aramaic instances. Since the self-reference theory has never ceased to have its partisans, it seems odd that Simon Légasse should be 'un peu surpris' by my attempt at 'reviving' it. Cf. 'Jésus historique et le Fils de l'Homme: Aperçus sur les opinions contemporaines', *Apocalypse et théologie de l'espérance*, 1977, pp. 273–4. The titular use has been maintained by Dalman, Bowman, Black and Sjöberg, but denied by Lietzmann and Campbell.

16. *Jesus the Jew*, p. 177.

17. *An Aramaic Approach*, pp. 327–28; *Post-biblical Jewish Studies*, p. 164; *Jesus the Jew*, pp. 171–72. It is on this point that the philologists and theologians appear unable to find a common language. For example, in his highly praised book, *The Origin of Christology*, C. F. D. Moule argues that the definite article used in the New Testament indicates that the phrase is 'demonstrative' because it expressly refers to 'Daniel's Son of Man' (p. 13). He is aware that his statement is contrary to the findings of Aramaic scholars who, in Professor Moule's words, claim it to be 'a mistake to assume that the Greek phrase with the definite article, *ho huios tou anthrōpou*, could have reflected a distinctively demonstrative form in the original language of Jesus'. 'This', he adds, '(though I am not an Aramaist) I would venture to challenge. I cannot believe that it was impossible to find a phrase that would unequivocally mean "the Son of Man" or "*the* Son of Man"' (p. 15). For a fuller exposition of his theory, see 'Neglected Features in the Problem of "the Son of Man"', *Neues Testament und Kirche* (für Rudolf Schnackenburg), ed. J. Gnilka, 1974, pp. 413–28.

18. E.g., 'Whoever says, "Here are five (pieces of money), give me something worth three" is a fool. But he who speaks thus, "Here are three (pieces of money), give me something worth five" is a *bar nash*' (*ySanh.* 26b).

19. Borsch, *The Son of Man in Myth and History*, p. 23, n. 4.

20. Colpe, article on *huios tou anthrōpou*, *TWNT* VIII, p. 406, *TDNT*, VIII, pp. 403–04. Cf. also A. Polag, *Die Christologie der Logienquelle*, 1977, pp. 104–5.

21. Jeremias, 'Die älteste Schicht der Menschensohn-Logien', *ZNW* 58, 1967,

p. 165 and n. 9. These early reactions to a study which appeared at the end of 1967 are attributable to the fact that already in 1966 a large number of advance off-prints were despatched to interested scholars, a matter explicitly mentioned by Jeremias.

22. *Ekhah Rabbati* 1.5 (ed. Buber, p. 67).

23. Bowker, 'The Son of Man', *JTS* NS 28, 1977, pp. 19–48.

24. Ibid., pp. 31–32. The text quoted is *yBer.* 5b. See *An Aramaic Approach*, p. 323; *Post-biblical Jewish Studies*, p. 160.

25. Casey, 'The Son of Man Problem', *ZNW* 67, 1976, pp. 147–54.

26. Ibid., p. 149.

27. R. Bultmann, *Theologie des Neuen Testaments*, ⁵1965, pp. 30–32; H. Conzelmann, *An Outline of the Theology of the New Testament*, 1969, p. 135, etc.

28. Review of *An Aramaic Approach* in *CBQ* 30, 1968, pp. 417–28; esp. pp. 424–28; 'The Contribution of Qumran Aramaic to the Study of the New Testament', *NTS* 20, 1974, pp. 382–407; 'Methodology in the Study of Jesus' Sayings in the New Testament', *Jésus aux origines de la christologie*, ed. J. Dupont, 1975, pp. 73–102.

29. Fitzmyer, art. cit., *CBQ*, p. 427.

30. Fitzmyer, art. cit., *NTS*, p. 397, n. 1. For his later opinion see above pp. 73–74.

31. Fitzmyer, art. cit., *CBQ*, p. 420.

32. Fitzmyer, 'Methodology', p. 85, n. 44.

33. Cf. G. Dalman, *Grammatik des jüdisch-palästinischen Aramäisch*, ²1905, pp. 57–58, 96–99.

34. Luke 16.20 etc.; John 11.1 etc.

35. *Jesus the Jew*, pp. 190–91, 261.

36. Fitzmyer, 'Methodology', p. 93, n. 69.

37. *BJ* v. 567: *Mannaios ho Lazarou*.

38. P. Thomsen, 'Die lateinischen und griechischen Inschriften der Stadt Jerusalem und ihrer nächsten Umgebung', *ZDPV* 44, 1921, no. 199, p. 118: *Lazarou*.

39. See for instance, the *Textkritischer Anhang* compiled by E. Güting in his edition of the tractate *Terumot (Priesterheben)* in *Die Mischna*, ed. K. H. Rengstorf and L. Rost, 1969, pp. 192–220.

40. Cf. P. Thomsen, art. cit., p. 113. The legitimacy of the use of these inscriptions is admitted by Fitzmyer, art. cit., *CBQ*, p. 420.

41. J.-B. Frey, *Corpus Inscriptionum Iudaicarum (=CII)* II no. 1296, 1952, p. 283.

42. *CII*, no. 1309, p. 290. The patronym is missing.

43. *CII*, no. 1337, p. 298. It is worth observing that not only the *aleph* but even the '*ayin*, is omitted. Nevertheless the shortening is not reflected in Greek.

44. This was already noted in *Jesus the Jew*, pp. 190–91, 261.

45. Dalman, op. cit., p. 97. For instance, *na* for '*ana*, *nan* for '*anan*, *tun* for '*attun*, *mar* for '*amar*, *nash* for '*enash*, *ta* for '*etha*. Apropos of the last example it should be remarked that if Fitzmyer's methodological principle were applied to I Cor. 16.14, the reading *Marana tha* (Come, our lord!) would not be permissible because of the missing *aleph*, for the imperative of the verb is spelt as '*etho* in Dan. 3.26. Yet cf. Fitzmyer, *Jerome Bible*, 1977, pp. 275, 812.

46. See 6Q8 8, line 1 in *DJD*, III, 1962, p. 118; Mur 19, lines 10, 24 in *DJD*, II, 1961, p. 105.

47. See Mur 18, line 3 (*DJD* II, p. 101).
48. Ibid., p. 103.
49. Cullmann, *The Christology of the New Testament*, 1959, p. 150. The original German edition appeared in 1957.
50. Tödt, *The Son of Man in the Synoptic Tradition*, 1965, p. 22. The German original was published in 1959.
51. Hahn, *The Titles of Jesus in Christology*, p. 20. The German text was issued in 1963.
52. Perrin, *Rediscovering the Teaching of Jesus*, pp. 164–73.
53. Leivestad in *Annual of the Swedish Theological Institute* 6, 1968, pp. 49–105.
54. Leivestad, 'Exit the Apocalyptic Son of Man', *NTS* 18, 1972, pp. 243–67.
55. Ibid., p. 244.
56. Winter, *Deutsche Literaturzeitung* 89, 1968, col. 784.
57. Hooker, *The Son of Man in Mark*, London 1967, p. 48.
58. Fitzmyer, art. cit., *CBQ*, p. 428.
59. See in particular his paper, 'Problèmes de la littérature hénochique à la lumière des fragments araméens de Qumrân', *HTR* 64, 1971, pp. 333–78, and above all, his edition of *The Books of Enoch. Aramaic Fragments of Qumran Cave 4*, Oxford 1976. Note in this respect Fitzmyer's changing opinions. 'If Milik's latest theory ... proves to be acceptable ... then the whole question of the conflated titles in the second part of I Enoch, including the "Son of Man", must be re-worked in the discussions of the material regarding the title as used by Jesus', *NTS*, 1974, p. 397. 'If ... Milik is correct ... we can no longer look to the second part of Enoch ... the so-called Similitudes, for the titular use of "Son of Man"', 'Methodology', 1975, p. 94.
60. Ullendorff, *Ethiopia and the Bible*, 1968, p. 61.
61. *Jesus the Jew*, pp. 169, 257–60.
62. Milik, *The Books of Enoch*, pp. 91–96.
63. Cf. *Jesus the Jew*, p. 176 and my recent volume, *An Introduction to the Complete Dead Sea Scrolls*, pp. 182, 234. M. Black, 'The Throne-Theophany, Prophetic Commission and the "Son of Man"', *Jews, Greeks and Christians, Religious Cultures in Late Antiquity. Essays in Honor of W. D. Davies*, ed. R. Hammerton-Kelly and R. Scroggs, 1975, p. 68.
64. Lindars, 'Re-enter the Apocalyptic Son of Man', *NTS* 22, 1975, p. 52.
65. Casey, in *JSJ* 7, 1976, p. 29.
66. Perrin, 'Son of Man', *IDBS*, 1976, p. 883.
67. Bowker, art. cit., *JTS*, p. 26.
68. Brown, 'The Son of Man: "This Fellow"', *Biblica* 58, 1977, p. 367.
69. *Jesus und der Menschensohn* (Anton Vögtle Festschrift), ed. R. Pesch and R. Schnackenburg, Freiburg 1975. Another tendency to evade the problem begins to show itself. 'It cannot be our purpose', writes J. D. Kingsbury, 'to ascertain what *bar nasha* may have meant to the historical Jesus. But as for Matthew, we believe that he does indeed construe the term *ho huios tou anthrōpou* as a christological title and not merely as a circumlocution for the personal pronoun.' *Matthew: Structure, Christology, Kingdom*, 1976, p. 118. Cf. also Fitzmyer, 'Methodology', pp. 93–94.
70. *Jesus the Jew*, pp. 177–86, 260–61.
71. C. H. Dodd, *The Founder of Christianity*, 1970, pp. 119–21, 184.

72. Roloff, *Das Kerygma und der irdische Jesus*, 1970, pp. 61–62 and n. 38. Cf. also Richard N. Longenecker, *The Christology of Early Jewish Christianity*, 1970, pp. 85 86.

73. Lindars, art. cit., *NTS*, p. 53.

74. Ibid., p. 54.

75. Ibid.

76. Bowker, art. cit., p. 44.

77. The interpretation put forward by C. F. D. Moule is in some ways akin to that of Bowker. Its literary Achilles heel, in addition to the philological weakness mentioned in n. 17 above, is exposed by Professor Moule himself: 'No doubt the position I have presented would stand more securely if, in each several strand of the Gospel traditions . . . "the Son of Man" carried all the associations of suffering, vindication and judgement simultaneously, and if Dan. 7 were more specifically cited in the Son of Man sayings.' *The Origin of Christology*, p. 19.

78. This translation has been directed by Luis Alonso Schökel and Juan Mateos and issued under the imprint of the Madrid publishing house, Cristianidad.

79. Attached to Matt. 8.20, we find a footnote indicating the translators' point of view but keeping other options open: '"este Hombre", lit. "el Hijo del hombre", locución aramea para designar a un individuo; a veces, alusión a la "figura humana" de Dn 7.13' (p. 1505).

80. The text of the original lecture was published under the title, 'The "son of man" Debate' in *JSNT* 1, 1978, pp. 19–32 and a rejoinder from J. A. Fitzmyer appeared in the following year: 'Another View of the "Son of Man" Debate', *JSNT* 4, 1979, pp. 58–68. See above p. 73.

The argument continues and the following studies have been published since 1978: J. A. Fitzmyer, *A Wandering Aramean: Collected Aramaic Essays*, Missoula 1979; M. D. Hooker, 'Is the Son of Man Problem really insoluble?', *Text and Interpretation*, ed. E. Best and R. McL. Wilson, 1979, pp. 155–68; Maurice Casey, *Son of Man: The Interpretation and Influence of Daniel 7*, 1979; Barnabas Lindars, 'Jesus as Advocate: A Contribution to the Christology Debate', *Bulletin of the John Rylands Library* 62, 1979–80, pp. 476–97; A. J. B. Higgins, *The Son of Man in the Teaching of Jesus*, 1980; James D. G. Dunn, *Christology in the Making: A New Testament Inquiry into the Origins of the Doctrine of the Incarnation*, 1980, pp. 65–97; Francis J. Moloney, 'The Reinterpretation of Psalm VIII and the Son of Man Debate', *NTS* 27, 1981, pp. 656–72; Barnabas Lindars, 'The New Look on the Son of Man', *Bulletin of the John Rylands Library* 63, 1980–81, pp. 437–62; Joseph Coppens, *Le Fils de l'Homme néotestamentaire*, 1981; F. F. Bruce, 'The Background of the Son of Man Sayings', *Christ the Lord: Studies in Christology presented to Donald Guthrie*, 1982, pp. 50–70; Ragnar Leivestad, 'Jesus – Messias – Menschensohn', *Aufstieg und Niedergang der römischen Welt* II, 25/1, 1982, pp. 221–64; Hans Bietenhard, 'Der Menschensohn', ibid., pp. 265–350; Joseph Coppens, *Le Fils de l'Homme vetéro-et intertestamentaire*, 1983; Barnabas Lindars, *Jesus, Son of Man*, 1983; C. C. Caragounis, *The Son of Man*, 1983; W. Horbury, 'The Messianic associations of "The Son of Man"', *JTS* 36 (1985); J. J. Collins, *Daniel*, Minneapolis, 1993, pp. 304–12; G. Vermes, 'Qumran Forum Miscellanea I' (The 'Son of God' fragment [4Q521]), *JJS* 43 (1992), 301–3; *The Changing Faces of Jesus* (2001), see index.

8. *The Jesus Notice of Josephus Re-examined*

Originally published in *JJS* vol. XXXVIII, no. 1, 1987, pp. 1–10.

1. F. C. Burkitt, 'Josephus and Christ', *Theologisch Tijdschrift* 47, 1913, pp. 135–44.

2. A. von Harnack, 'Der jüdische Geschichtsschreiber Josephus und Jesus Christus', *Internationale Monatsschrift für Wissenschaft, Kunst und Technik* 7, 1913, pp. 1037–68.

3. B. Niese, *De testimonio Christiano quod est apud Josephum ant. Iud. XVIII, 63 sq disputatio*, 1893/4.

4. E. Schürer, *Geschichte des jüdischen Volkes im Zeitalter Jesu Christi* I ³1901, pp. 544–9.

5. E. Norden, 'Josephus und Tacitus über Jesus Christus und eine messianische Prophetie', *Neue Jahrbücher für das klassische Altertum, Geschichte und Literatur* 16, 1913, pp. 637–66; reprinted in A. Schalit (ed.), *Zur Josephus-Forschung*, 1973, pp. 27–69.

6. J. Juster, *Les juifs dans l'empire romain* II, 1914, pp. 127–69.

7. E. Meyer, *Ursprung und Anfänge des Christentums* I, 1921, pp. 206–11.

8. S. Zeitlin, 'The Christ Passage in Josephus', *JQR* NS 18, 1927/8, pp. 231–55.

9. Th. Reinach, 'Josèphe sur Jésus', *REJ* 35, 1897, pp. 1–18.

10. A. Pelletier, 'L'originalité du témoignage de Flavius Josèphe sur Jésus', *RSR* 52, 1964, pp. 177–203.

11. L. H. Feldman, *Josephus* (Loeb) IX, 1965, p. 49.

12. P. Winter, 'Josephus on Jesus', *Journal of Historical Studies* I, 1968, pp. 289–302; cf. E. Schürer, ed. G: Vermes and F. Millar, *The History of the Jewish People in the Age of Jesus Christ* I, 1973, pp. 428–41.

13. A.-M. Dubarle, 'Le témoignage de Josèphe sur Jésus d'après le témoignage indirecte', *RB* 80, 1973, pp. 481–513.

14. E. Bammel, 'Zum Testimonium Flavianum', in O. Betz et al. (eds.), *Josephus-Studien* [Otto Michel Festschrift] (1974), pp. 9–22. Bammel accepts the authenticity of the whole Testimonium apart from a few textual alterations.

15. O. Betz, 'Probleme des Prozessen Jesu', *ANRW* II.25, 1, 1982, pp. 580–96.

16. G. H. Twelvetree, 'Jesus in Jewish Traditions', in D. Wenham (ed.), *Gospel Perspectives* V, 1985, pp. 285–341.

17. In *Contra Celsum* I 47, 6–7 Origen writes: 'For Josephus . . ., although he did not believe in Jesus as Christ (*kaitoi ge apistōn tō Iēsou ōs Christō*), sought for the cause of the fall of Jerusalem and the destruction of the temple. He ought to have said that the plot against Jesus was the reason why these catastrophes came upon the people, because they had killed the prophesied Christ; however, although unconscious of it, he is not far from the truth when he says that these disasters befell the Jews to avenge James the Just, a brother of "Jesus the so-called Christ", since they had killed him who was a very righteous man.' (Cf. H. Chadwick, *Origen, Contra Celsum*, 1953, p.43, n. 2.)

18. Art. cit. (in n. 8), p. 237.

19. *Epitome of Antiquities*, ed. Niese, 1896, p.304; Zonaras, *Epitome Historiarum*, ed. Dindorf, 1869, II, 12.

20. The Syriac version of the Testimonium occurs in Michael the Syrian's Chronicle and in the Syriac translation of *The Ecclesiastical History* by Eusebius. Both texts are reproduced by S. Pines, *An Arabic Version of the Testimonium Flavianum and its Implications*, 1971, pp. 24 and 26. For the Arabic version contained in Agapius' *Universal History*, see ibid., pp. 14 and 16. *sophos anēr* is rendered as *gabrā ḥakima* and *rajul ḥakim*, respectively.

21. The Syriac uses the adjective *šbiḥ*.

22. Pines comments: 'The words *and his conduct was good – wa-kānat lahu sīra ḥasana* might be interpreted – though perhaps not very convincingly – as not being essentially very different from the Syriac words . . . which may be translated . . . as . . . *for he was the worker of fine deeds*. Indeed it might be argued (though the contention does not seem to be very probable) that the Arabic words in question are a free paraphrase of the Syriac text.' (p.34)

23. This phrase, although not un-Josephan, may represent ordinary Greek usage.

24. Cf. art. cit. (in n. 12), p.293. By greatly enlarging on the unsuitability of the designation 'wise *man*', the Slavonic version of the Testimonium places what seems to be an early Greek gloss ('if indeed one might call him a man') in proper perspective: 'At that time there appeared a man, if it is permissible to call him a man. His nature and form were human, but his appearance was more than that of a man and his works were divine. He worked wonderful and mighty miracles. Therefore I cannot call him a man.' See *Josephus* (Loeb) III, p.648; V. Istrin, A. Vaillant and P. Pascal, *La prise de Jérusalem de Josèphe le Juif* I, 1934, pp. 148–49.

25. Cf. Matt. 23:34; I Cor. 6:5; Eph. 5:15; Jas. 3:13.

26. Art. cit. (in n. 9), p.10, n. 4.

27. Art. cit. (in n. 10), p.188.

28. Exod. 8:22; 9:4; 11:7; Deut. 28:59.

29. Cf. also Wisd. 5:2; 19:5; Jud. 13:13; II Macc. 9:24: III Macc. 6:33; IV Macc. 2:14; 4:14. Among the oddities recorded by the second century BC paradoxographer Apollonius in his *Marvellous Tales* are the following. Epemenides slept for fifty-seven years; Pythagoras bit and thus killed a poisonous snake; he was seen simultaneously in two different places, and had a golden thigh. See O. Keller (ed.), *Rerum naturalium scriptores graeci minores* I, 1879, reproduced in David Lenz Tiede, *The Charismatic Figure as Miracle Worker*, 1972, pp. 18, 313, 316.

30. Cf. e.g. *Vita Mosis* I, 143, 203, 212; II, 125.

31. *Ibid.* II, 213; *Migr.* 47; *Decal.* 46. Cf. Nikiprowetzky, *De Decalogo (Les oeuvres de Philon d'Alexandrie* 23), 1965, pp. 136–37.

32. *Vita Mosis* I, 212.

33. On Josephus' inconsequential stand vis-à-vis the biblical miracles, vacillating between Jewish faith and Hellenistic rationalism, see Gerhard Delling, 'Josephus und das Wunderbare', *NT* 2, 1958/9, pp. 291–309; G. MacRae, 'Miracle in the Antiquities of Josephus', *Miracles*, ed. by C. F. D. Moule, 1965, pp. 127–47; K. H. Rengstorf, *Sēmeion* B II, 2, *TDNT* VII, 1971, pp. 223–25; O. Betz, 'Das Problem des Wunders bei Flavius Josephus', *Josephus-Studien*, ed. by O. Betz, K. Haacker and M. Hengel, 1974, pp. 23–44.

34. Each Synoptic evangelist describes the reaction of the witnesses in his own way. Compared to Luke's *paradoxa*, Mark has 'We have never seen anything like

this' (2.12). Matthew, by contrast, instead of quoting the onlookers, explains why they glorified God: (because) 'he had given such authority to men' (9.8). It is not without interest to note the introductory words of the evangelists:

Mark	Matt.	Luke
They were all amazed and glorified God	They were afraid and glorified God	And amazement filled them and they glorified God and they were filled with awe

In Luke, the first two phrases are missing from D, W and other codices. The absence of the glorification of God seems to imply that the *paradoxa* were not acknowledged as supernatural miracles.

35. See for instance G. MacRae, art. cit. (in n. 33), p.143; cf. also A. E. Harvey, *Jesus and the Constraints of History*, 1982, p. 98.

36. Cf. O. Betz, art. cit. (in n. 33), p. 28.

37. As is well known, Josephus several times insinuates that he does not necessarily believe in the reality of some of the Bible stories; he certainly did not expect his Gentile readers to be persuaded: 'On these matters let everyone decide according to his fancy' (*Ant.* i 108 – longevity of the patriarchs). 'On these matters everyone is welcome to his own opinion' (*Ant.* ii 348 – crossing of the Red Sea). 'Of these happenings each of my readers may think as he will; for my part I am constrained to relate them as they are recorded in the sacred books' (*Ant.* iii 81 – portents surrounding God's manifestation on Sinai. 'On this readers are free to think what they please' (*Ant.* iv 158 – the Balaam story). 'Now I have written about these matters as I have found them in my reading; if, however, anyone wishes to judge otherwise of them, I shall not object to his holding a different opinion' (*Ant.* x 281 – the Daniel story). Cf. Dionysius of Halicarnassus, *Roman Antiquities* i 48, line 4; ii 40, 3; 74, 5; iii 36, 5 – *krineto de ōs ekastos tōn akouontōn bouletai*; see also Pliny, *Hist. nat.* ix 18 – *De his opinetur ut cuique libitum est*.

38. Art. cit. (in n. 10), p. 189.

39. Op. cit. (in n. 35), p. 98.

40. *The History of the Synoptic Tradition* (1963), p. 31.

41. Mark 6:4–5. Matt. 13:57–8 rewords the final section: *kai ouk epoiēsen ekei dunameis*. The Marcan statement *ouk edunato* is unlikely to be a church formulation.

42. Cf. the healing stories in the Acts of the Apostles and tḤul. 2:22–4 in connection with Jacob of Kefar Sama proposing to cure R. Eleazar ben Dama in the name of Jesus.

43. *Contra Celsum* I 6, 17–18.

44. Mark 3:22–7; Matt. 12:24–30; Luke 11:15–23.

45. The larger unit of Mark 3:22–30 contains a more indirect statement: to say that Jesus' exorcisms are done under the influence of an unclean spirit is tantamount to a blasphemy against the holy spirit.

46. I do not think that the hypothesis that the Testimonium Flavianum is a Christian revised edition of an originally hostile notice by Josephus requires serious refutation although it has been put forward by Th. Reinach (art. cit. in n. 9), Robert Eisler (*The Messiah Jesus*, 1931, p. 61), E. Bammel (art. cit. in n. 14, pp. 9–22), Morton Smith (*Jesus the Magician*, 1978, p. 45), and G. H. Twelvetree

(art. cit. in n. 16, pp. 303, 310). In my opinion, if Josephus had included a genuine anti-Christian statement in *Antiquities*, it would have simply been deleted and not emended. More likely still, in that case not only would we be without a Testimonium Flavianum, but also without the *Antiquities*. The survival of Josephus is entirely due to Christian copyists and editors. Would these writers have salvaged the work of a Jew who was the author of a wicked slander concerning Christ, who for these apologists was a divine being?

For a detailed bibliography of the Testimonium, see L. H. Feldman, *Josephus and Modern Scholarship*, 1984, pp. 679–703.

9. A Summary of the Law by Flavius Josephus

Originally published in *Novum Testamentum*, XXIV, no 4, 1982, pp. 289–303.

1. *Ant.* iv 198.
2. *Ant.* 268. On further references to the project, see Louis H. Feldman's note *d* on p. 531 of the Loeb *Josephus* IX (1965), drawing on H. R. Moehring, *Novelistic Elements in the Writings of Flavius Josephus* (1957), pp. 11–12. Cf. also David Altshuler, 'The Treatise "On Customs and Causes" by Flavius Josephus', *JQR* 69, 1979, pp. 226–32.
3. *Ant.* i 17.
4. The principle figures in Scripture (Deut. 4.2; 13.1) as well as in rabbinic literature (*bBer.* 34b: 'You have neither detracted from it nor added to it'). It is also attested in Greek historiography: cf. W. C. van Unnik, *Flavius Josephus als historischer Schriftsteller* (1978), pp. 26–40. The interpretation offered by van Unnik, viz., that Josephus seeks to reassure his readers concerning the reliability of his account of the biblical story (ibid. p. 39), is more satisfactory than those of H. P. Kingdon ('The Origins of the Zealots', *NTS* 19, 1972–73, p. 78: 'Josephus counted on his largely non-Jewish readership's ignorance of the Bible and their unwillingness to check his statements against the Greek Scripture'), and L. H. Feldman ('Hellenizations in Josephus' Portrayal of Man's Decline', in *Religions in Antiquity* – E. R. Goodenough Festschrift – 1968, p. 338: Josephus held that the Bible and interpretative tradition formed an undivided whole).
5. On this first-century BC writer from Rhodes see Menahem Stern, *Greek and Latin Authors on Jews and Judaism* I, 1974, pp. 148–49.
6. Acts 13.15; 15.21.
7. *Hypothetica* in Eusebius, *Praeparatio evangelica* viii 7, 12.
8. *Quod omnis probus* 81–82.
9. Cf. *mMeg.* 3.6; 4.1; *Mekhilta* on Ex. 15:22 (ed. Lauterbach II 90); *yMeg.* 75a: 'Moses ordered to Israel that they should read the Torah on sabbaths'.
10. Two further matters, priestly government and transgression in thought alone, will be discussed later, the former at (193–94) and the latter in the conclusion of this paper.
11. *De Decal.* 154. On the relation of Josephus' account to the Decalogue, see Ehrhard Kamlah, 'Frömmigkeit und Tugend – Die Gesetzapologie des Josephus in cAp 2, 145–295', in O. Betz, K. Haacker, M. Hengel (eds.), *Josephus-Studien – Otto Michel Festschrift*, 1974, pp. 220–32.

12. *Gen.R.* 81:1 (ed. Theodor-Albeck, 971). For an extensive treatment of 'the beginning and (the middle and) the end' as a designation of God in Greek, Hellenistic, Jewish-Hellenistic and early Christian literature, see W. C. van Unnik, 'Het godspredikaat "Het Begin en het Einde" bij Flavius Josephus en in de Openbaring van Johannes', *Mededelingen der Kon. Ned. Akademie van Wetenschappen*, Afd. Lett., NS 39, no. 1, 1976.

13. Th. Reinach (*Flavius Josèphe: Contre Apion*, 1930, *in loc.*) remarks that the letter *mem* is not the middle of the Hebrew alphabet, but the thirteenth in a series of twenty-two, and advances the theory that *aleph, mem* and *taw* represent, in fact, the initials of the Greek words, *archē, meson* and *telos*. However, if the five final letters are also included in the count in their proper order, the initial *mem* occupies the fourteenth place out of a total of twenty-seven!

14. The excerpt survives in the *Aegyptiaca* of Diodorus Siculus: Cf. M. Stern, op. cit. (in note 5) I, pp. 26–7, 31. E. Kamlah, art. cit. (in note 11), pp. 226–7, holds it, somewhat over-enthusiastically, as a certainty that Josephus directly depends on Hecataeus in the relevant part of his account.

15. Cf. *IQS* 5.2–3; *IQSa* 1.27–2.3, etc.

16. The same view is expressed at Qumran in regard to the royal Messiah who is to be instructed by the priests (*4QpIs* 8–10, 23). The Temple Scroll, in its turn, portrays the king as obliged to follow the advice of his council of twelve priests, twelve Levites and twelve Israelites, 'who will sit with him in judgement and in (proclaiming) Torah. His heart will not rise above them and he will do nothing without them in regard to any counsel' (*11Q Temple* 57.13–15).

17. Cf. Jacob Neusner, *A History of the Mishnaic Law of Holy Things* VI, 1980, pp. 273–5.

18. Cf. *m Yeb.* 6:6; *mGit.* 4.5, etc.

19. *War* ii 161. Note that according to *Ant.* iv 290 eunuchs who have emasculated themselves are to be banned from Jewish society because they have deprived themselves of the God-given power 'to increase our race' and should be counted as 'destroyers of children'. Cf. also Tacitus, *Hist.* v 5, 3: *augendae multitudini consulitur.*

20. Ibid.

21. For similar ideas see the accounts of the Essenes (*War* ii 121; *Ant.* xviii 21 and Philo, *Hypoth.* 7, 14–17) and the New Testament (Eph. 5.22; Col. 3.18; I Cor. 14.34; I Pet. 3.1).

22. In rabbinic law, the killing of a viable foetus is forbidden: cf. *Mekhilta* on Ex. 21.13 (ed. Lauterbach III 33). Ps.-Phocylides contains the following prohibition: 'A woman shall not destroy the foetus in her womb, nor shall she throw it, after giving it birth, before the dogs or the vultures as a prey' (184–85). Cf. P. W. van der Horst, *The Sentences of Pseudo-Phocylides*, 1978, pp. 232–34.

23. See the discussion of the concept of *merismos* in H. Schreckenberg, *Rezeptionsgeschichtliche und textkritische Untersuchungen zu Flavius Josephus* (1977), pp. 166–8. For the Essene eschatology, cf. *War* ii 154–55.

24. It is of interest to note that Josephus (like Matt. 22.24 and *bBB* 109a) describes levirate marriage as one that follows a childless union rather than one without a male offspring as in the case of Deut. 25:5.

25. Cf. also i 60, 178; *Ant.* iv 211; Philo, *Legat.* 210.

26. Cf. *yKil.*32b; *yKet.* 35a; *Gen.R.* 100.2.

27. See also *Letter of Aristeas* 228; *Ps.-Phocyl.* 8; *Aboth de-R. Nathan* A (ed. Schechter 119).

28. As will be seen, the Law forbids charging interest to friends (208). Deut. 23. 20–21 specifies that this prohibition applies only to Jews, and not to foreigners.

29. Cf. Josephus' account of Essene secrecy in *War* i 141.

30. See e.g. Th. Reinach, op. cit. (in note 13), *in. loc.*, suggests that this refers to the exclusion of foreigners from the Passover meal. Lucio Troiani, *Commento storico al 'Contro Apione' di Giuseppe*, 1977, 192, thinks of Judaeophile Gentiles who have not become full proselytes.

31. Cf. Tacitus, *Hist.* v 5, 1: *adversus omnes alios hostile odium*. Josephus cleverly points to Spartan xenophobia (259) in contrast to Jewish philanthropy (261).

32. On the contrary, according to *Ant.* iv 265, they must bury them.

33. Cf. *Ant.* iv 257–58.

34. See also *Ant.* 276.

35. *Sat.* xiv 103. See however David Goldenberg, 'The Halakha in Josephus and in Tannaitic Literature', *JQR* 67, 1976, p. 38.

36. See the Fragmentary Targum, Ps.-Jonathan and Neofiti margin.

37. The word itself figures in (146), (213), (261).

38. For the fruit trees see (212) above.

39. Cf. Philo, *Hypoth.* 7, 7 and 9.

40. Lev. 20:10. – *Ant.* iii 275.

41. Cf. Deut. 22.23 (dealing with a betrothed girl). But *Ant.* iv 252 refers to the case of an unattached virgin.

42. Lev. 20.13 – *Ant.* iii 275.

43. On the question of idolatry, see my paper, 'Leviticus 18:21 in Ancient Jewish Bible Exegesis' in E. Fleischer and J. J. Petuchowski (eds), *Studies in Aggadah, Targum and Jewish Liturgy in Memory of Joseph Heinemann*, 1981, pp. 108–24.

44. Cf. *Ant.* iv 207. Philo also adopts a similar viewpoint: *De vita Mosis* ii 205; *De spec. leg.* i 53.

45. See *C. Ap.* i 43; ii 223; *War* ii 152–53 (concerning the Essenes).

46. On Jewish heroism see (234–35): 'There should be nothing astonishing in our facing death on behalf of our laws with a courage which no other nation can equal. For even those practices of ours which seem the easiest others find difficult to tolerate: I mean personal service, simple diet, discipline which leaves no room for freak or individual caprice in matters of meat and drink, or in the sexual relations, or in extravagance, or again the abstention from work at rigidly fixed periods. No; the men who march out to meet the sword and charge and rout the enemy could not face regulations about everyday life. On the other hand, our willing obedience to the law in these matters results in the heroism which we display in the face of death.'

47. See also *War* iii 374; *Ant.* xviii 14.

48. *War* ii 155.

49. The Pharisees believed in the eternal punishment of the wicked. Cf. *War* ii 163; *Ant.* xviii 14.

50. How original Josephus' summary is cannot be assessed without further study of its presumed sources. As I have noted earlier (p. 100), it does not depend

structurally on *Antiquities*; in fact, it departs from it more than once. Th. Reinach, op. cit. (in note 13), p. 86, n. 5, postulates an unidentified source to which the word 'theocracy' may be assigned. E. Kamlah, as has been indicated, claims that Josephus uses Hecataeus (cf. note 14) and another anonymous Hellenistic–Jewish apologetical source. However, the only demonstrable connection with a known writing occurs in Philo's *Hypothetica*. Similarities between the extract preserved in Eusebius' *Praeparatio evangelica* viii 7–20, and the introductory part and section III of Josephus' summary, have already been signalled by F. H. Colson in his edition of *Hypothetica* in the Loeb Library: *Philo* IX, 1960, p. 409, note *a*; pp. 422–37, *passim*. They are also regularly pointed out by L. Troiani, op. cit. (in note 30). Already in 1931, A. D. Momigliano put forward the theory that Josephus had access to Philo's work ('Intorno al Contro Apione', *Rivista di Filologia* 59, reprinted in *Quinto contributo alla storia degli studi classici e del mondo antico*, 1975, p. 768) and that *Hypothetica* should be considered the direct source of the summary of the Law in *Contra Apionem* ('Un' apologia del giudaismo: il "Contro Apione" di Flavio Giuseppe', *Rassegna mensile di Israel* 5, 1931 – IX, p. 9). Indeed, when some of the correspondences are closely analysed, e.g. 7, 3 – (202); 7, 8 – (207); 7, 9 – (213), etc., the verbal similarity (it never amounts to identity) can be shown to be such that the only reasonable inference must be that either Philo and Josephus both borrow freely from a common source (as Kamlah conjectures), or that Josephus actually paraphrases Philo. If the second alternative is the correct one, it could be argued that *Hypothetica*, not *Contra Apionem* ii 164ff, is the earliest surviving abridged version of Judaism. Yet this is by no means obvious. For even if a direct Philonic influence on Josephus is agreed, it concerns only section III, leaving intact the first two parts and the appendices. On the other hand, as *Hypothetica* is available only in the form of excerpts, it is impossible to prove that the chapters now lost did not contain the whole account of Josephus. Be this as it may, *Contra Apionem* ii 190–219 may still be acknowledged as one of the earliest and possibly the oldest, theological précis compiled by a contemporary of the New Testament writers.

51. On contempt of death, see note 46 above and *War* ii 152 concerning the Essenes.

52. Art. cit. (in note 11), *passim*, especially pp. 230–32.

53. See above, p. 43, notes 31–32.

54. *bMak.* 24a. According to another recension, the final word was spoken by Habakkuk: 'The righteous shall live by his faith' (Hab. 2.4).

10. New Light on the Sacrifice of Isaac from Qumran

Originally published in *JJS* vol. XLVII, no. 1, 1996, pp. 140–6.

1. The volume in fact did not appear until the spring of 1995.

2. Cf. E. Schürer, G. Vermes, F. Millar, M. Goodman, *History of the Jewish People in the Age of Jesus Christ* (*History*) III, 1986, pp. 308–18.

3. Cf. *History* III, pp. 312–13.

4. Jub. 17.15–16.

5. The decision to order the test occurred on the 12th of the first month (Jub.

17.15) and the site of the sacrifice was reached on the third day, i.e. 15 Nisan (Jub. 18.3).

6. The editors deserve credit for their efforts even though their handling of the non-Qumran evidence is occasionally somewhat clumsy.

7. God is to test Abraham because Prince Mastemah accuses the patriarch on account of Isaac. This is an abridged version of Jub. 17.15–18.1: on hearing the heavenly praises of Abraham for his love of God and faithfulness in trials, Mastemah suggests to God the idea of ordering Abraham, who was doting on Isaac, to sacrifice his son. God was certain that Abraham would pass the test as he had been faithful on all the previous occasions. Hence the command taken from Gen. 22.2.

8. The author possibly interprets Beer Sheba as seven wells.

9. Since I,14 ends with 'And Abraham lifted up', the reconstruction of the damaged beginning of Col. II is bound to be 'his eyes' (cf. Gen. 22.4).

10. After a short lacuna, the reading *'esh* is clear. The editors remark that Targum Pseudo-Jonathan on Gen 22.4 helps to understand this reference to 'fire'. Ps.Jon. speaks of a 'cloud of glory' (i.e. a shining cloud) identifying the mountain. [Cf. also Gen. Rabbah 56.1–2, where it is specified that the vision of a cloud was observed by both Abraham and Isaac. GV] Better still, Pirqe de-R. Eliezer 105 reads: 'He saw a pillar of fire (*'mwd sl 's*) (rising) from the earth to heaven'.

11. The text of lines 1–4 is inspired by an abridged version of Gen. 22.4–8. There seems to be no room for reference to the two servants or the knife.

12. This address of Isaac to Abraham is lacking in Genesis 22. By contrast, as the editors note, the Targumic account (Ps.Jon., Neofiti [=N],[and Fragmentary Targ.=FT, GV) as well as Gen.R. 56.8 [not 7 as in DJD]) testify to such an additional speech by Isaac. Of Isaac's opening word only a single letter, clearly a *kaph*, is legible in 4Q225, but there is space for 15 more letters. However, all the Targums begin with the imperative *kpwt*: ('Bind my hands properly'). Cf. also Gen.R. 56.7, *kptny yph yph* ('Bind me very well'). Hence the reconstruction [*kpwt*] proposed by the editors enjoys an extremely high degree of probability.

13. No presence of the holy angels is found in the biblical version of the sacrifice of Isaac. But it is a standard feature in the Palestinian Targums. The editors cite Ps.Jon. on Gen. 22.10 ('The eyes of Isaac were looking on the angels on high'; cf. also FT and N. GV) and Gen.R. 56.5 and 7, both passages alluding to the weeping or tears of the ministering angels.

14. The Targums (on Gen. 22.14) and Gen.R. 56.10 associate the sacrifice with the future deliverance of the children of Isaac from all distress. The phrase [not allowing Mastemah to destroy] 'his sons from the earth' may have a similar connotation.

15. Mastemah's party rejoices in the prospect of Isaac's death.

16. Probably Isaac, unable to live up to his intention to serve as the victim of the sacrifice.

17. *khs* may mean 'false' as opposite to faithful, thus alluding to Abraham. This is however unlikely because of the mention of 'A[braham]' five words further on. *khs* has also the sense of 'failing' or 'meagre' (as opposite to firm or strong), in which case the self-sacrificing Isaac may be the subject.

18. The editors imply that the caller is Mastemah. In Gen. 22.11 the speaker is

'the Angel of the Lord', i.e. God himself. There is no reason to suppose that 4Q225 has changed the subject.

19. The editors assume that Mastemah is still speaking and propose the odd-sounding and far too short reconstruction, 'N[ow I know that] he will not be loving.' The missing words are more likely to be those of God to Mastemah, e.g. 'Now I know that you have lied that he is not a lover (of God).' Gen.R. 56.7 positively formulates the statement: 'I have made it known to all that you (Abraham) love me.'

20. Milik's reading of *yṣ*[*ḥq*] seems correct. In Gen. 22.17 Abraham is blessed. The change of subject in 4Q225 corresponds to the stress in early post-biblical exegesis of the story on the positive part played by Isaac in the event.

21. See Israël Lévi, 'Le sacrifice d'Isaac et la mort de Jésus', *REJ* 64, 1912, pp. 161–84; Hans-Joachim Schoeps, 'The Sacrifice of Isaac in Paul's Theology', *JBL* 65, 1946, pp. 385–92; Shalom Spiegel, 'Me'agadot ha'aqedah', *Alexander Marx Jubilee Volume*, 1950, pp. 471–547.

22. Shalom Spiegel, *The Last Trial - On the Legend and the Lore of the Command to Abraham to Offer Isaac as a Sacrifice: The Akedah*, 1969.

23. J. E. Wood, 'Isaac Typology in the New Testament', *NTS* 14, 1968, pp. 583–94; N. A. Dahl, 'The Atonement - An Adequate Reward for the Aqedah?', *Neotestamentica et Semitica* (eds E. E. Ellis and M. Wilcox), 1969, pp. 15–29; Robert J. Daly, 'The Soteriological Significance of the Sacrifice of Isaac', *CBQ* 39, 1977, pp. 45–75; M. Wilcox, 'Upon the Tree - Deut. 21.22–23 in the New Testament', *JBL* 96, 1977, pp. 97–9; P. R. Davies and B. D. Chilton, 'The Akedah: A Revised Tradition History' *CBQ* 40, 1978, pp. 514–46; P. R. Davies, 'Passover and the Dating of the Akedah', *JJS* 30, 1979, pp. 59–67; Bruce Chilton, 'Isaac and the Second Night: A Consideration', *Biblica* 61, 1980, pp. 78–88; C. T. R. Hayward, 'The Present State of Research into the Targumic Account of the Sacrifice of Isaac', *JJS* 32, 1981, pp. 127–50; James Swetnam, *Jesus and Isaac*, 1981, pp. 4–80; Alan F. Segal, 'He who did not spare His only Son', *From Jesus to Paul* (ed. Peter Richardson, 1984), pp. 169–84; Bruce Chilton, 'Recent Discussion of the Aqedah' in *Targumic Approaches to the Gospels*, 1986, pp. 39–49; C. T. R. Hayward, 'The Sacrifice of Isaac and Jewish Polemic against Christianity', *CBQ* 52, 1990, pp. 292–306; Jon D. Levenson, *The Death and Resurrection of the Beloved Son*, 1993, pp. 173–219, 245–49.

24. *Scripture and Tradition*, pp. 194–95.

25. Cf. *Sifra* (ed. Weiss), 102c; *yTaan.* 65a; *Mekh.* (ed. Lauterbach) I, 57, 87–88.

26. Cf. *Mekh.* I, 57, 88, 222–23.

27. FT and Ps.Jon. on Lev. 22.27. For Mount Moriah=Temple Mount, see II Chron. 3.1; Jub. 18.13; *Ant.* i, 226.

28. PT on Ex. 12.42; *Mekh.* I, 57, 88.

29. *bRosh ha-Shanah* 16a.

30. Cf. *Scripture and Tradition*, pp. 197–202.

31. Cf. ibid. pp. 218–27.

32. P. R. Davies and B. D. Chilton, see n. 22. For the separate responsibilities of the co-authors, see Chilton, *Targumic Approaches*, (cf. n. 23 above), p. 47, n.1.

33. *CBQ*, 515.

34. As regards IV Macc., Martin Goodman, having provided linguistic and historical arguments in favour of the commonly held date, concludes that 'suggestions of a date in the early second-century (Dupont-Sommer; Breitenstein) should be dismissed'. Cf. *History* III, p. 591.

35. This is a hint at Gen.R. 56.3. 'It comes as a shock when we hear the Amoraim compare Isaac to a condemned man bearing his cross.' Cf. art. cit., p. 539, and n. 68 where E. R. Goodenough is quoted as observing: 'This detail so strikingly brings to mind the crucifixion of Jesus that it seems impossible that there was no relationship.' As though Jesus had been the only crucified person who had to carry the cross to the place of crucifixion! On the Roman method of crucifixion, which often entailed the carrying of the beam of the cross by the condemned man, cf. Martin Hengel, *Crucifixion in the Ancient World and the Folly of the Message of the Cross* (London, 1977); Art. 'Crucifixion', *Anchor Bible Dictionary* I, 1992, pp. 1208–9. The old *Jewish Encyclopedia*, 1905, vol. IV, p. 368, displays its usual common sense in its article on 'Cross'. '(Crucifixion) was so familiar to the Jews in New Testament times that they spoke frequently of "men carrying their cross before them while going to be executed".'

36. *CBQ*, pp. 516–17.

37. This is an argument made to stand on its head because the midrashic texts unanimously assert that the atoning-redemptive virtue of the lamb sacrifices in the Jerusalem sanctuary derived from the fact that they reminded God of the binding of Isaac!

38. C. T. R. Hayward, 'The Present State of Research into the Targumic Account of the Sacrifice of Isaac', *JJS* 32, 1981, pp. 127–50; James Swetnam, *Jesus and Isaac* (1981), pp. 18–21; Alan F. Segal, art. cit. (cf. n. 23 above); C. T. R. Hayward, *CBQ* (cf. n. 23 above).

39. Scholars still exercised by the problem of methodology relative to the use of rabbinic literature in New Testament exegesis are invited to consider items 2 and 7 in the table below.

40. In a thorough study, 'The sacrifice of Isaac in Qumran literature' (Biblica 83, 2002, 212–29) Professor Joseph A. Fitzmyer re-examines 4Q225. In the course of his discussion, he expresses surprise several times on finding items in my synoptic table, especially nos. 1, 3, 11 and 12, which have no attestation in 4Q225. He calls them 'dubious evidence for the interpretation of the Qumran text' (see pp. 222 and 225). Fitzmyer's objection seems to reveal a misunderstanding of the purpose of my study. In fact the title of the piece and the subtitle make clear that my aim was to determine the impact of 4Q225 on the history of the ancient Jewish exegesis of Genesis 22. Items 1, 3, 11 and 12 are those aspects of this exegesis on which the new document does not shed fresh light. Professor Fitzmyer judges my contribution through the prism of his agenda and not mine.

11. The Dead Sea Scrolls Fifty Years On

First published in *The Jewish Year Book 1999* (Vallentine Mitchell, London, 1999) pp. xlii–li.

12. Jesus the Jew and his Religion: Autobiographical Reflections

First published in G. Vermes, *Providential Accidents: An Autobiography*, 1998, pp. 211–24.

1. Rudolf Bultmann, *Jesus and the Word*, 1934, p. 14. (The original German edition, *Jesus*, appeared in 1926.)

2. Of the other two designations investigated in the book, on the basis of my earlier research (cf. pp. 81–90 above) I excluded 'son of man' from among the original titles during the lifetime of Jesus, although I accepted it as a Christian midrash, a theologico-exegetical product of the Greek-speaking early church. As for 'Messiah', I argued that because of its most generally held sense of a liberating king of the last days, Jesus was disinclined to apply the notion to himself and that the so-called 'messianic secret' of the Gospel of Mark, i.e. the prohibition by Jesus to be proclaimed Messiah, was inspired by his unwillingness to be seen as fulfilling that role. And when questioned, his elliptic reply, 'It is you who say so', needs to be completed by 'but not I'.

3. He first voiced his unease in a conversation, and repeated it in an evaluation of the book on the BBC's Third Programme under the somewhat depressing title, 'A rather pale Galilean'.

4. I remember Robert Shackleton's comment that he infinitely preferred talking about Voltaire, on whom I consulted him, to discussing the hourly wages of cleaning women which he, *qua* Bodley's Librarian, had ultimately to decide.

5. In Belfast, my hosts were nervous that the followers of the Reverend Ian Paisley might disturb the lectures (which for them were anti-Christian). Their fears were unfounded. In Dublin, by contrast, the large Roman Catholic audience insisted that I should not fudge my answers: 'Did I think Jesus was God? Yes or no, no double talk, please!'

6. By that time I had new publishers, SCM Press in London, who also rescued *Jesus the Jew* from Collins, and Fortress Press in the United States.

7. 'We are so accustomed . . . to make Jesus the object of religion that we become apt to forget that in our earliest records he is portrayed not as the object of religion, but as a religious man' (T. W. Manson, *The Teaching of Jesus*, 1935, p. 101).

8. J. P. Meier, *A Marginal Jew* II, 1994, p. 14, n.7.

9. See above, pp. viii–x.

10. Apparently the book was a publishing success in Hungary and the first printing was sold out on the day it reached the bookshops.

11. To name a few: A. E. Harvey, *Jesus and the Constraints of History*, 1982; E. P. Sanders, *Jesus and Judaism*, 1985; *The Historical Figure of Jesus*, 1990; M. J. Borg, *Jesus: a New Vision*, 1987; J. H. Charlesworth, *Jesus within Judaism*, 1989; *Jesus' Jewishness*, 1991; J. D. Crossan, *The Historical Jesus*, 1991; J. P. Meier, *A Marginal Jew*, I III, 1991–2001, etc.

12. Since 1971, the Commission has been associated with the Sacred Congregation of the Doctrine of the Faith, and is presided over by the head of that Congregation, Cardinal Joseph Ratzinger.

13. *Scripture and Christology: A Statement of the Biblical Commission*, translated with a commentary by Joseph A. Fitzmyer, SJ (1986).

14. 'If to understand Jesus studies are conducted *only* along these lines, there is always the danger of mutilating his personality, precisely at the moment when stress is being put by such studies on his Jewish background and character' (p. 23).

15. S. Safrai, 'The Teaching of Pietists in Mishnaic Literature', *JJS* 16, 1965, pp. 15–33; 'Jesus and the Hasidim', *Jerusalem Perspective* 42–44, 1994, pp. 3–22.

16. The French Catholic Bishops' 'repentance' at the end of September 1997 for their Church's failure to condemn the persecution of the Jews during the Second World War preceded the statement by the Pope promised for the end of 1997.

Acknowledgements

Chapter 1, 'Jesus the Jew', represents my Claude Goldsmid Montefiore lecture delivered at and published by the Liberal Jewish Synagogue of London in 1974. Chapters 2, 3, and 4 transcribe my three Riddell Memorial Lectures given in the University of Newcastle upon Tyne in 1981 under the title 'The Gospel of Jesus the Jew'. Chapter 5, 'Jewish Studies and New Testament Interpretation', contains the text of a public lecture in Oxford delivered in 1979 (see *Journal of Jewish Studies*, vol. XXXI, no. 1, 1980, pp. 1–17). Chapter 6, 'Jewish Literature and New Testament Exegesis', corresponds to my presidential address to the First Congress of the European Association for Jewish Studies, held in Oxford in 1982 (see *Journal of Jewish Studies*, vol. XXXIII, nos. 1–2, 1982, pp. 361–376). Chapter 7, 'The Present State of the "Son of Man" Debate', is an expanded version of a paper read in Oxford in 1978 at the Sixth International Congress of Biblical Studies (see *Journal of Jewish Studies*, vol. XXIX, 1978, pp. 123–134). Chapter 8, 'The Jesus Notice on Josephus Re-examined', was written for the Festschrift intended to celebrate the seventieth birthday of Professor Alexander Scheiber (1913–1985) who, alas, died before the volume was ready for publication (see *Journal of Jewish Studies*, vol. XXXVIII, 1987, pp. 1–10). Chapter 9, 'A Summary of the Law by Flavius Josephus', appeared in *Novum Testamentum* (vol. XXIV, no. 4, 1982, pp. 289–303). Chapter 10, 'New Light on the Sacrifice of Isaac from Qumran', is a re-examination of the problem of the Akedah with the help of a Dead Sea Scroll (see *Journal of Jewish Studies*, vol. XLVII, 1996, pp. 140–146). Chapter 11, 'The Dead Sea Scrolls Fifty Years On', is a general survey of half a century of Qumran research, first published in *The Jewish Year Book 1999* (Vallentine Mitchell, London, 1999, pp. xlii–li). Chapter 12, 'Jesus the Jew and his Religion', is a personal account of my long involvement with the problem of the Jesus of history. It is borrowed from my autobiography, *Providential Accidents*, published in 1998 (SCM Press, London, and Rowman & Littlefield, Lanham, MD).

Bibliography

Abrahams, I., *Studies in Pharisaism and the Gospels*, I–II, 1917.

Alexander, P. S., Review of G. Vermes, *Post-biblical Jewish Studies, JTS* 27, 1976, p. 172

Allegro, J. M., *Discoveries in the Judaean Desert* V, 1968

Baillet, M., *Discoveries in the Judaean Desert* III, 1962

Banks, Robert, *Jesus and the Law in the Synoptic Tradition*, 1975

Barr, James, *The Semantics of Biblical Language*, 1961

— *Fundamentalism*, 1977

Barthélemy, D., and Milik, J. T., *Discoveries in the Judaean Desert* I, 1955

Becker, Joachim, *Messianic Expectation in the Old Testament*, 1980

Betz, Otto, *What do we know about Jesus?* 1968

— et al. (eds), *Josephus-Studien*, 1974

Bishop, E. E., *Jesus of Palestine*, 1955

Black, M., *An Aramaic Approach to the Gospels and Acts*, [3]1967

— *The Scrolls and Christian Origins*, 1961

Black, M. (ed.), *The Scrolls and Christianity*, 1969

Borg, M. J., *Jesus: A New Vision*, 1987

Bornkamm, G., *Jesus of Nazareth*, 1960

Borsch, F. H., *The Son of Man in Myth and History*, 1967

Bousset, Wilhelm, *Die Religion des Judentums im späthellenistischen Zeitalter*, [2]1926

Brandon, S. G. F., *Jesus and the Zealots*, 1967

Braude, W. G., *Pesikta Rabbati* I–II, 1968

Buber, Martin, *Two Types of Faith*, 1951

— *Israel and the World – Essays in a Time of Crisis*, 1963

— *The Kingship of God*, 1967

Büchler, Adolf, *Types of Jewish Palestinian Piety from 70 B.C.E. to 70 C.E.*, 1922

Bultmann, Rudolf, *Jesus*, 1926 = *Jesus and the Word*, 1934, 1958

— *The History of the Synoptic Tradition*, 1963

— *Theologie des Neuen Testaments*, [5]1965 = *Theology of the New Testament* I–II, 1952–55

Carmignac, Jean, *Recherches sur le 'Notre Père'*, 1969

Casey, Maurice, *Son of Man: The Interpretation and Influence of Daniel 7*, 1979

Cassidy, Richard J., *Jesus, Politics and Society*, 1978

Catchpole, D. R., *The Trial of Jesus*, 1971

Chadwick, H., *Origen, Contra Celsum*, 1953

Charles, R. H., *The Apocrypha and Pseudepigrapha of the Old Testament* I–II, 1912–13

Charlesworth, James H., *The Pseudepigrapha and Modern Research*, 1976, ²1981
— (ed.), *John and Qumran*, 1972
— (ed.), *The Old Testament Pseudepigrapha* I–II, 1983, 1985
— *Jesus within Judaism*, 1989
— *Jesus' Jewishness*, 1991
Chilton, B., *Targumic Approaches to the Gospels*, 1986
Colson, F. H. and Whitaker, G. H., *Philo* I–X, 1929–62
Conzelmann, Hans, *An Outline of the Theology of the New Testament*, 1969
Coppens, J., *Le Fils de l'Homme néotestamentaire*, 1981
— *Le Fils de l'Homme vétéro- et intertestamentaire*, 1983
Cranfield, C. E. B., *The Gospel according to St Mark*, 1959
Crossan, J. D., *The Historical Jesus*, 1991
Cullmann, O., *The Christology of the New Testament*, 1959
Dalman, Gustaf, *Jesus-Jeschua*, 1922 = *Jesus-Jeshua: Studies in the Gospels*, 1929, 1971
— *Die Worte Jesu* ²1930 = *The Words of Jesus*, 1902
Danby, H., *The Mishnah*, 1933
Daube, D., *The New Testament and Rabbinic Judaism*, 1956
Davidson, Robert, and Leaney, A. R. C., *Biblical Criticism*, 1970
Davies, W. D., *The Setting of the Sermon on the Mount*, 1964
Derrett, J. M. D., *Law in the New Testament*, 1970
Dodd, C. H., *The Parables of the Kingdom*, 1935, 1978
— *The Founder of Christianity*, 1970, 1971
Dunn, James D. G., *Christology in the Making*, 1980
Eisler, R., *The Messiah Jesus*, 1931
Eissfeldt, Otto, *The Old Testament: An Introduction*, 1965
Feldman, L. H., *Josephus* (Loeb) IX, 1965
— *Josephus and Modern Scholarship*, 1984
Fiebig, P., *Der Menschensohn*, 1901
Fitzmyer, J. A., *The Dead Sea Scrolls. Major Publications and Tools for Study*, 1977
— *The Genesis Aprocryphon of Qumran Cave* I, ²1971
— *Essays on the Semitic Background of the New Testament*, 1971
— *A Wandering Aramean: Collected Aramaic Essays*, 1979
Fleischer, E. et al. (eds), *Studies in Aggadah, Targum and Jewish Liturgy*, 1981
Foerster, W., 'Epiousios', *TDNT* V, pp. 590–99
— 'Exousia', *TDNT* V, pp. 562–75
Fortna, R. T., 'Redaction Criticism, NT', *IDBS*, 1976, pp. 733–35
Fredriksen, P., *Jesus of Nazareth, King of the Jews*, 1999
Freyne, Seán, *Galilee from Alexander the Great to Hadrian*, 1980
Garcìa Martìnez, F., and D. W. Parry, *A Bibliography of the Finds in the Desert of Judah (1970–1995)*, 1996
Gerhardsson, Birger, *Memory and Manuscript: Oral Tradition and Written Transmission in Rabbinic Judaism and Early Christianity*, 1961, ²1964
— *Tradition and Transmission in Early Christianity*, 1964
— *The Origins of the Gospel Tradition*, 1977
Goodblatt, D. M., *Rabbinic Instruction in Sasanian Babylonia*, 1975
Goodenough, E. R., *Introduction to Philo Judaeus*, ²1962

Grant, Michael, *Jesus: An Historian's Review of the Gospels*, 1977

Grässer, E., *Das Problem der Parousieverzögerung in den synoptischen Evangelien und in der Apostelgeschichte*, ²1960

Gray, J., *The Biblical Doctrine of the Reign of God*, 1979

Green, William S., 'What's in a Name? The Problematic of "Rabbinic Biography"', *Approaches to Ancient Judaism: Theory and Practice*, 1978, pp. 77–96

— 'Palestinian Holy Men: Charismatic Leadership and Rabbinic Tradition', *Aufstieg und Niedergang der römischen Welt*, ed. W. Haase, II. *Principat*. 19.2 *Religion (Judentum: Palästinisches Judentum)*, 1979, pp. 619–47

Hahn, F., *The Titles of Jesus in Christology*, 1969

Hamerton-Kelly, R., *God the Father: Theology and Patriarchy in the Teaching of Jesus*, 1979

Hanson, P. D., *The Dawn of Apocalyptic*, 1975

Harvey, A. E., *God Incarnate: Story and Belief*, 1981

— *Jesus and the Constraints of History*, 1982

Heinemann, J., *Prayer in the Talmud; Forms and Patterns*, 1977

Hengel, Martin, *Judaism and Hellenism*, I–II, 1974

— *Die Zeloten*, ²1976

— *Crucifixion in the Ancient World*, 1977

Hering, J., *La royaume de Dieu et sa venue*, 1959

Higgins, A. J. B., *The Son of Man in the Teaching of Jesus*, 1980

Horst, P. W. van der, *The Sentences of Pseudo-Phocylides*, 1978

Hübner, H., *Das Gesetz in der synoptischen Tradition*, 1973

Idelsohn, A. Z., *Jewish Liturgy and its Development*, 1932

Isaac, J., *Jésus et Israël*, 1946

Istrin, V. et al., *La prise de Jèrusalem de Josèphe le Juif*, 1934

Jacobs, Louis, *A Jewish Theology*, 1973

Jeremias, Joachim, 'Grammateus', *TDNT* I, pp. 740–42

— *New Testament Theology* I, 1971

— *The Parables of Jesus*, ²1972

— *The Prayers of Jesus*, 1977

Joüon, P., *L'évangile de Jésus-Christ*, 1930

Judéo-Christianisme. Recherches historiques et théologiques offertes en hommage au Cardinal Jean Daniélou, 1972

Juster, J., *Les juifs de l'empire romain*, 1914

Käsemann, E., *Essays on New Testament Themes*, 1964

Kautzsch, E., *Die Apokryphen und Pseudepigraphen des Alten Testaments* I–II, 1900

Kittel, G., and Friedrich, G., *Theologisches Wörterbuch zum Neuen Testament* I–X, 1933–76 = *Theological Dictionary of the New Testament* I–X, 1964–76

Klausner, J., *Jesus of Nazareth*, 1925

Klein, Charlotte, *Anti-Judaism in Christian Theology*, 1978

Klostermann, E., *Das Markusevangelium*, ⁴1950

Knibb, M. A., *The Ethiopic Book of Enoch* I–II, 1978

Kohler, K., *Jewish Theology*, 1918

Kümmel, W. G., *Promise and Fulfilment*, 1957

— *The Theology of the New Testament*, 1969

— *The New Testament: The History of the Investigation of its Problems*, ²1970

— *Introduction to the New Testament*, [2]1975
— 'Ein Jahrzehnt Jesusforschung', *Theologische Rundschau* 40, 1975, pp. 283–336; 41, 1976/77, pp. 198–258, 295–363
— 'Jesusforschung seit 1965', *Theologische Rundschau* 43, 1978, pp. 105–61, 232–65; 45, 1980, pp. 48–84, 293–337
Ladd, G. E., *The Presence and the Future*, 1974
Lagrange, M.-J., *L'évangile de Jésus-Christ*, 1929
Lehmann, Paul, *The Transfiguration of Politics: Jesus Christ and the Question of Revolution*, 1975
Leo XIII, *Providentissimus Deus*, 1893
Levenson, J., *The Death and Resurrection of the Beloved Son*, 1993
Lietzmann, H., *Der Menschensohn*, 1896
Lindars, Barnabas, *Jesus Son of Man*, 1983
Machoveč, Milan, *A Marxist looks at Jesus*, 1976
McKnight, E. V., *What is Form Criticism?*, 1975
Maier, J., *Geschichte der jüdischen Religion*, 1972
Manson, T. W., *The Teaching of Jesus: Studies of its Form and Content*, 1931, [2]1935
Marmorstein, A., *Studies in Jewish Theology*, 1950
Meier, J. P., *A Marginal Jew* I–III, 1991–2001
Metzger, Bruce M., *The Early Versions of the New Testament*, 1977
Meyer, A., *Jesu Muttersprache*, 1896
Meyer, E., *Ursprung and Anfänge des Christentums*, 1921
Meyers, Eric M., and Strange, James F., *Archaeology, the Rabbis and Early Christianity*, 1981
Milik, J. T., *The Book of Enoch: Aramaic Fragments of Qumran Cave 4*, 1976
— *Discoveries in the Judaean Desert* I, 1955; III, 1962
Moehring, H. R., *Novelistic Elements in the Writings of Flavius Josephus*, 1957
Momigliano, A. D., *Quinto contributo alla storia degli studi classici e del mondo antico*, 1975
Moore, A. L., *The Parousia in the New Testament*, 1966
Moore, G. F., *Judaism in the First Centuries of the Christian Era* I–III, 1927–30
Moule, C. F. D. (ed.), *Miracles*, 1965
— *The Origin of Christology*, 1977
Mowinckel, S., *He That Cometh*, 1956
Murphy-O'Connor, J. (ed.), *Paul and Qumran*, 1968
Neill, S. C., *The Interpretation of the New Testament 1861–1961*, 1963
Neusner, Jacob, *The Rabbinic Traditions about the Pharisees* I–III, 1971
— 'The Present State of Rabbinic Biography', *Hommage à Georges Vajda*, ed. G. Nahon and Ch. Touati, 1980, pp. 85–91
— *A History of the Mishnaic Law of Holy Things* VI, 1980
— *Judaism: The Evidence of the Mishnah*, 1981
— *Judaism in Late Antiquity*, 1995
Niese, B., *De testimonio Christiani quod est apud Josephum ant. Iud. xviii 63 sq disputatio*, 1893–94
Oppenheimer, Aharon, *The 'Am Ha-Aretz*, 1977
Otto, Rudolf, *The Kingdom of God and the Son of Man*, 1943
Parkes, J., *The Conflict of the Church and the Synagogue*, 1934

Perrin, Norman, *The Kingdom of God in the Teaching of Jesus*, 1963
— *Rediscovering the Teaching of Jesus*, 1967
- *What is Redaction Criticism?* 1969
— *The New Testament: An Introduction*, 1974
— *Jesus and the Language of the Kingdom*, 1976
Pines, S., *An Arabic Version of the Testimonium Flavianum and its Implications*, 1971
Piper, John, '*Love your Enemies': Jesus' Love Commandment in the Synoptic Gospels and the Early Christian Paraenesis*, 1979
Przybilski, B., *Righteousness in Matthew and his World of Thought*, 1980
Reinach, Th., *Flavius Josèphe: Contre Apion*, 1930
Richardson, P. (ed.), *From Jesus to Paul*, 1984
Riches, John, *Jesus and the Transformation of Judaism*, 1980
Rigaux, B., *Les épîtres aux Thessaloniciens*, 1956
Rivkin, Ellis, 'Pharisees', *IDBS*, 1976, pp. 657–63
— *A Hidden Revolution*, 1978
Russell, D. S., *The Method and Message of Jewish Apocalyptic*, 1964
Sanders, E. P., *Paul and Palestinian Judaism*, 1977
— *Jesus and Judaism*, 1986
— *The Historical Figure of Jesus*, 1990
Schechter, S., *Some Aspects of Rabbinic Theology*, 1909
Schlatter, A., *Der Evangelist Matthäus*, 1929
Schlosser, J., *Le Règne de Dieu dans les dits de Jésus* I–II, 1980
Schnackenburg, Rudolf, *New Testament Theology Today*, 1963
— *The Moral Teaching of the New Testament*, 1965
Schoeps, Hans Joachim, *Theologie und Geschichte des Judenchristentums*, 1949
— *Urgemeinde, Judenchristentum, Gnosis*, 1956
Schreckenberg, H., *Rezeptiongeschichtliche und textkritische Untersuchungen zu Flavius Josephus*, 1977
Schrenk, G., see Quell, G.
Schürer, Emil, *Geschichte des jüdischen Volkes im Zeitalter Jesu Christi* I–III
    $^{3/4}$1901–9
Schürer, E., Vermes, G., Millar, F., Black, M., Goodman, M., *The History of the Jewish People in the Age of Jesus Christ* I–III, 1973–87
Schürmann, H., 'Eschatologie und Leibesdienst in der Verkündigung Jesu' *Vom Messias zu Christus*, ed. K. Schubert, 1964, pp. 203–32
Schweitzer, Albert, *Von Reimarus zu Wrede*, 1906 – *The Quest of the Historical Jesus*, 1910, ^{3}1954, 2000
Simon, Marcel, *Verus Israel*, ^{2}1964
— 'Reflexions sur le Judéo-Christianisme', *Christianity, Judaism and Other Greco-Roman Cults* II, ed. J. Neusner, 1975, pp. 53–76
Simon, Marcel, et al., *Aspects du Judéo-Christianisme*, 1965
Simon, Marcel, and Benoit, A., *Le judaisme et le christianisme antique*, 1968
Smith, Morton, *Jesus the Magician*, 1978
Souter, A., *Text and Canon in the New Testament*, 1913
Spicq, C., *Agapè dans le Nouveau Testament* I–III, 1958–9
Spiegel, S., *The Last Trial*, 1969

Stauffer, E., *New Testament Theology*, 1955
Stendahl, K., *The School of St Matthew*, 1954, ²1968
— *The Scrolls and the New Testament*, 1958
Stern, M., *Greek and Latin Authors on Jews and Judaism* I–III, 1974–84
Strack, Hermann, and Billerbeck, Paul, *Kommentar zum Neuen Testament aus Talmud und Midrasch* I–IV, 1922–28
Strange, James F., see Meyers, Eric M.
Strobel, A., *Untersuchungen zum eschatologischen Verzögerungsproblem*, 1961
Swetnam, James, *Jesus and Isaac*, 1981
Talmage, F. E., *Disputation and Dialogue: Readings in Jewish-Christian Encounter*, 1975
— *Kerygma und Apokalyptik*, 1967
Tiede, D. L., *The Charismatic Figure as Miracle Worker*, 1972
Tödt, H. E., *The Son of Man in the Synoptic Tradition*, ET 1965
Troiani, L., *Commento storico al 'Contro Apione' di Guiseppe*, 1977
Ullendorff, Edward, *Ethiopia and the Bible*, 1968
Urbach, E. E., *The Sages: Their Concepts and Beliefs* I–II, 1975
Vermes, Geza, *Jesus the Jew: A Historian's Reading of the Gospels*, 1973, 1981, 1983, 1994, 2001
— *Post-biblical Jewish Studies*, 1975
— *The Dead Sea Scrolls in English*, ²1975
— *The Dead Sea Scrolls: Qumran in Perspective*, 1977, rev. 1981
— *The Complete Dead Sea Scrolls in English*, 1997, 1998
— *Providential Accidents: An Autobiography*, 1998
— *An Introduction to the Complete Dead Sea Scrolls*, 1999, 2000
— *The Changing Faces of Jesus*, 2000, 2001
— *The Authentic Gospel of Jesus*, 2003
Vermes, Pamela, *Buber on God and the Perfect Man*, 1980
Volz, Paul, *Eschatologie der jüdischen Gemeinde im neutestamentlichen Zeitalter*, ²1934
Weber, Ferdinand, *Jüdische Theologie*, 1897
Wellhausen, Julius, *Einleitung in die drei ersten Evangelien*, 1905
Westerholm, Stephen, *Jesus and Scribal Authority*, 1978
Winter, Paul, *On the Trial of Jesus*, 1961, ²1974
Wrede, Wilhelm, *Messiasgeheimnis in den Evangelien*, 1901 = *The Messianic Secret*, 1971
Yoder, J. H., *The Politics of Jesus*, 1972

Index of Names and Subjects

CPSIA information can be obtained at www.ICGtesting.com
229030LV00007B/1/A

9 780800 636234